A G<small>IFT</small> F<small>OR</small>

⊹ FROM ⊹

ANGEL

WISDOM

Angel

*W*isdom

365 MEDITATIONS AND INSIGHTS FROM THE HEAVENS

TERRY LYNN TAYLOR AND MARY BETH CRAIN

Hallmark
BOOKS

BOK 3006

HarperSanFrancisco

ANGEL WISDOM: *365 Meditations and Insights from the Heavens*.
Copyright © 1994 by Terry Lynn Taylor and Mary Beth Crain.
All rights reserved. Printed in the United States of America. No
part of this book may be used or reproduced in any manner
whatsoever without written permission except in the case of
brief quotations embodied in critical articles and reviews. For
information address HarperCollins Publishers, 10 East 53rd
Street, New York, NY 10022.

Published under license from HarperCollins Publishers, Inc.

The Library of Congress has cataloged the original edition of
this title as follows:

Taylor, Terry Lynn.
    Angel wisdom : 365 meditations and insights from
the heavens / Terry Lynn Taylor and Mary Beth
Crain.
        p.   cm.
    ISBN 0-06-251067-3 (pbk: alk. paper)
    1. Angels—Prayer-books and devotions.
2. Devotional calendars. I. Crain, Mary Beth.
II. Title.
BL477.T373   1994
291.2'15—dc20   94–8050
                                                 CIP

ISBN 0-06-0953918 (Hallmark edition)

    01 02 03 RRD 10 9 8 7 6 5

*A*NGELS ARE OFTEN THOUGHT OF AS AGENTS—OF CHANGE, loving concern, encouragement, humor, intelligence, and, of course, light.

This book is dedicated to our agent, Loretta Barrett, who embodies all of these qualities. Thanks to her guidance, talent, and overwhelming confidence in this project, *Angel Wisdom* became a reality.

ACKNOWLEDGMENTS

The authors would like to thank their publisher, Tom Grady, for his angel vision and angelic ability to quietly make wonderful things happen; and their editor and kindred spirit, Barbara Moulton, for her angel wisdom, support, and excitement for this project. Thanks also to Lisa Bach and Priscilla Stuckey for their excellent editing and input, and to our top-notch production editor, Mimi Kusch. And, last but not least, we thank each other—and the angels.

The wonderful experience of doing an angel book makes one appreciate the angels in one's life even more. Many thanks to:

My husband and computer widower, Adam Shields, for his love, support, wonderful sense of humor, pride in my work, and saintly patience as I disappeared into my office for days at a time;

My twin brother, David Gersten, who inspired a number of these meditations and who has always had faith in his not-always-sensible sister;

My mother, Hazel Gersten, for bragging about me to all of her friends, even when half the time she has no idea what project I'm working on now;

My dear friend, Deborah Tracy, for always being there;

My sister-in-law, Christine Shields, for her love, kindness, and generosity;

My cousin, Claire Bucalos, for her excitement in and enthusiasm for all things metaphysical;

John Spalding, for his suppport, encouragement, and general all-round good friendship;

My four cats—Rhonda, Petie, White Sox, and, of course, Angel—for providing untold hours of humor and unbearable cuteness of being just when I seemed to need it most;

And everyone else who helped me, either wittingly or unwittingly, along the way.

MARY BETH CRAIN

I thank the following people for becoming my protective support system and helping me maintain a life outside while I spent so much time within.

To each member of my immediate family, thank you once again for your love, support, and understanding. Thank you to Tim Gunns for helping me tame my creative surges without breaking my spirit, and for his love and patience. I would not have been able to write this book and keep up with any of my other "stuff" if it hadn't been for the help, support, integrity, and grounding of Ellen Rayme. I am so grateful she came into my life. Once again I thank Shannon Melikan for her patience, loyalty, and understanding, and for helping me shape and develop certain ideas before I wrote about them. I thank Linda Kramer for supporting my creative energy in a way no one else can, and for always being there when I need a little boost of confidence. I am grateful to Sally Allen for walking her talk with the angels and for sharing her insight into this recent boom of angel interest in ways that help me laugh about things that would otherwise make me sad. Thanks also to Karyn Martin-Kuri for sharing her knowledge and wisdom.

TERRY LYNN TAYLOR

INTRODUCTION

$\mathcal{W}$E WROTE this book because it was time.

At virtually every workshop or lecture Terry has given, someone has always requested her to sign their much-used copy of *Messengers of Light*, *Guardians of Hope*, or *Creating with the Angels*. Invariably she notices the dog-eared pages; invariably the owner informs her that he or she has come to rely upon the book as an oracle, opening it up at random for a "message" from the angels concerning some problem or question. And of course guidance always comes as a message that proves to be of uncanny service.

We found this so fascinating that we began to toy with the idea of writing a book with this end in mind. But we didn't really take the plunge until Carlos Santana told Terry that when he was ill in Germany, he took *Messengers of Light* into the bathtub with him and spontaneously opened it up to the part about healing. "The angels give us better and quicker answers than those X-rays," he mused.

And so we decided to collect some of those answers in the form of *Angel Wisdom*.

Everyone has a guardian angel. Your guardian angel is a guardian not only of you, but of the limitless capacity for happiness and potential for the positive that you have within you.

Angels—divine messengers of light—have always been among us, to give us hope and inspiration, to light our paths and make our steps lighter, to remind us that where there is life there is joy. And being human, we all need that reminder. Life can be confusing; as we encounter what we perceive to be obstacles or difficulties, as our paths become obscured by the shadows of our unlived dreams and unrealized desires, we occasionally need a flashlight and a nudge in the right direction.

This book is that nudge. You see, all of us have the "answers" to life's problems and caprices within us. *Angel Wisdom* is just the flashlight, beaming in on our intuition and illuminating our inner wisdom. *Angel Wisdom* contains angel-inspired meditations that can help you to better understand why certain things are happening in your life and how to harness the creative energy within you that will help you to make each of your experiences an exciting exercise in growth and change.

Angel Wisdom is designed to help you tune in to your "angel consciousness." When you have angel consciousness—the consciousness that we are divine, that we have a higher wisdom that will always operate for the good, that life is meant to be enjoyed, not endured—you actually develop a whole new way of seeing the world. As you develop angel consciousness, you begin to want to keep near you things that help the fires of that consciousness to burn brightly. A book like this does that. It gives us messages of hope, messages of light, a fresh and encouraging perspective on life.

The authors have a hard time staying in a bad mood, because we're always getting messages that remind us of how stupid we're being. "You don't have to be feeling this way," the angels remind us.

"But what if we want to?" we gripe.

"You can if you want to, but it's completely unnecessary," they good-naturedly inform us. And we have no choice but to listen. Because once you become angel conscious, you can't stay cranky. You just won't allow yourself to, because the angels won't allow you to.

We can always find meaning and joy in life, no matter how down we are, no matter what we've suffered. The key is to choose to find it. We hope that *Angel Wisdom* will help you to tap into your angel consciousness—to become more aware of the fun in things, to see the glass as half-full instead of half-empty, to regard life as a never-ending mystery and delight that you always have the power to make even more mysterious and more delightful.

MARY BETH CRAIN AND TERRY LYNN TAYLOR

HOW TO USE THIS BOOK

$\mathcal{Y}$OU MAY use this book, of course, any way you wish. You can read it as a daily meditation. You can read it as you would any other book, from beginning to end or, as an odd uncle of Mary Beth's used to do, from end to beginning. (He hated suspense of any kind.) You can keep it on your bookshelf without reading it at all, meaning to get to it one of these days, and we guarantee that, as someone—was it Orson Welles?—said he would "drink no wine before its time," so the proper time for you and this book to connect with each other will present itself, not a moment sooner or later. You can loan it out, and it will come back to you if and when it's supposed to. The angels are like that.

If, however, you'd like to use this book as a meditational tool, a workbook or an oracle, we offer the following suggestions.

As a meditational tool. You may simply wish to meditate or reflect upon the thoughts in this book. You can do this by reading it as your daily inspiration, or you can take a concept and focus simply on the word itself, using it as a sort of mantra. Sit with the word and let it become part of you—your breath, your blood, your consciousness, your unconsciousness. See what thoughts and connections come up for you as you meditate on this word.

After your meditation, you can go on to read the written meditation in the book. When you come to the exercise, you may indeed discover that through meditation your unconscious has provided many helpful suggestions as to the meaning of the concept in your life.

As a workbook for your issues. You may simply want to turn to a concept that you feel relates to a specific problem or question in your life. For example, if you want to feel more prosperous, you can turn to "Prosperity" and use the meditation and exercises accordingly. Or you can, each day, pick a concept that relates to an area of your life that you'd like to improve on, using that as your meditation/awareness guide for the day.

As an oracle. Oracles have existed since ancient times, either in the form of a person with the powers of a seer, or as methods of divination—such as the Chinese I Ching or the Norse Runes—that people could consult in order to be able to "see" into the future and plan their lives accordingly.

Angel Wisdom is not intended as a predictive device. It won't tell you the future; it is simply a method of bringing clarity to the issue at hand. But you may use it as an oracle of sorts if you open it at random, accepting the guidance that you receive as an "answer" to your immediate question, whatever it may be.

However you decide to use this book, we hope you enjoy it and profit by it.

ANGEL

WISDOM

$\mathcal{W}$ORTHINESS

An Angel Reminder: We are all worthy of attention from the angels.

Some people want to connect deeply with the angels, but they keep themselves at a distance because they feel they are not worthy to receive notice from such holy beings. Judging oneself as unworthy to receive what is rightfully ours by human birth is a very limited and egoistic way of seeing things. We must never forget that we are not just our minds or bodies. We are also souls that are in constant contact with the angels. The angels do not judge, they do not look for faults, they do not measure our holiness, and they would never ask us to prove our worth to them or to the world. We are worthy whether we know it or not.

If you feel a lack of worthiness at times, what things could you do to feel worthy and deserving? This is a trick question, because there really is nothing we can do to prove or attain worthiness. We don't need to change or do things differently. We only need to recognize and acknowledge that we already have value and we have the choice to make ourselves useful. Don't punish yourself for something that doesn't exist. Give yourself a break and know in your heart that you are more than worthy of divine attention.

An Angelic Reflection: I know that I stand on holy ground, always worthy of angelic attention.

$\mathcal{T}$HE SILENCE AFTERWARDS

An Angel Reminder:

"Be done and come home
To the silence afterwards . . .
The silence that lives in the grass
On the underside of each blade
And in the blue space between the
stones. . . ."

Rolf Jacobsen, The Silence Afterwards

How familiar are we with real silence? The "silence afterwards" that Norwegian poet Rolf Jacobsen describes is perhaps a metaphor for the silence of the soul united at last with God in profoundest contemplation. Making quiet spaces in our lives gives us a chance to move beyond the demands and limitations of our physical and mental selves and reconnect with the divine center. We can always find a few moments in our day to be silent and still, to quiet our minds and listen instead to the rustle of the leaves, the chirping of the birds, the whisper of the wind. Should we wish to, we can continue deeper into the silence afterwards, the mysterious quiet at the core of our beings that rejoices in the soundless sound of the universal heartbeat resonating deep within each of us.

Have some fun with silence. Grow still and become aware of the sounds around you. Listen to your breathing; see if you can hear your own heartbeat. Now try to grow even quieter. Become your breath and your heartbeat. Hear the sounds around you begin to fade, and see if you can move even deeper, into the silence afterwards.

An Angelic Reflection: In the silence afterwards I experience the bliss of divine perfection.

BEGINNING

An Angel Reminder: There are no endings, only new beginnings.

Beginnings are not always easy. But without them life would not exist. Sometimes we wish we could bypass the beginnings—the confusion, the frustrations that always come with just starting out, not being sure of the way, and knowing how far we still have to go. But if we remember that everything has a beginning—indeed, everything *is* a beginning—we can calmly move forward at our own pace. We can enjoy the process and understand that when we master one thing or attain one goal it must lead us directly on to the new challenge, where we begin all over again to learn, achieve, and live. The angels know, after all, that although we may think we want endings, completion, attainments, what we are really seeking is the excitement of a life in which each day is a new beginning.

What things in your life are at the beginning stage?
A new job? New relationship? New home? New personal
improvement program? Do you feel overwhelmed by
uncertainties? Or are you eager to explore all the
exciting possibilities that exist for you at this
wonderful time of beginning?

An Angelic Reflection: I accept each new beginning in my life as a new joy waiting to be experienced.

$\mathcal{A}$TTUNEMENT

An Angel Reminder: We can easily tune in to the frequency of the angels.

To attune means to bring into accord or harmony, to tune in to a frequency so that you can connect with a pure tone and eliminate interference. When we become attuned to the angelic frequency, we discover that there are many angels to listen to. We each have a personal guardian angel. There is a special angel for the country and state that we live in, the city, the street, even the trees around us. Some angels are in charge of groups, and others embody specific qualities like protection, courage, and wisdom and dispense them accordingly. Tuning in to the angel airwaves isn't as difficult as you may think. Sometimes all it takes to establish communication is the thought of an angel or the desire to connect with one. The most important thing to remember in attuning ourselves to the angels is that as our motives and desires become clarified and purified, our connections to the angels will become clearer and more refined.

Pick an angel to attune to. Have some writing paper nearby, in case a message comes through that you want to record. Close your eyes and mentally tune in to the angel of your choice. Do this simply by thought. Take your time and pay attention to the thoughts that begin to come to you. You may think that some of them are just your imagination, but what is your imagination if not the place where you discover and play with the truths of the universe?

An Angelic Reflection: I have the ability to attune myself to any angel for messages and guidance.

$\mathcal{G}$RACES

An Angel Reminder: Without gracefulness, all labor is in vain.

Greek philosophy

In Greek mythology the Graces were the goddesses associated with the sweetness and beauty of nature. They were virginal young maidens who embodied the qualities of gracefulness, charm, beauty, goodwill, and fun, and their job was to spread the spirit of enjoyment and appreciation of life. They were depicted as happy and free; they danced, sang, frolicked in fields and fountains, and by their very natures inspired poetry, music, art, and other elevated pursuits of the soul. They were also on call to the mighty Athena, goddess of storms and battles, for help in handling the heavier aspects of existence, both mortal and immortal. In other words, the Graces knew how to have a roaring good time, and the Greeks considered this knowledge essential to the smooth running of life.

Think about the different meanings of the word grace: *to be in a state of grace, a condition of being in tune with and favored by the Divine; saying grace, an expression of gratitude to God; the quality of grace—gentleness, delicacy, elegance, and harmoniousness of movement. How can you make your life more grace-full?*

An Angelic Reflection: I bring the spirit of grace to all that I do.

SHARING

An Angel Reminder: The angels are always sharing God's love with us.

In understanding the concept of sharing, it's important to distinguish between sharing and giving. Pure giving is the process of bestowing a present or part of ourselves on someone else, expecting no reciprocation. The recipient of our giving is free to use our gift in any way he or she chooses. When we share, however, we bond with another to become an equal part of the energy exchange. We often say of a couple that they are sharing a life together. People come together to share ideals and causes. Roommates share a house. A meal can be shared. We are meant to share the earth with all of life. There is, of course, an element of giving in sharing: sharing what we possess in the true spirit of graciousness means offering what we can spare, with a pure heart free of expectation, to benefit the whole. If you share something with the desire to control others or to create a need in them, you will not benefit anyone. The angels share with no strings attached. And when we respond by sharing our energy, love, and gratitude, we are strengthening the bond between earth and heaven.

Think about the things we can't really own that we share with others—the birds, the sun, the moon, the stars, the air, God's love. When the universe shares with you, do you share in kind?

An Angelic Reflection: All of life involves sharing. Even breathing is an act of sharing between the earth and myself. I will become more aware of what is being shared with me and more open to sharing with others.

ℬOOKMARK

An Angel Reminder: No strength is greater than calmness, no power greater than peace.

The angels have a favorite poem, written by St. Teresa of Avila, that they pass on to us. Entitled "Bookmark," it is, in fact, a reference point, a page to return to whenever we have allowed our fears to intrude upon our serenity.

> Let nothing disturb thee
> Nothing afright thee;
> All things are passing;
> God never changeth;
> Patient endurance
> Attaineth to all things;
> Who God possesseth
> In nothing is wanting;
> Alone God sufficeth.

Remember that there is a naturally calm place within you where you can always find the peaceful energy of God and the angels. Whenever you are worried or fearful, know that you can always return to that bookmark in the pages of your life.

An Angelic Reflection: I draw on the angels' calmness to keep my perspective balanced.

WHO AM I?

An Angel Reminder: Knowing yourself is a taller order than you think.

If someone were to ask you, "Who are you?" what would you reply? Would you give your name, address, and Social Security number? Would you state your occupation? Would you list your most appealing qualities? To the angels, the question "Who am I?" has both an infinite number of answers and a single answer. We are, on the one hand, constantly changing entities, responding to different forces around us. We are never the same from one moment to the next; we have varying moods and sides to our personalities; our beliefs are altered by our experiences; we may at any moment discover new talents and abilities that completely alter the way we perceive ourselves. On the other hand, we are no self at all but rather part of the Divine Self, the universal oneness in which all ego disappears. In other words, say the angels, don't become attached to any one idea about yourself, and give your ego an occasional rest from having to carry the burden of your identity.

Reflect, if you like, upon the following Sufi meditation on our essential human nature:

> *I am not the body; I am not the senses*
> *I am not the mind*
> *I am not this; I am not that*
> *What then am I? What is the self?*
> *It is in the body; It is in everybody*
> *It is everywhere; It is the All*
> *It is Self. I am It. Absolute Oneness.*

An Angelic Reflection: I am more than the sum of my parts.

LEGACY

An Angel Reminder: What we take with us is what we leave behind.

A woman whose beloved husband of thirty-two years died of cancer found that her terrible sense of loss began to diminish when people she ran into would talk of her husband. Everyone who knew him, it seems, had a beautiful story to tell of his kindness and compassion. He had given money, unasked, to those he knew were undergoing hardship. He had given his services as a mechanic free of charge to others. Many of these stories were completely new to her, for, being a modest man, her husband had never mentioned them. But the more people she talked to, the more present her husband seemed to become, as she realized that bits and pieces of him were continuously living on in the lives and memories of others.

What stories of you would you like to leave behind when you exit the earth? Begin planning your "living legacy," becoming more conscious of the effect you have on others and how the things that you do live far beyond the moment and can touch the lives of more people than you could know.

An Angelic Reflection: The seeds of my actions take root in the hearts and lives of everyone with whom I come in contact.

$\mathcal{E}$BB AND FLOW

An Angel Reminder: "To everything there is a season, and a time to every purpose under heaven."

Ecclesiastes 3:3 (King James Version)

Ideally we want everything to go smoothly. Wouldn't life be great, after all, if we were always on a roll and never had to worry about impediments to our progress? But the angels know that the secret to progress is being able to accept the natural rhythm of the universe, which is ebb and flow. Flow is a time of action and visible productivity; ebbing away signals a decrease in active energy and a time to retreat and incubate. Ebb and flow correspond to the Chinese symbol of the two complementary energies of the universe, the yin/yang or the receptive/creative. One is not negative, the other positive; they just *are,* and each has its appropriate time under heaven. For instance, in times of decreased energy and activity it may look as though we aren't being productive, but we may, in fact, be even more productive on another level. Allowing ourselves to rest and rejuvenate helps us to forge a deeper connection to the angels, who often speak more clearly to us when we are in a state of stillness.

Reflect upon situations of ebb and flow in your life. If there are days when you just "can't seem to get anything done," don't try. If it's at all possible, relax, rest, and let thoughts and ideas come to you. Realize that the energy of "ebb" is just as valuable in its own way as the energy of "flow," and get into it!

An Angelic Reflection: I work with, not against, the natural rhythm of the universe.

COMPLETION

An Angel Reminder: In completion we discover both liberation and personal power.

When life starts getting out of hand, it is often because of things left undone. We start one project and another intrudes. We mean to get to something but are forever, it seems, distracted by other, more immediate concerns. Before we know it, the pileup of unfinished business has become an avalanche. The angels believe wholeheartedly in completion, for it is only by tying up the loose ends that the unraveling can stop and the renewal can begin. Once we make the commitment to do the undone, the angels will be more than happy to help us become more disciplined, patient, optimistic, and trusting in ourselves and the natural order of things.

Do you have things that need to be completed? List them in terms of priorities. Don't become discouraged or paralyzed; instead, resolve to take just one action a day that will bring you closer to your goal. Ask the angels to inspire you with ideas and free you from fear and concern, and know that it will all get done.

An Angelic Reflection: As I learn the secret of completion, I harness the power that enables me to realize all of my desires and objectives.

GOSSIP

An Angel Reminder: "Be kind, for everyone you meet is facing a hard battle."

Plato

There is no way to get away from gossip; people are interested in one another, and regardless of what you do there is a good chance you are the topic of a gossip session somewhere. Even if all you do is avoid people and stay in your house, that fact alone can provide grist for the neighborhood gossip mill. Many problems come from gossiping. Gossip can hurt others and damage their reputations if it involves vicious rumors. Our TV news is basically gossip these days, and it is good to be aware of that. People who gossip might be a lot better off using the time improving themselves or at least looking at why they are so interested in someone else's life. Look beyond gossip and realize that things are not as bad as they seem and people are not as horrible as the gossip mongers make them out to be.

The angels would never gossip, but if they ever did, what would they be saying about you? Use your imagination and pretend you are listening in on two angels talking about you. The best way to avoid the pitfalls of gossip is to learn to process wisely the information that comes out of your mouth. And it never hurts to remember that others you gossip with won't really trust you because there is always the chance that you will do it to them.

An Angelic Reflection: I honor and respect the people around me by gossiping about their positive qualities.

SHORTCUTS

An Angel Reminder: The fastest and cheapest course may turn out to be the most expensive to repair.

Shortcuts are designed to get us to a destination in less time. The question the angels want us to ask is, what are we gaining—or losing—in the process? Sometimes a shortcut is, indeed, a more efficient use of our time and effort, conserving energy that can better be applied elsewhere. But taking shortcuts can sometimes cost us more. If we use a shortcut to avoid necessary expenditure—if our saving in minutes and dollars results in an inferior product—we are likely to find ourselves back where we started. Then we will have less than we started with in terms of time, energy, money, and credibility. The angels approve of efficiency and frugality, but they caution us never to make them into gods, paying homage to them at the expense of quality and substance.

What kinds of shortcuts have been helpful to you? Which ones have you regretted? Reflect upon when and why you have taken shortcuts and what you learned from the experience.

An Angelic Reflection: I am aware of the difference between a shortcut and shortchanging myself and others.

$\mathcal{T}$ALENT

An Angel Reminder: Each and every one of us is born with talent.

Is talent given selectively by God, bestowed upon some people, while others come into the world empty-handed? The angels and God do not favor some of us over others. Each and every one of us has some sort of talent, a special ability in some area. While society may place a high value on certain abilities and skills, the angels view all talents with equal appreciation. To them, a talent for compassion, cheerfulness, thoughtfulness, honesty, humor, and any other angelic quality that improves life is just as, if not more, valuable than the highest artistic or athletic accomplishments or the greatest business success. And we can always develop talent, as long as we do not allow ourselves to become inhibited by labels or criticism. Even if certain people have put us down or discounted our potential, the angels are always there to applaud our efforts and give us positive reinforcement for having the courage to discover and improve our best selves.

What are your main talents? Do you think that you were born with them? Or did some of your talents develop with time and practice? Do you wish you were more talented at certain things? Remembering that we are what we think, call upon the angels as your talent agents, and ask them to send you inspiration to improve your abilities in any area of your choosing.

An Angelic Reflection: I appreciate my abilities in all areas and I am open to exploring the full range of my talents.

UNPREDICTABILITY

An Angel Reminder: "Scientific progress depends heavily on the unplanned collision of ideas."

Eli Sercarz, UCLA immunologist

Many of us feel uncomfortable with the idea of unpredictability. We want to be able to plan our lives; if we don't know what's ahead, we feel helpless, lost, too vulnerable. But the angels honor unpredictability as the source of new vision, insight—and order. In science, for instance, the "unplanned collision of ideas" gives way to planned formulas for improving the lot of humankind. It is often through the unpredictable that the angels do their best work; we may, for instance, find the ideas and answers we've been seeking in the most unlikely places. So the angels encourage us to welcome the lively energy of unpredictability into our lives, to remain open to the unplanned inspirations and solutions that might, if we're not too scared to take a peek, be just around the corner.

Think about the role the unpredictable has played in your life. What wonderful experiences have you had that were never planned? How much do you think you can really predict— that is, control—in terms of your future?

An Angelic Reflection: I seek not to predict, but to know through experience.

$\mathcal{R}$EPAIR

An Angel Reminder: In the eyes of the angels, no human being is ever damaged beyond repair.

The word *damaged* is often used to describe people who had a horrible childhood or who, as adults, have been treated treacherously by another and have not been able to get over the emotional pain. But to the angels, *damage* is not a word to be used for human beings. When something is damaged it loses its value and usefulness. This never happens to a human being, because all of us are valuable and useful. Those who are led to believe they are damaged may never try to repair their lives. *Repair* means to put into good or sound condition, to put right. We are all capable of repairing any damage that has been done to us, and we can begin by calling in the angels, who are top quality repair people. They know how to spiritually compensate us for loss, how to heal and renew us, as soon as we start believing in wholeness instead of damage. And remember: when something has been repaired, the weak link becomes even stronger and more useful than it was originally.

If you consider yourself damaged and worn-out by the world, ask the angels to help you design a personal repair kit. It may include meditation, Twelve-Step programs, completing a creative project, volunteering service, and so forth. Make your first step changing your belief in damage into a belief in repair, and your second step a commitment to your future of strength and wholeness.

An Angelic Reflection: With each step forward on the path of spiritual restoration, I will be not only repaired but also renewed.

$\mathcal{T}$HE NEXT WORLD

An Angelic Reflection: We can't be there until we can be here.

Some people spend a lot of time thinking and planning for the trip to that ultimate one-way destination, the next world. They see the beyond as a place of eternal joy, beside which the earth pales in comparison. So they try to renounce earthly "pleasures" or even to welcome suffering as redemption insurance. Or they may simply adopt an attitude of waiting it out here in the "vale of tears," bags packed and ready to go, not a moment too soon. But the angels warn us that if we haven't taken the time to live to our fullest, we may be in for a big surprise when we alight from that sweet chariot and discover that we're back in school, repeating the classes we unwittingly flunked in Earth College. It is only when we understand that the kingdom of heaven is indeed within—in our capacity to create love, joy, peace, and awareness on earth—that we can take our rightful places in paradise.

If the universe were to hand you a report card, how do you think you'd be doing so far in the courses of joy, humor, love, light, kindness, and gratitude? Don't be afraid to give the angels a call if you need some tutoring to get your grades up.

An Angelic Reflection: I'm aiming to graduate from Earth College magna cum laude—with highest praise.

𝒫HILOSOPHERS

An Angel Reminder: When we search for truth with the angels, an extra light has been turned on in our minds, and we will find that we understand a new common sense.

Each of us in our own special way is a genuine philosopher. Philosophy by definition is the search for understanding of the basic truths and principles of the universe, of life, of morals, and of human perception. The word *philosophy* comes from the Greek word *philosophos,* which means to love wisdom. If you love wisdom and seek truth and a deeper understanding of the universe, then you are a philosopher. The angels see us all as philosophers, and they like us to seek higher truth. Begin to think of others as philosophers. In this way you will respect each person as a great and original thinker and learn many new things about loving wisdom.

Take a moment to philosophize with the angels. Visualize an extra light being switched on in your mind, allowing you to see things in a new and deeper way. When we seek understanding with the angels, we will get to know ourselves as true philosophers. Accept your role as a philosopher and take time to philosophize at least twice a day. Seek others with interesting philosophies.

An Angelic Reflection: As I search for my own understanding of truth and wisdom, I will never forget that others have their own search and we can respect one another on the way.

Giveaway

An Angel Reminder: The Lord giveth; the Lord taketh away; the Lord giveth back in new form.

The Native American practice of the giveaway is an exercise in gratitude and faith. In the giveaway ceremony, a family gives all of its possessions up to the rest of the tribe and the Great Spirit. The tribe then replenishes the necessities they so freely relinquished. The giveaway symbolized people's acknowledging that their possessions are not really their own. Everything belongs to the Creator, and it is up to the Creator to decide when we will receive and when we will have to give back to the universe. But God will never leave us wanting, for in taking something back from us, God will always give us something new in its stead.

Try practicing the spirit of giveaway in your life. If someone admires something of yours, such as a piece of clothing or jewelry, give it to that person. If someone needs something from you, give it freely. As you give away in gratitude, try to understand that what you have really belongs to all, and do not seek anything in return. Then note what is given back to you and in what form.

An Angelic Reflection: I am happy to be able to give back to the universe even a small bit of what has been given to me.

IT'S A WONDERFUL LIFE

An Angel Reminder: We are continually searching for truth and continually finding it in the noble actions of others.

Most of us are undoubtedly familiar with what has probably become the most popular Christmas movie of all time, *It's a Wonderful Life.* This inspirational classic follows the path of George Bailey, a human who throughout his life has sacrificed his own desires for the betterment of others. When George finds himself facing prison and financial ruin because of the business error of his bumbling uncle, he decides to make the ultimate sacrifice of his own life to spare his family shame and make sure they receive his life insurance policy. But God, hearing the prayers of the many who love George, sends an angel to prevent him from committing suicide and to show him how much poorer a place the world would have been had he never been born. *It's a Wonderful Life* relates several eternal truths. One is that our mere presence has a vast influence on the world. Another is that by aspiring to love and compassion, not wealth and power, we acquire the riches of heaven on earth. And a third is that the angels are always listening to the most urgent pleas of our souls.

Pretend that you are the main character in It's a Wonderful Life. *How have you influenced the lives of others? How much poorer would the world be if you had never been born? What effect would you like to have on the world from this moment forth?*

An Angelic Reflection: I value and respect my singular presence here on earth.

𝒫OSITIVE THINKERS

An Angel Reminder: Positive thinking requires seeing life in a clear light, without lies or pretense.

Norman Vincent Peale wrote a groundbreaking book in 1951 entitled *The Power of Positive Thinking,* and for the last forty years we've heard a lot about the power that positive thinking brings. Positive thinkers have to be creative and intelligent in their thinking. Positive thinkers look beyond difficulties for creative solutions, seeing the difficulties in a clear light so that clear solutions will surface. On the other hand, negative thinkers see difficulties in dark hues of hopeless despair and become overwhelmed and defeated by difficulties. We always have the choice to turn the lights on and take a good look at what we are dealing with, and we are always free to assume the best.

Positive thinkers do not lie to themselves. Often people set out to practice positive thinking, and they end up denying difficulties, disregarding pain, and practicing grandiose wishful thinking. All this is only a form of positive lying. Think about how positive your own thinking is and find ways to strengthen your resolve against the negative, without lies or pretense. The angels will help you.

An Angelic Reflection: I see the world around me in bright reflections of hope and angel light. I have the power to know what is best.

$\mathcal{F}$ORTUNE-TELLING

An Angel Reminder: The future is not ours to see, but it is ours to create.

On television and in magazines these days we find many advertisements for psychic hot lines. In an uncertain world it may seem comforting to have someone predict your future, but the angels see it another way. They know that true comfort comes from imagination, creativity, and trust. If we live imaginatively and creatively and leave the rest to heaven, we will be too busy in the present to have time to worry about the future. Seeking information about the future from another human may mean we are avoiding the responsibility of making our own decisions. The angels may not give you past-life information or foretell future events, but they will give you all the guidance and inspiration you need to make this moment count.

If you want insight into a problem or you feel you need to know future events, give yourself a psychic reading. Write down your questions and answer them the way you might want the future to turn out. Put this paper away for a few months or even a year. When you get it out again, have a good laugh with the angels, as you notice that some of the things you wanted no longer appeal to you and you realize that, with trust, patience, imagination, and determination, we always eventually get what we really want.

An Angelic Reflection: As I live in the present to the best of my ability, I create the future I am meant to have.

REUNION

An Angel Reminder: What a gift it is to be reunited with the angels.

If we feel separated from nature, and if we believe that we are separate from heaven, then our lives will become a quest to be reunited with that to which we know we belong. Love is the bridge that allows us to feel we have finally been reunited. When we fall deeply in love with another human it feels as if we knew that person before and now have a sacred reunion. To become reunited with heaven and nature we must learn to love them again. The feeling of separateness that we experience is an illusion; we have never been separated from nature, since that is impossible. And heaven is always present in our hearts.

Think of any area in your life that you feel you have been separated from and yearn to be reunited with. It may be that you long to have those fresh and innocent thoughts that you did as a child, or it may be that you long for a reunion with your true love. Remember that what or whom you wish to be reunited with is still within you. Even if you have not yet met your true love on the earth, you are still a part of him or her. The angels will help you reunite with your true self and true path, and all other parts of your life will unite in joy.

An Angelic Reflection: I will unite my spirit with the angels and remember those sweet feelings I had as a child, when the angels were my favorite playmates.

ZEN THERAPY

An Angel Reminder: The less self-centered, the more centered.

A story is told by Paul Reps in his book *Zen Flesh, Zen Bones:* A pompous university professor once had tea with the Japanese Zen master Nan-In, who proceeded to fill his cup—and then to keep on pouring. When the horrified professor pointed out that the cup was overflowing, Nan-In replied, "Like this cup, you are full of your own opinions and speculations. How can I show you Zen unless you first empty your cup?"

Many people today go into therapy. Those who truly desire to receive insight into their behaviors will benefit from the experience. But others may use therapy as an excuse to become even more self-absorbed. The Zen masters had no patience for those who wasted their time and were only interested in discussing themselves or their own viewpoints. If one was genuinely interested in becoming enlightened, one first had to empty the cellar of one's mind of the old junk of preconceptions and narcissistic fascination. Only then could the light of new awareness penetrate one's being.

If you are active in or considering therapy, a Twelve-Step program, or any other consciousness-raising endeavors, take a moment to examine your motivations and expectations. Do you really want to change and improve your life? Or do you more enjoy the sound of your own voice? Would you be angry or grateful if your therapist filled your teacup until it overflowed back onto you?

An Angelic Reflection: I try not to be too full of myself.

$\mathcal{W}$ISHES

An Angel Reminder: Be careful what you wish for when the angels are within earshot.

Witnessing the first star of the night or a shooting star is a good time to make a wish. On our birthdays we make a wish when all the candles on the birthday cake are blown out. Who can resist throwing a coin into a wishing well? This is a ritual of following a wish with an offering. Wishes were quite important to us in childhood. We still wish, even when our intellectual minds tell us that wishing is childish. When we wish for something we are acknowledging that we feel worthy to receive the fulfillment of our deepest desires. Wishing is like a magical prayer, and we must be conscious and careful of what we wish for and how.

Step out in the early evening when the first stars appear in the twilight. Find the brightest star and make a wish. Hold a vision of your wish for a moment in your mind, then thank the stars in the heavens and know that your highest good will always be done.

An Angelic Reflection: I wish for peace and goodwill to run rampant in the world.

COMPETITION

An Angel Reminder: Let us cheer one another on instead of trampling one another down in competition.

Competition is an affront to creative energy; it limits our vision and narrows our choices. Competition, contrary to popular belief, does not bring out the best in us. Rather, it causes us to see people as obstacles, mere blocks to something we are trying to achieve or win, and this way of thinking is dehumanizing. If winning is our only goal, we cannot possibly enjoy the process of an activity because our minds are set on doing something better than the next person. Life is not a competitive journey, and those who think so never find out who they really are; they find out only how they compare to others. The angels don't understand why humans would do any activity designed to make one person happy at the expense of making everyone else sad and unsure of themselves.

Greatness comes from going at one's own pace, not from forcing oneself to do better than someone else. Think about the last time you were involved in a competitive situation. Did you feel extra creative and worthy? Probably not. Try giving up a competitive situation in your life. You will be surprised at the fun you will have. Then pity the poor souls who keep trying to compete with you; they'll have nothing to win.

An Angelic Reflection: I do not need a competitive spirit; I welcome originality and cooperation into my life.

Separation

An Angel Reminder: Absence makes the heart grow not only fonder but also stronger.

Sometimes we are forced to be apart from what we desire. At these difficult times the angels are always near us to help us grow stronger in patience, faith, and trust in the self. When we are called upon to experience separation from someone or something to which we are greatly attached, it can be a call to regeneration. As a snake sheds its old skin and emerges in new form, as a caterpillar must break free of its cocoon in order to become a butterfly, so we may have to discard what is no longer useful in order to make room for the new. If the separation is only temporary, it may be an opportunity to pause and reevaluate our attachments, to take a break and attend to other duties and dreams we may have been neglecting—in short, to become reacquainted with ourselves.

If you are undergoing a painful separation in your life, try to listen to its message and adapt to the new demands on your soul. You may need to retreat a bit, to go inward and reflect upon why this has occurred and what opportunities might open up for you as a result. Resist the urge to cling to the past, and wait patiently for reasons to reveal themselves.

An Angelic Reflection: Separation may give me the chance to rediscover myself.

$\mathcal{D}$EVOTION

**An Angel Reminder: "People think I am disciplined. It is
not discipline—it is devotion. There is a great difference."**

Luciano Pavarotti

Luciano Pavarotti explains that in order to be a great
artist, one must set priorities. "Many times I would like to
go out with my friends, to have dinner, wine. But if I have
a concert the next day I stay home. I do not spend time on
the phone; I give my voice rest, and I stay quiet. If one
wants to be a singer, one must be devoted to it. Not disciplined, but devoted." What a wise distinction Pavarotti
makes. Discipline is a system of regulation; devotion is the
ultimate dedication to someone or something that you
love. Of course, devotion may require discipline; when we
put energy into the object of our devotion we cannot afford to waste it on other, less important activities or to
allow others to drain our most valuable resource. But devotion does not mean total self-denial or self-flagellation.
Pavarotti knows that there is a time to be with friends, to
talk on the phone, to relax—but that time is not before a
concert. The angels encourage becoming devoted to the
thing we strive for above all, for then, sooner or later, it
will surely be ours.

*Is there anything that you are devoted to? Anything you
would like to become devoted to? What things would you
have to sacrifice? What would you gain as a result?*

**An Angelic Reflection: I am willing to set the necessary
priorities to achieve the goals that are most important
to me.**

EXPECTATIONS

An Angel Reminder: Don't expect anything from an ass but a kick.

Old Irish saying

The wisdom of the old Irish saying on expectations has a down-to-earth ring to it. But the problem with expectations is that they too often are not down to earth. Rather, they are the result of our own hopes, wishes, and projections. We want people to be a certain way and so we have our own agenda for their behavior, which is a sure way to guarantee our eventual disappointment. If people don't live up to our expectations, it isn't their fault— it's ours, for expecting them to be something they aren't. The angels caution us to ground our expectations in reality, to base them on what we see, not what we want to see. That way we will not only spare ourselves disillusionment, we will also allow others the freedom and right to be themselves, whether they be asses or angels.

If you often find yourself disappointed by others, reflect upon how your expectations may be setting you up for disappointment. How can you change the situation? Ask the angels to help you become more realistic in your expectations and less attached to your perceptions of how people should behave.

An Angelic Reflection: I see people for who and what they are and create beneficial, not disappointing, scenarios for myself and others.

$\mathcal{F}$AITH

An Angel Reminder: "Faith is the state of being ultimately concerned . . . and the acceptance of the promise of ultimate fulfillment."

Paul Tillich

Many of us don't understand what faith is, confusing it with belief or with rigid adherence to religious doctrine. But faith goes far beyond concept or definition; it is an experience—a calling, in fact—that takes us out of the realm of intellect and into the realm of inner knowing. When theologian and philosopher Paul Tillich speaks of faith as "ultimate concern," he is talking about the thing that is of all-consuming value to a human being, the object of his or her spiritual passion, the thing that produces "the centered movement of the whole personality to something of ultimate meaning and significance." Whatever we have faith in, we put our energy and commitment into. If you have faith that you will lose weight, you will direct your energy toward that goal, knowing that you will meet it. If the angels and living an angelic life are your ultimate concern, you will direct your energy toward that purpose, not fearing disillusionment but expecting fulfillment.

What are your ultimate concerns? In what areas would you like your faith to be strong? Clarify your desires and what you want out of life. Then use your imagination to visualize the fulfillment of these desires, and practice the art of effortless knowing, asking the angels to help you cast out doubts and worries and keep you filled with clarity, positive energy, and commitment.

An Angelic Reflection: I have faith in divine love and wisdom, and I trust the angels to connect me to it.

ENJOYMENT

An Angel Reminder: Enjoyment of life is the ultimate gratitude to God.

The capacity for enjoyment is natural to us. But how often is our potential for enjoyment marred by the nagging voice of guilt? We should be working, should be worrying, should be exercising. After we get the shoulds out of the way, then we can enjoy ourselves. This attitude amuses the angels, who know, of course, that as long as we subscribe to the theory of the shoulds, we will never eliminate them from our lives. Enjoyment is not a reward for shoulds accomplished; it is a necessary activity that, when regularly engaged in, maintains our connection to divine love. The angels suggest that we take the time each day to practice enjoyment, until it becomes a natural part of our lives and our interactions with others. Who knows—that may turn out to be our greatest contribution to humanity.

To keep yourself emotionally and spiritually fit, set aside some time each day for an enjoyment workout. Instead of getting all the shoulds out of the way, do something you enjoy first and refuse to feel guilty about it. Note how your attitudes about life begin to change.

An Angelic Reflection: As I make enjoyment a priority, my life becomes even more balanced and productive.

CONTENTMENT

An Angel Reminder: Things can always be worse.

The angels define contentment as follows: A man loses his paycheck and says, "Thank God I still have my job." He loses his job and says, "Thank God for my home, which is paid for." He loses his home and says, "Thank God for my wonderful wife." He loses his wife and says, "Thank God for the time we had together." He loses a leg and says, "Thank God I still have one good leg." He loses the other leg and says, "Thank God I am still alive." He dies in his sleep and says, "Thank God I died in peace." *That* is contentment.

What are some of the things you are contented with in your life? What are some of the blessings you haven't noticed? Notice what happens when you start taking some time each day to simply be contented.

An Angelic Reflection: I know that while I strive for greater joy, I can still be happy with what I already have.

$\mathcal{P}$OLITE

An Angel Reminder: Politeness can be a power tool.

Polite behavior means acting in a way that is courteous, refined, and shows good manners. We can use politeness at those very times we feel like being the opposite to deflect an otherwise messy situation. When you find yourself with a person who rubs you the wrong way or who lives life in a way that repels you, try being extremely polite. It may feel uncomfortable at first, but the more you practice and see the amazing results, the more fun you will have doing your polite act. The power comes in keeping the situation light and considerate no matter what happens—and who could fault you for that? The angels truly enjoy polite actions, and they will always provide a little extra humor when needed. If being polite feels phony to you, remember that you will have plenty of opportunities to be your real self around the real people you adore. If you try politeness and it seems to fail, use the next best thing—your feet—and walk away.

Next time you find yourself around people who are less than pleasant, practice being polite. If an issue comes up that is contentious, simply agree. If someone throws you an insult, catch it and say thank you; then offer a cup of tea. Remember that killing with kindness, in the long run, will make you feel much better than uttering a sarcastic or angry remark that brings only fleeting relief. Ask the angels to help you have fun in all situations regardless of who is there.

An Angelic Reflection: In a situation that feels out of control because of the behavior of others, I can be truest to myself by blocking negative energy with the power of politeness.

$\mathcal{Y}$OUR QUESTION

An Angel Reminder: A question is a re-quest for information or a quest for an answer.

We all have our own questions of life, and we must learn to live with our questions, remaining alert for the information that will pull the pieces of our puzzle together. Your answers and the information you quest after will come to you in many interesting ways, especially with the angels active in your life. Each person you meet, each problem you encounter, and your everyday experiences of life hold answers to your request. The angels hold the answers to many of our questions, and their answers can surprise us when we discover them.

You have a question that is yours and yours alone. It is the question of your life and your purpose here on earth. Don't be afraid to ask it. Look for answers in your dreams, in the beauty of the clouds, and wherever fine books are sold. Play with information, live with your questions, let each new answer lead to a new question. If you do this your mind will stay forever young.

An Angelic Reflection: I will never stop asking my questions.

STAMINA

An Angel Reminder: The angels give our minds true staying power.

Stamina means not just the power of physical endurance, but also moral endurance. The word comes from a Latin word meaning thread, *stamen,* also known as the pollen-producing reproductive organ of the flower. Physical stamina comes from a well-cared-for body that circulates energy well. Moral stamina comes from a well-cared-for mind and also from the angels. The angels are the thread of energy that allows us stamina. With stamina we are able to withstand prolonged mental and physical strain without losing our power. The moment power is lost and our morale is dampened, we no longer have stamina, we simply have strain. Keeping things as simple as you can in your life will allow you all the stamina you need to produce great things.

Real staying power comes from knowing how much we can do and paying attention to signals our bodies and minds send to us when it is time to quit. If we push beyond our own limits of stamina, then whatever we are doing will suffer. Two keys for increased stamina are living simply and living consciously. And it never hurts to practice and exercise to keep yourself in shape physically and mentally.

An Angelic Reflection: I will create the energy I need to do my personal best by keeping my life simple and full of angel love.

CHILDREN

An Angel Reminder: And a little child shall lead them.

It has been said that children are closest to the angels because they still remember them. Many believe that the reason children often have angel experiences is that they were with the angels before they were born and that their minds and souls, not yet scarred by the adult afflictions of skepticism and cynicism, are still receptive to their old friends. The angels want us to treat our children as they do—to respect their pure wisdom, allow their imaginations to soar, and honor their individuality. We do not, after all, own our children. They are neither our possessions nor our security. We are here to love them, guide them, learn from them—and to let them go when it is time.

How might the children you have or know be close to the angels? What can you learn from them in the way of lightheartedness, curiosity, fun, honesty, imaginativeness, and other angelic attributes?

An Angelic Reflection: As I strengthen my connection to my children—and to the child within—I grow closer to the angels.

$\mathcal{P}$RAYER

An Angelic Reminder: "The only way to reach God through prayer is to cleanse your mind of all negation . . . and fill it with thoughts of love, service, and joyous expectation."

Paramahansa Yogananda

An endless array of books explain what prayer is and how to pray. Should it be a communal or a personal affair? Is petitionary prayer permissible or selfish? Should we pray for miracles or only for what God wants for us? All of these questions may be valid, but the bottom line, to the angels, is that prayer is, first and foremost, a creative means of expressing ourselves to God and, in so doing, communicating with our higher selves. How and where to pray is up to us. We may have specific requests we'd like to share with God. We may want to reflect upon the Bible or meditate on some aspect of the Divine. We may want to pray in church or synagogue, in the woods, on the beach, in our bedrooms. One famous prayer enthusiast, the evangelist Frances Gardner, fervently maintained that her best praying was done in the bathtub! The important thing is that prayer should be a positive, energy-renewing force in our lives, bringing us closer to the joyful reality of divine love.

Call a prayer meeting with the angels. Invite your guardian angel, or any angels you like, to join with you. Pray in any way you like, and be aware of any images, words, and ideas that come to you.

An Angelic Reflection: Through prayer my mind, heart, spirit, and soul are acquainted with the divine truths that bring joy, clarity, and peace.

*S*PIRITUAL FUEL

**An Angel Reminder: Light is our spiritual fuel. The
more light we radiate from the centers of our souls, the
closer we travel to the realm of heaven.**

The soul imprint, the essence of who we are, is a vari-
able of light. God's word is said to be light unto our
path. God and the angels are often thought of in terms
of light. When people "see" angels they actually experience the effects of divine light. True angel consciousness is a matter of turning on the lights in our minds,
bringing our lives to light, and living in the light of
truth. Choices involving love strengthen our light;
choices made out of fear dim our reflections. Our own
frequency of light depends upon our conscious spiritual choices. The higher the choice, the higher
frequency of light we radiate.

*When we need strength and spiritual fuel in any situa-
tion, what we need to do is concentrate on the light that is
within us. Meditate on the light that makes up your
third eye. See the light in your mind and learn how to
control it. We can direct this light throughout our beings
and allow it to vibrate at a high enough rate to make us invisible to others who are not vibrating in love and light. If
you believe in unlimited possibilities, then you will want
to believe that you can raise your vibration high enough to
see into the angels' realm.*

**An Angelic Reflection: Light is my spiritual fuel. I will
choose actions that will increase my light and take me
closer to heaven.**

*A*BUNDANCE

An Angel Reminder: True abundance is the ability to see the abundance that is already ours.

The philosophy of all banks may be reduced to an old saying: "What's yours is mine, and what's mine is me own." The Bank of Angels, however, operates on the principle that there is a never-ending supply of abundance in the universe and that it belongs to each and every one of us. From the beauty and majesty of the earth itself to the various riches, both little and big, that all of us have acquired simply through being alive, abundance is a daily, infinite reality. And through the qualities of awareness, appreciation, imagination, discipline, and expectation—all of which are free for the taking at the Bank of Angelica—we can create abundance whenever we need it. Of course, we sometimes yearn for abundance or envy it in others. That's okay with the angels, who know that every once in a while, being human, we will experience feelings of emptiness, frustration, and deprivation—until we agree to accept the abundance that is already ours and the power that's within us to increase its existence in our lives.

Think of the abundance that already exists in your life— love, good friends, talents, good health, beautiful home. In which areas would you like to feel more abundant? Close your eyes, breathe deeply, and see abundance coming to you in these areas. Ideas and ways to realize this vision will begin to come to you.

An Angelic Reflection: Before me is a banquet table laden with marvelous dishes, prepared and served by the angels. If I feel deprived, it is only because I haven't allowed myself to taste life's possibilities.

CONTENTS UNDER PRESSURE

An Angel Reminder: Open carefully.

Have you ever felt like the contents of your life have been dumped on the ground before you? That everything you believed in and depended on has suddenly been turned upside down? If so, you have been given a wonderful gift, because now you can choose which items to keep in your life and which ones to leave on the ground to be recycled and transmuted. Maybe you have been carrying some items around for too long and the heavy load finally broke open, causing the contents of your life to scatter. Every once in a while life seems to shake us up and knock loose a few things we have become too attached to. Next time it happens, ask the angels to help you pick up the pieces.

We can take stock of the contents we are carrying around before they are dumped out before us. Think of what contents in your life may be under pressure and think of ways you could relieve the pressure or get rid of it. The angels want you to lighten your load and enjoy some levity.

An Angelic Reflection: I will seek to relieve the pressure in my life in natural ways.

$\mathcal{T}$AKING CARE OF OUR OWN

An Angel Reminder: The angels take care of their own.

One question often raised in value clarification classes is, if you had to choose who was going to be saved from a fatal accident and you were given three choices, what would you do? One, you could save an entire airplane full of five hundred people you don't know who live halfway around the world; two, a busload of twenty people from a nearby community, whom you probably don't know; and three, a car with the father of a family that you know well. Of course this is just speculation, and it is designed to be a dilemma. Most people choose the airplane because it involves the most lives saved. There is no correct answer, but the answer that is chosen least often is the father in his car. Choosing to save the father would mean we are taking care of our own. And if each of us took care of our own, the quality of life would improve tremendously, and lives would be cherished.

A cliché circulating these days says, "Think globally and act locally." We could use this to think about the above dilemma. What do you think is right in the above example? Do you take care of your own? It may not be glamorous, especially if the people close to you are not always your favorites. Know who makes up your own and take care of them first. The angels don't march away from us if there is a bigger event happening when we need them; the angels take care of their own.

An Angelic Reflection: I will recognize where I am needed most. I will look beyond popular thought or numbers and look for ways I can improve the quality of life in my own backyard.

QUALITY

An Angel Reminder: The sucker born every minute is the sucker who believes that there's a sucker born every minute.

P. T. Barnum thought he had a finger on the pulse of the human psyche when he made his famous observation about a sucker being born every minute. And so he created a world that confirmed his beliefs. He gave what he assumed was a stupid public the "greatest show on earth," and he laughed at their gullibility. The Barnum approach to the public lives on in today's media, which decrees that people want sensationalism, not quality, and which subsequently dishes out huge portions of tastelessness and mediocrity. But the truth is that quality can and does prevail, that when people are given the best they will respond to it and uplift their level of awareness accordingly. The angels choose to see people as seekers rather than suckers, and they will always help us connect to our higher natures.

What is your attitude toward quality? Do you demand the best from and for yourself and others? Or do you sometimes take the easy way out, sacrificing quality for quick-fix mediocrity?

An Angelic Reflection: I seek from and give to the world the best that is in me.

$\mathcal{D}$RAGONS

An Angel Reminder: Dragons are messengers of wisdom.

In Western culture, dragons are regarded as evil and fearsome. But in Eastern traditions, the opposite is true. The Chinese, for instance, view dragons as beneficial creatures. In Tibetan culture, the dragon represents inscrutability—the silent power of unwavering intelligence and confidence in one's place in the world. In our own lives, dragons can represent the parts of ourselves we are trying to avoid or destroy. These parts of ourselves may appear in the guise of dragonlike people or problems that follow us around, breathing fire down our necks. Or they may be revealed in things that we do or don't do that cause us shame. But since we can never really destroy a part of ourselves, our only real choice lies in confronting our dragons head-on. When we try to deny or repress aspects of ourselves, we only give them more power. But when we acknowledge the parts of us that we fear, accepting them simply for what they are, we can then begin to understand them and tame them. The angels offer natural assistance in dragon taming and want us to know that in facing our dragons we allow them to become our friends and teachers.

Envision or draw a single dragon that represents all the dragons in your life. Now think of your dragon as a special pet with tremendous power to help you gain insight and power in any situation.

An Angelic Reflection: In facing my fears, I divest them of their power over me.

$\mathcal{F}$UTURE

An Angel Reminder: There is no need to go into shock over the future.

The future is the time that comes after the present. By the time you think about that, you will be in the future. The future of humankind looks pretty bleak right now, especially if you know anything about the conditions in Third World countries. Some predict changes on earth in the near future, and again the picture is not bright. Most futuristic scenarios feature humans acting like programmed computers and everything being saved by technology. Is this really what we are striving for? Think about your vision of the future. Don't get attached to it, and don't forget that the angels are now a large part of your future.

Brighten your future with the angels' light. The opposite of bleak is joyful, happy, colorful, bright, and full of life. There is no reason that the future for you has to be bleak. Statistics are silly inventions from humans looking for certain outcomes. Don't buy into statistics; buy into the future of life.

An Angelic Reflection: I welcome the future with a joyful heart and a hope-filled mind.

COMPANION

An Angel Reminder: Your guardian angel is your companion; the two of you go together.

When God looks at you, God sees two beings: you and your guardian angel. Your guardian angel is your spiritual traveling companion through life. A companion stays with us through thick and thin, through work and play, through the highs and lows. A companion is a friendly notion, a welcome friend who is with us to make our lives easier. Our guardian angels can be our true companions through life. With the angels as our companions and by thinking of ourselves as spiritual beings having a human experience, then we can be true friends in life.

Your guardian angel has known you from the very beginning of your existence. Your guardian angel knows what you came here to do. The goals you set before taking the leap of faith into your current body are fresh in your angel's mind. Getting to know your guardian angel will help you get to know yourself. Think of the relationship you have with your guardian angel as you would any other relationship. What things help it grow? What natural stages does your relationship go through? Like any relationship, the one with your guardian angel requires respect and reciprocation.

An Angelic Reflection: I will enjoy the companionship of my guardian angel and respect our special relationship.

$\mathcal{B}$LOCKAGES

An Angel Reminder: We must allow others the right not to accept our love.

Sometimes we expend a lot of energy that doesn't seem to be returned in kind. We may be trying to reach a certain person—to get his or her attention, gratitude, or love—only to be ignored or even rejected completely. When this happens the angels counsel us to step back and examine why we continue to give our best to those who are neither ready nor willing to accept it. Love and connectedness can come to us only when the other person desires the same thing and is open, not closed, to our energy. If we experience repeated psychic blockages in a relationship, we first need to withdraw our energy from it so that it can breathe and we can heal. Then we need to reconnect to our strong centers and reaffirm our value, our goodness, and our right to have genuinely loving relationships.

Are your relationships generally fulfilling and energizing or frustrating and draining? Is there anyone in your life who is not accepting the energy you are sending? If so, ask yourself why you continue to put out the energy, allow the person the right not to receive it, and reflect upon where you could better direct your effort.

An Angelic Reflection: I am learning the secret of how much to give and receive in my relationships.

$\mathcal{F}$ORGIVENESS

An Angel Reminder: Forgive yourself and you will forgive others; forgive others and others will forgive you.

A pithy soul once observed, "I bury my hatchets, but I never forget where they're buried!" The angels want us to know that we don't have to forget in order to forgive. Instead, they urge us to release our attachment to what has been done to us and to increase our awareness so that we don't allow it to happen again. Of course, because forgiveness always involves the release of the energy-draining emotions of anger, hurt, and revenge, it is ultimately for our own benefit. When we hope for a positive response from someone who has hurt us, we risk further attaching ourselves to them. When we truly practice forgiveness, we simply let go—of our indignation, of the other person, even of our desire to control the situation. In so doing, we join the divine cleanup brigade, helping the angels to keep our lives free of the litter of bitterness and the sludge of grudge so that a clear river of happiness and peace can flow through us.

Think of a hurt you have experienced that seems to plague you. Ask the angels to help you release your attachment to being right, and to help you forgive this person and move on. If you don't feel immediately forgiving, don't worry. Just let go, and let the angels do the rest.

An Angelic Reflection: Forgiveness is the surest route to the inner peace the angels want for me.

SHRINE

An Angel Reminder: An angel shrine can focus attention so that each time you see it you are reminded of how much the angels love and help you.

A shrine is a hallowed place with a special association. Many of us have shrines in our homes without even realizing it. Do you have a special place where you collect things, such as family pictures, that remind you of a special association? Some of us have intentional shrines devoted to a great teacher. Shrines are places of focus; they may be as large as a cathedral or as small as a picture. The important part of the shrine is its special association, that which makes it sacred to us. Many people who are living in angel consciousness create special shrines to remind them of the angels.

Creating a shrine is fun and a good way to use your imagination. Think of some items that hold a special meaning for you. Find a place in your home where you could display these items in an interesting and inspiring way. A bookshelf, dresser top, small round table, whatnot shelf, and even a windowsill can house a shrine. Have a ceremony to honor your shrine. Light a candle and invite the angels in to enjoy the energy you cocreate with them.

An Angelic Reflection: I have a special association with the angels, and I have made a shrine in my heart to honor their love.

$\mathcal{M}$OON

An Angel Reminder:

"And of the white moon ...
Praised be my Lord, by the flame
Whereby night groweth illumined
In the midst of its darkness ..."

St. Francis of Assisi

The moon is the symbol of the intuitive, psychic self. Shrouded in the shadows of the night, yet illuminating the darkness, the moon reminds us of the secret, powerful knowledge within us that can, if we heed it, bring the subconscious to light and illuminate our earthly path. Mythologically and metaphysically the moon embodies the qualities of intuition, receptivity, and desire for harmony and wholeness. Unlike the sun, it continually changes character, moving, in its various phases, from abundance to scarcity to complete seclusion. So when we look at the moon, we behold a mysterious unity of light and darkness, visible and invisible, known and unknown—a unity that echoes in the deepest recesses of our own ever-changing, ever-mysterious selves.

How do you see the moon? Write down some images and phrases that come to mind. These images and phrases may reflect how you perceive your inner self. The next time you look at the moon, try for a moment or two to become one with it, to sense its essence. Then note what images and feelings emerge as you begin to open to the intuitive part of your nature.

An Angelic Reflection: I am in tune with my inner knowing.

*G*LORIOUS OPPORTUNITY

An Angel Reminder: Glorious opportunities are constant companions on the spiritual path.

Glorious opportunities are those times in our lives when we are faced with a decision that will bring transformation. Glorious opportunities are chances for us to change for the better. If we find ourselves in a situation where we feel everyone has abandoned us, then we have the glorious opportunity to become self-reliant. If we hit rock bottom and feel that we can't go on, we have the glorious opportunity to learn about the miraculous power of prayer and surrendering to a higher power. The angels are always close at hand when we are faced with a major crisis. Next time you are at a crossroads in life, remember that you have been given a glorious opportunity to bond closer to the angels and transform your life.

Think back in your life and recall the glorious opportunities that have presented themselves to you. Did you come out a winner, or did you miss the chance and have to repeat the lesson?

An Angelic Reflection: I welcome the inherent possibilities for transformation in all my experiences.

$\mathcal{B}$LAME

An Angel Reminder: Blame achieves no purpose in the eyes of the angels.

Often we are tempted to look for blame when something happens that we don't like. But what good ever came out of blame? When we blame the government for society's many ills, does this solve the problems? Could it ever really be fair to blame other people for our own unhappiness, when all they are doing is living their own lives? The angels promote a life free from blame. This means neither pointing a finger nor taking on blame yourself, which is a largely discouraging and unproductive pastime. Blame is intimately related to another useless and completely nonangelic activity: guilt. The angels encourage us instead to take responsibility for our own happiness or unhappiness. If things aren't going right in our lives, we can "take the bull by the horns" and use our own ingenuity to change the situation. If we have done something wrong or hurt someone else, either intentionally or unintentionally, we can take responsibility for our actions, not only in the sense of owning up to them, but also in trying to understand what motivated us and how we can learn from the experience.

The angels regard blamers the same way we viewed tattletales in grade school—as annoying. And since we wouldn't want to annoy the angels, the next time you feel the urge to place blame, try promoting understanding and right action instead. You will be amazed at how productive your observations will soon become.

An Angelic Reflection: In my life, the natural antidotes to blame and guilt are awareness and understanding.

LIGHT

An Angel Reminder: Let your life be like an angel food cake—sweet and light.

The angels are depicted as beings of light, which is appropriate on several levels. Their shining halos are symbolic of heaven, a place of total light where the bliss of truth reigns and darkness cannot enter. They radiate the light of divine love and wisdom, illuminating our consciousness and bringing us enlightenment. They are also light in the sense that they are weightless, free spirits that soar without effort to all regions of the universe. And they maintain an attitude of lightheartedness, bringing humor and *delight* into our lives and teaching us that God is not only love, but joy.

Reflect upon the multileveled meanings of the word light. How can you become more like the angels, bringing the light of love and understanding to others, replacing the heavy burdens of worry and negativity with the freeing consciousness of hope and trust, scattering seeds of laughter and lightheartedness wherever you go?

An Angelic Reflection: Like the angels, I too am a being of light.

$\mathcal{U}$NCONVENTIONALITY

An Angel Reminder: The angels are anything but conventional.

When we follow established customs, play by the rules, and try not to make waves or act in ways that draw undue attention to us, life attains a state of comfortable predictability that is commonly termed security. Of course there is nothing wrong with security; when, however, it becomes complacency, we deprive ourselves of the excitement of discovery that should be a natural part of life. After all, we were born being unconventional. As infants we were far too absorbed in the excitement of self-discovery to worry about convention. So being even the slightest bit unconventional helps us to reconnect to the delightfully unexpected parts of ourselves with which we may have lost contact. Life becomes an adventure in exotic cuisine rather than a prepackaged frozen dinner. We see things from different perspectives; our minds stretch to embrace freedom of expression. And as we risk opening up to new possibilities, we encourage others to explore their own untapped creativity.

Have you dreamed of being unconventional but have been too inhibited by societal norms or others' expectations of you? If so, give yourself permission to express some parts of yourself that you've kept hidden, and note the effect on your life and relationships.

An Angelic Reflection: The more I am willing to express who I really am, the better I will know myself and the better others will know me.

RECOVERY

An Angel Reminder: The angels want us to regain use of the divine inner peace we were born with.

Most addictive behavior starts in an attempt to regain inner peace, yet ends up doing quite the opposite. Addictive patterns are not necessarily a weakness or a disease; they result from not using our mental ingenuity to solve problems and from forgetting to recognize that spiritual help is always available from the angels. With the angels as recovery agents we are guided to regain our mental peace, which will bring us out of the recovery trap of illness and disease and send us into living with lighthearted and positive feelings as our natural state of being.

Most of us start our day hoping it will be good and productive. Many obstacles get in the way, but if we recognize that we have the mental strength and the help from the angels to deal with little problems quickly and carefully, we can regain control of our mental peace each time the bombardments of the day catch up with us. We can create happy moments free from past memories of illness and weakness. Wake up with the angels and choose to recover your mental peace at every turn in your day.

An Angelic Reflection: I will use my mental ingenuity and the angels to help me recover the beauty and truth I was born with.

ℬOREDOM

An Angel Reminder: We can never be bored as long as we are in love with life.

When we're bored, we feel at a loss for something to do. We think, mistakenly, that the antidote to boredom is busyness. But to the angels—who, by the way, are never bored—the true antidote to boredom is "beingness." As long as we are alive, we have something to be interested in—and something to be working at—in every moment. To be truly alive means to be actively engaged in life. This does not mean running around in a whirlwind of activity but rather approaching life as a lover: with curiosity, enthusiasm, passion, concern, and constant awareness of the part we play in the other's development or disintegration. Boredom, on the other hand, is the result of passive involvement in life. People who are bored seek to be entertained or distracted—to escape, essentially, from themselves and their planetary duties. The cure for boredom, then, is not to fill our lives with distractions but to become acquainted with our beingness, our real working and loving relationship to the universe.

If you feel bored and restless a lot of the time, practice seeing life as your lover. What do you give to each other? What do you love about each other? How can you make the relationship more exciting and fulfilling? One sure cure for boredom is getting in touch with your creativity. Ask the angels to guide you in discovering the singularly beautiful things that you can create to enhance life and connect you to your beingness.

An Angelic Reflection: As I enter into the creative spirit of life, I have neither the time nor the inclination to be bored.

*S*TAY IN YOUR BODY

An Angel Reminder: Your body is a nice place to be.

Sometimes when we are in tense and difficult situations we tend to leave our bodies. This doesn't mean we are astral traveling; it means we get uncomfortable with our present situations and take off in our minds. If our minds are nervously off somewhere else, our bodies will not be able to cope with the present. Our bodies work best when we stay in them and treat them well. Our minds are actually quite comfortable being in our bodies, when we can accept what is happening in the now. The angels probably can protect us more easily when we stay in our bodies.

Next time you encounter an uncomfortable situation, stay with it. Even if you get sweaty palms and want to faint, stay in your body and let these sensations pass. Rarely will you pass out, and if you do the angels will take care of you. Pain can be altered when you stay in your body and seek understanding of how to cope with it. To stay conscious of the present, practice staying in your body. Staying in your body is a practice of centering and being mindful of the moment. Be here now.

An Angelic Reflection: I love my body, and I will honor it by staying with it through thick and thin.

Cheating

An Angel Reminder: Cheating can get you expelled from the school of life.

In many ways we humans cheat ourselves out of true, authentic lives. Each time we avoid working through a fear we cheat ourselves out of self-respect. Compromising our values cheats us out of integrity, and sticking to selfish desires cheats us out of loving others. One reason cheating appeals to us is because it takes blood, sweat, and tears to get through many of the rough spots we face, and when we hit rock bottom we may feel that we can't afford to lose any more blood, sweat, or tears. Never forget that the angels are always with us. They want us to know that we will gain much more self-worth if we quit cheating our way through life. If you make the effort to work through your fears and rough spots without using denial, the blood, sweat, and tears that you lose will make room for many gratifying blessings.

Are you cheating yourself out of good health by eating, drinking, or smoking too much when you experience emotional pain? Could it be that you cheat yourself out of a satisfying career because you have an easy job with good money? Remember that the easy way out is usually much more trouble in the long run. Next time you feel like cheating, stop and ask the angels for a boost in courage, then face that painful emotion, fear, or challenge and come out glorious on the side of self-respect.

An Angelic Reflection: Cheating is for weaklings; I will go the path of courage and come forth with true angelic blessings.

Wanted

An Angel Reminder: The angels want you.

One thing we share with all human beings is the desire to feel wanted by others. The greatest gift parents can give their child is the sense that she or he is wanted. All the material and social privileges in the world are useless if a child feels unwanted. It is okay to need and want others to be around. And it is nice to be needed and wanted. The key is for us to fill certain needs and wants within ourselves before we go to someone else with our requests for help. We must also give others the choice of whether or not they want to help us, and defining what we really need helps them make a clear choice.

Do you feel wanted? You are wanted here on earth. Learning to feel good about your own needs and wants and to feel good about being needed by others is a process of learning to know yourself. Know that you have most of the resources inside you that you need to make life a wonderful experience. Know that one of your most valuable resources is your guardian angel.

An Angelic Reflection: I feel wanted and loved by the angels.

$\mathcal{R}$EMOTE CONTROL

An Angel Reminder: We are not even remotely in control of the universe.

We are an impatient society. We want things to happen yesterday. We have become accustomed to instant gratification, from fast food to fast-forward; we even find it difficult, these days, to sit through a movie we cannot orchestrate by remote control. But sooner or later we inevitably discover that life cannot be rewound or fast-forwarded, that we cannot control the timing of the universe. Sooner or later we must confront delays, obstacles, blocks that stand in the way of instant gratification. The angels want us to be aware that these blocks have been created for our own good so that we are not robbed of the chance to reap the rewards of patience, perseverance, pondering, creative problem solving, and all the other strengthening qualities that are the true keys to mastery and control in our lives.

If you are often tempted to fast-forward through problems and difficulties or to rewind your life to an easier time, try handing your remote over to the angels. Then tackle your difficulties with the powerful tools of thoughtfulness, imagination, and creativity. If you feel you need a remote around just in case, make more use of the "pause" and "mute" functions.

An Angelic Reflection: I prefer the lasting rewards that come with patience and perseverance to the fleeting satisfaction of instant gratification.

ON BEHALF

An Angel Reminder: We are here on behalf of God.

Many of us live to help others. We want
our lives to inspire love in others. To
think about how we help ourselves
and others, we can consider what we do
on behalf of others. What qualities do we
put forth and represent in our lives? When
we do something on behalf of another we
can think of ourselves as being half of it.
That means we do not sacrifice ourselves or hurt
ourselves to help another. It means we become
part of the help and receive help in the process.

*Think of the knowledge and the qualities cultivated in your
own life that could be used on behalf of others. Think of how
the angels give love on behalf of us. What can we do on behalf
of the angels?*

**An Angelic Reflection: I will do what I do on behalf of God
and the angels.**

*I*MAGINATION SHIFT

An Angel Reminder: "It's my conviction that slight shifts in imagination have more impact on living than major efforts at change."

Thomas Moore

We receive images, mental pictures, and thoughts all day long. Thinking and imagining are voluntary actions. We create our psychological experiences by the way we are thinking, and we take them a step further in the way we use our imaginations. We also have the choice of perspectives. As Joseph V. Bailey, author of *The Serenity Principle,* puts it, "If you focus on the smashed bug on the windshield of your car, you will definitely miss the scenery and likely have an accident. Wisdom is like looking through the windshield, not at it." If we can remember and fully realize that we are thinkers in charge of our thoughts and captains of our perspectives, then we will be able to make slight shifts in our imaginations that will gently reposition us to receive a glimpse of heaven.

If you want to have a more imaginative response to life, you must be willing to accept that your thoughts are your creation and not be attached to them. Too many thoughts means not enough insights. Insights are seeded in our imaginations, and when we allow our minds to have quiet time, the seeds will begin to germinate and our insights will grow. Insights bring change without the effort of changing.

An Angelic Reflection: I will choose my perspective and begin to notice the angels in the beautiful scenery of life.

$\mathcal{M}$OMENTS

An Angel Reminder: "I found that the nature of life itself is joyful, that deep within the core of each one of us is the joy that indeed surpasses understanding. This is a joy beyond polarity—a joy that includes sorrow, a hope that embraces despair."

Dorothy Maclean

Moments are brief intervals of time. Right now, as you read this, people all over the world are giving birth to babies and experiencing a moment of bliss that will remain in their memories for all time. At the same time, others are experiencing moments of sadness and sorrow. We may not all experience bliss at the same time, but just knowing that bliss is occurring right now means that life goes on. Moments go on and will continue on into infinity. Time is the structure in which we organize our moments. Time heals the painful moments, and time is always on our side.

What if all our moments were happening simultaneously? Could you grasp that possibility? Could it be that bliss and sorrow are partners? If you want to explore moments, keep a journal of what you feel in the moment by writing in a stream-of-consciousness manner—writing down whatever comes into your mind. Then study what you wrote at a later time.

An Angelic Reflection: I will accept all the moments of my life as gifts wrapped in bright colors.

$\mathcal{A}$NGEL ENTHUSIAST

An Angel Reminder: Angel enthusiasm is not merely a hobby; it is a way of life.

We probably all know a sports enthusiast or a hobby enthusiast. But how many true angel enthusiasts do you know? Maybe it is time for you to become one. Typical angel enthusiasts read a variety of books on angels. They may also wear angel pins to remind others of the angels, and their environments tend to include beautiful pictures or posters of angels and a few tasteful angel figurines. An angel coffee mug helps the angel enthusiast wake up and smell the angels (who, by the way, don't smell like coffee). Most importantly, angel enthusiasts do at least one thing each day to promote angel consciousness in the world around them. The angels don't need armchair enthusiasts; they need an army of fans willing to go out in the world as representatives of humor, happiness, love, light, and beauty.

Take a break from your usual routine at least once a day to renew your angel enthusiasm. You may want to take a stroll down the street and smile at all you meet, sending them a secret blast of angelic radiance. Or you may just want to get comfortable, close your eyes, and ask the angels for peace. Take an action personal to you that will increase your angel enthusiasm. Above all, allow yourself to have fun *with your enthusiasm for the angels.*

An Angelic Reflection: My enthusiasm for the angels is more than just a passing phase. It is a daily way of being that encourages life, love, and laughter in the world around me and represents the angels' most noble causes.

*T*EACH WITHOUT WORDS

An Angel Reminder: "Wherever the sage is, he teaches without words."

Lao-Tzu, Tao Te Ching

We probably know many people—ourselves included—who are inspired to teach, preach, or otherwise enlighten others, but who are the ones most in need of their own lessons. Somehow it is much easier to know what to do than to do it, and certainly it is much more interesting to distract ourselves from ourselves by focusing on the faults and problems of others. Few among us live lives of inner and outer congruence, walking our talk and practicing what we preach. Even fewer among us don't talk at all but rather enlighten and inspire others purely by the example of day-to-day living. The next time we set out to teach someone the right way to do something or try to change their behaviors, we might try setting an example instead, living the conduct we would like to see in others.

Are some people in your life adept at telling you how to live your life yet not able to run their own properly? How about you? Are you an expert at giving advice? Could some situations in your life be helped by taking your own advice? How do you think your life would change if you began teaching without words?

An Angelic Reflection: My purpose is not to teach, but to inspire.

SHOULD

An Angel Reminder: Shoulds reflect either a judgment or a hindsight.

Have you ever pondered the true meaning of *should?* It is a word we hear often, and it is a word that will secretly drive us crazy if we aren't careful. *Should* expresses duty, judgment, and obligation: "You should have done it this way." In this way *should have* expresses something that has passed and causes us to hang on to what could have been. And *should* can take us into the future as well: "We should get there by ten." *Should* reminds us of what we are not. You should be thin, you should be heavier, you should go here, you should stop doing that, you should be nice. But the truth is, you should stop using the word *should!* Would you ever think of telling the angels what they should have done?

Next time you hear yourself or someone else use the word should, *examine what is really being said. Are you discussing something you won't do or something you will do? Does the statement make you feel guilty? Does it take you into the past or the future? What good does telling people they should do this or that bring? Using the word* should, *with its vast repertoire of guilt, is a habit that might be difficult to break. Lose the tendency to be tormented by the guilt-inducing world of shoulds, and you will become more aware and happy.*

An Angelic Reflection: I will make a conscious effort to ban the word should from my verbal and spiritual vocabulary.

$\mathcal{A}$CT AS IF

An Angel Reminder: Act happy and you will be happy.

Each of us has probably dreamed about being an actor or actress at some point in our lives. Acting can be very helpful when you need a little extra confidence or faith. If you are feeling helpless or dependent on others and want to change that, start acting *as if* you are self-reliant and capable. People respond to how we act in a situation, not always to how we feel. By acting something out, you are actually doing it; you are taking the steps to build up the confidence and faith you feel you are lacking. Each time you "act as if," you change the if into a reality.

Act as if the angels are with you all the time, guiding you into the flow of happiness. If you want to be happy, act happy. Discover your innate acting talents and use them creatively. Act as if you were a great person, because you are.

An Angelic Reflection: I will act as if I am living the life I want, and I know that it will be so.

$\mathcal{L}$UCK

An Angel Reminder: We were all born under a lucky star.

Luck is a funny thing. By definition it means the chance happening of either a good or bad event. Those of us who seek to live in angel consciousness know that all events can bring about spiritual growth, and the real chance is that nothing is left up to chance. Luck is something we want to believe in. It seems as if it were a gift from the universe, but it is actually a game that we play with ourselves. Sometimes we judge what is lucky. For example, you may think that someone killed suddenly was unlucky, but maybe death is the most wonderful gift humans receive, a truly lucky and fortunate event. We fear death because it is unknown, and fear makes us uncomfortable, but we don't really know the fate of others. There is no need to project luck onto something that most likely has nothing to do with chance.

Are you superstitious? Superstitious behavior causes us to feel separated from the angels, because it causes us to be less trusting of the ways of the universe. Superstition and luck have one result, and that is a feeling of being haunted. A superstition is a belief, not a knowing. If you look deeper into your superstitions they will disappear because they have no substance. Begin to live life free from the issue of luck and superstition, and the angels will bring you such a sense of good fortune you will feel like you have won the greatest lottery ever.

An Angelic Reflection: Good fortune looks upon my life; I know that God does not play dice with the universe.

REFINEMENT

An Angel Reminder: Taming the personality does not mean breaking the spirit.

Refinement is very different from repression, especially in terms of the personality. To refine means to remove defects or impurities and to cultivate elegance. To repress means to ignore our imperfections and push them into a corner where they retain their power. When we refine our personalities we learn to keep what is pure and positive for us and discard the negative impurities. In the process of refining our personalities we don't want to throw the baby out with the bathwater, meaning the goal is not always to remove certain traits but to bring them out of the corner to refine and improve them. The goal of refining the personality is to bring it into alignment with our inner selves.

Think of your imperfections as gifts; they are what make you interesting. Refine your imperfections by pouring love into them. That way you will have a better and clearer view of what you are dealing with. The important part of refinement is purity. Think about purifying your life. It doesn't mean going to a lot of work fasting or forcing yourself to be different. It means being purely you, and that is what the angels are here to help you do.

An Angelic Reflection: I will visit the angel refinery and bring the pure essence of love into my soul to refine my brilliance.

RAISON D'ÊTRE

An Angel Reminder: "Let us love one another, for love is from God; and everyone who loves is born of God and knows God. The one who does not love does not know God; for God is love."

1 John 4:7, 8 (New American Standard Bible)

God is the angels' raison d'être, and God is love. Love is our *reason for being,* and we are born of God's love and the angels watch over us. We are part of a wonderful trinity or triangle of love—God, the angels, and us. To understand how God loves us we must understand that this love exists for free. God does not love us because of our good deeds or because of how much we love God; God's love for us is always the same regardless of what we do, where we live, or what we look like. We are loved whether we like it or not. You could spend your whole life trying to find ways to live and actions to take that would please God, but really you only need to find a way to be your whole self: body, mind, and spirit. Remember: God loves us even when we don't love ourselves.

Do you think of love as an accumulative force or as a free energy? Do you feel love is your raison d'être? Do you think you could increase God's love for you? Think about your feelings about love and God. Realize that the angels behold the face of love at all times. We too have God within us at all times, for we have love in our hearts always, regardless of whether or not we are allowing it to show. The angels say, "Relax. God is love."

An Angelic Reflection: I feel God's unconditional love for me and I pass it on to others.

$\mathcal{W}$INGS

An Angel Reminder: "If you listen to your inner voice, I think that you awaken enthusiasm and imagination, which is vision. And I think that these are the two wings that we need to fly. Enthusiasm and imagination."

Carlos Santana

Wings are symbols of the angels' divine mission. They did not appear in Christian art until A.D. 312, when artists began to understand that angels functioned as God's messengers. Angels then began to be pictured with wings, like the winged god Hermes, messenger to the Greek gods. Wings symbolize the quickness with which angels carry messages from God to humans. Wings are also a symbol of freedom. What child hasn't dreamed of sprouting wings and flying away into the clouds in search of his or her true home?

Each time you help heaven in a way that is personal to you, imagine your wings growing a little bigger. Close your eyes and focus your attention on your back, where the wings are sprouting, and feel the process. Have some fun with your wings. Maybe someday they will grow big enough to carry you on the wind, up through the clouds for a glimpse of your true home.

An Angelic Reflection: I feel my wings expanding as the angels touch my life with their light and love.

GOOFING OFF

An Angel Reminder: Reserve time in your schedule to goof off with the angels.

If we don't give ourselves a break once in a while from the struggle to live a perfect spiritual life, we are going to become stale and boring. First of all, there is no perfect way to be spiritual. Children are spiritual by nature; we wouldn't want to force them to live up to perfection. Children delight in nature, they talk with angels, they contemplate God, and they spend most of their time playing. The angels don't want to force us to be perfect or spiritual. They want us to delight in life, talk with them, and think about God. They also want us to goof off once in a while, to take a break from the usual adult routine we are in and enter childhood again.

The dictionary's definition of goofing off is wasting or "killing" time. There is no way to waste or kill time; we don't have that power. And goofing off is positive because it renews our sense of play and allows us to relax more. As soon as you are able, take some time to goof off with the angels. It may feel difficult at first, but the more you practice the easier it will get. No one said it was going to be easy being a human, but the angels want us to be easy on ourselves. All work and no play makes us dull and boring, regardless of how spiritually right we may be.

An Angelic Reflection: I will reserve time to joyfully goof off with the angels. I know in my heart that there is no such thing as wasting time and that everything I do is right on time.

SAINTS

An Angel Reminder: Saints are here to help us mind our manners.

One of the loveliest concepts in Judaism concerns the hidden saints. According to legend, a secret number of saints are walking the earth, and we might encounter any of them at any moment. Unfortunately, however, they don't wear signs proclaiming their sainthood. Instead, they move among us anonymously and unobtrusively; they may be disguised as anything from a beggar to the kid behind the counter at McDonald's. So in order not to be rude or condescending to a saint, we must treat everyone we contact with care and respect, just in case. The angels know that universal respect is possibly the most useful talent we could develop. Not only will it keep us from getting into a jam if we should happen to run into a saint, but it just may make saints out of us. After all, we don't know who the hidden saints are, which means that one of them could be you.

Have you run into any possible hidden saints lately? If so, did your attitude and actions pass the test? How do you treat people in general? Some better than others? From now on, be on the lookout for saints, and see if you begin to view humanity from a different perspective.

An Angelic Reflection: I see and treat everyone, including myself, as a potential saint.

$\mathcal{R}$ENAISSANCE

An Angel Reminder: We are in the midst of a revival. Let us help revive that which feeds the human soul.

A renaissance is a time of renewal and rebirth of the arts as influenced by classical forms. The famous European Renaissance during the fourteenth to sixteenth centuries left us with the most memorable art depicting angels. Many familiar images from the Renaissance period grace greeting cards, the walls of our living rooms, and covers of the books we read. Why are humans so strongly attracted to images painted hundreds of years ago? Because the art is classical. Classical form is an innate component of our sensitive human nature. A renaissance is happening now; the current interest in angels is no mistake. And, with the angels' help, we will renew and revive interest in the most classical of all forms: love.

To renew your own sense of the classical, surround yourself with angel art and make a point of listening to music reminiscent of the Renaissance period. Support local arts and crafts fairs. Find a craft you enjoy doing and allow the angels to inspire you through classical form. Remember you are part of a special revival going on. Think of the mark our time period will make in human history and how crucial it is that we keep the arts alive with the energy of love. Be a renaissance person.

An Angelic Reflection: I will be an ever-present part of the renewal of love through art. My ancient memories hold the classical vision.

Wonderfully Wrong

An Angel Reminder: The wrong way is often the right track.

Isn't it wonderful to be wrong once in a while? It is especially wonderful to be wrong about people you oppose. Mistakes are gifts. Admitting when we are wrong is a boost to our souls, and being wrong most of the time means that we are living full lives. The reason being wrong is so right is that wrong allows change and change is the fuel that we burn to evolve. Great people are able to change their course when they get stuck with a "right way" that is not good for all. Pride is the only block to admitting when we are wrong or recognizing when it is time to change directions.

Lighten up and admit that life is more fun when you can accept your mistakes as gifts. That is your first step in freeing yourself from the confines of always having to be right. Being right takes so much energy, and the energy would be more creatively spent focused somewhere else. Who really knows who is right? Why take on a burden that doesn't belong to you?

An Angelic Reflection: I have no investment in being right all the time, so I can never lose anything by admitting when I am wrong. Instead, I will gain the joy of being more human.

$\mathcal{T}$HROES

An Angel Reminder: There is no need to remain in the throes of life's struggles.

A throe is a severe pang or spasm of pain. To be in the throes of something means to be caught up in a great and agonizing struggle. As humans we find ourselves dealing with throes over which we feel we have no control. *Throes* is a term used often in relation to feelings like jealously—feelings that make us extremely uncomfortable and bring us pain. Jealously is not easy to get rid of, but it doesn't have to control us. Life brings along its struggles, but we are the ones who create the agony by locking our minds up in the illusion of pain. Remember that with time and angels, pain is released and transmuted. Feelings like jealously, hurt, resentment, and bitterness are not permanent. The angels will help free us from the throes of life and lift us up and beyond the agonizing struggle.

Next time you feel that you are entangled in a throe, take the time to break free. Often we don't take the time it requires to disentangle ourselves; we just start reacting and making everything worse. Look at a throe as a big net that has dropped over you. If you panic and try to run, you only become more entangled in it. The angels have a view of the net from above. They can guide you out, step by step, until you are free. Just remember to ask them for help.

An Angelic Reflection: My heart is free from the throes of life's struggles. I will know when to release my pain before it becomes agonizing and entangling.

LEVELING

An Angel Reminder: Let's stop leveling one another and begin building one another up.

Leveling behavior is born from a feeling of incompleteness or low self-worth. It is a choice that some humans make when they feel they are not quite as grand as someone close to them. So instead of praising the other, they seek to bring that person down to their level. Of course there are no levels. All people have the capacity to shine brightly; we all have the light within us. The key is to allow people their right to shine in situations that warrant notice without trying to compete or take it away from them. If we succeed in allowing another to shine bright and cease the leveling game, then both parties are helped immensely.

It is difficult to notice when we seek to level, but it is a good thing to become aware of. A level is an imaginary line; it doesn't exist. How could humans be measured in rank or level of importance? Do not seek to find your level; seek to abolish the need for a level. The angels will help you; they live beyond levels. They are here with us now yet live in the highest dimension in the universe.

An Angelic Reflection: I know that in angel consciousness there are no levels of importance against which to judge and compare.

SIGNIFICANCE

An Angel Reminder: Taking a step back for a wider perspective always helps in times of troublesome thoughts.

Sometimes when we are overwhelmed by a problem in our lives, it helps to stop and ask ourselves how significant our problem really is in the scheme of things. Is the problem of major proportions? Would it stop any world events from happening? When held up next to the problem of a starving child in India, would it sink in comparison? Are you the only person in the universe with this problem? Should God stop the world from turning and take care of your little problem immediately? Remember, this is only meant as a humorous game to play when little problems get blown out of proportion in a big way. The angels know that the larger we allow our perspective to be, the more significantly happy we will be. They want to guide us in feeling significant without inflating our problems.

Close your eyes and hook up with your guardian angel. Imagine the two of you going way out into the universe to a point where you can look back at our beautiful planet earth. Think of all the billions of humans back on earth. At this point of reference we are one big blob of color. Think about what really matters to you and to the angels. On your way back to earth realize that in the whole scheme of things our little problems may not amount to much, but our positive choices that heal the earth amount to a lot.

An Angelic Reflection: I know that my significance is based on the part I play in the angels' scheme of bringing heaven to earth; it is not based on the little problems that trip me up once in a while.

$\mathcal{H}$EART

An Angel Reminder: "For God sees not as man sees, for man looks at the outward appearance, but the Lord looks at the heart."

1 Samuel 16:7 (New American Standard Bible)

The heart has always been a symbol of love, courage, and devotion. *Heart* and *soul* are two words often found together, and for good reason. It is through the heart that the soul expresses itself. The heart is the organ that keeps us alive physically, and it is the central source of our emotions and feelings. We know when someone is speaking from the heart, and we know when our hearts have been touched. It has nothing to do with logic or being rational; knowing is a feeling. When we say that someone's heart is in the right place we know that regardless of the outward appearance of that person's life, his or her intent is soul-felt and honest.

How is your heart feeling? Is it sad, happy, light, or burdened? Is your heart in the right place? To know what is in our hearts takes effort and time, for we must practice listening to the voice within. Don't go to sleep at night with a sad heart; take time to lighten your heart with the angels. Open your heart to the angels each night before you go to sleep, and they will bring joy to your soul and wings to your ideas.

An Angelic Reflection: My heart is happy, light, and full of love.

*H*UMAN ANGELS

An Angel Reminder: God works in mysterious and creative ways.

Many people believe that other humans have acted as angels in their lives. This is different than an angel appearing as a human and then disappearing. The human angels are humans that sometimes help the angels by relaying a message or a thought to someone when it is needed the most. The funny thing is, most human angels don't even know when they are acting as angels. They may never know they said the one thing that changed another's life. What this means is that there is no way to try to be a human angel. You can only increase the likelihood by being yourself and seeking to live by your higher power. Human angels feel comfortable with what they are here to do, and they allow themselves to be guided into situations where they can be of help in a noninterfering way—where they can help the angels relay a moment of pure love to another soul.

Have you been touched by a human angel? Ask these questions: Did the person give you a sense of hope, a knowing that there is much more to life than the material world? Did you feel safe and comfortable in that person's presence? Was the other's laugh inviting and warm? Did he or she say the one thing you needed to hear to open your mind and send you off on the right track? Was the person humble and kind? Do you want to be a human angel?

An Angelic Reflection: My life is a voyage of hope. I will forever be surprised by the angels' message that comes to me through loving humans.

SPRING

An Angel Reminder: We are continually called to new life.

Spring is a time of rebirth and renewal. In the spring fresh seeds can be planted in the rich earth that has melted from its icy winter hardness into a receptive and fertile field. In the spring we feel the surge of new life, the urge perhaps to begin new projects and relationships or to see the old ones in a new light. After the long, dark, cold winter, we feel the hope and promise of warmer days, as the earth readies itself for the celebration of summer and the coming to fruition of all that has been carefully and lovingly sown.

Where is the springtime in your life? Are there new beginnings, new ideas, new surges of energy in any direction? Feel the power of the angels' love warming the world, bringing new light into your being, and filling you with the energy of the spring.

An Angelic Reflection: In the ground of my life I plant seeds of love, light, and hope.

*C*OMFORT

An Angelic Reminder: The angels help us feel at ease and content in being who we are.

All of us have our particular ways of experiencing comfort. One person feels a great sense of comfort in a library, surrounded by books. Another gets comfort from taking a long hike, while another's source of comfort comes from making beautiful needlepoint pillows. Others create comfort for themselves through less productive means, such as overeating or indulging in too much sex, alcohol, or drugs. In all our searching for comfort, the goal is the same: we want to make life enjoyable rather than painful; we want to feel secure. Being all in favor of joy, the angels agree with this goal and want to help us feel comfortable while we are here on earth. But they also want us to recognize the difference between comfort and addiction, and they are always ready to help us find strong and lasting sources of comfort that will provide us with contentment while improving our lives. True comfort comes from knowing that our real security is found in our own infinite supply of inner resources—and knowing that the angels are always nearby, waiting to supplement those resources with an infinite supply of love.

Take time to notice the things you do to make yourself comfortable. Make a list or discuss these things with a friend so you can become more conscious of what you do for comfort. Ask the angels for help each time you feel a bit uneasy, and notice how your awareness of comfort begins to change.

An Angelic Reflection: I know that when I do things with ease and calmness, great rewards come my way.

$\mathcal{W}$ALKING

An Angel Reminder: If in doubt, take a walk.

The best way to change the chemistry of a situation is not by taking a chemical but by taking a walk. Walking is one of the best ways to think. Your body is busy using energy so that your mind can sort things out in a reasonable way. Walking is great because we do it so naturally, and we can always find a nice place to stroll. Walking gets us out of the house and out of our minds. You can use a good walk either to think or to release yourself from thinking, to exercise and to calm your nervous system. The angels love to take walks with you; it is a great time to get to know them. Next time you have a disturbing thought pattern, go out and take a walk with the angels. When you come back your perception will be changed, and so will the situation.

Walking with the angels is easy. Simply go out and start walking without any real destination in mind. Ask your guardian angel to lead you. Feel a force of energy coming from your solar plexus that leads you along; you follow. As you are led, allow thoughts to come and go. If your guardian angel is walking fast, then think fast. If your guardian angel slows down, slow down your thoughts and notice the beauty around you. Most of all, have a good time and remember there are no set rules. All you need is a willingness to get out and let your legs move you forward.

An Angelic Reflection: I will walk and talk with the angels.

Toys

An Angel Reminder: Toys bring children closer to adulthood and adults closer to the angels.

We may discount toys as childish holdovers from a time no longer relevant to our present lives, but in reality toys belong to all ages. Just as toys are the life tools of childhood, so they can be meaningful learning equipment in our adult lives. Toys fuel our natural creativity. They afford us temporary escape from the burdens of daily reality, into the rejuvenating realm of fantasy. They invite us to peep into all the forgotten nooks and crannies of our imaginations; they reunite us with our childhood capacity to find happiness in the simplest of pleasures. When we allow ourselves to play with toys, we are honoring the wisdom of both children and the angels, who understand that the shortest distance between the two points of childhood and adulthood may indeed be a direct flight into fancy.

Today, tomorrow, this week, buy yourself a toy that may help you gain a new perspective on a specific situation in your life. For instance, if you are lonely, get yourself a cuddly stuffed animal who can be your unconditionally loving companion. If you feel like you've been talking too much, or perhaps not enough, about a particular topic, a set of wind-up false teeth could be just what's needed to help you lighten up. Just visit a toy store; the toy you need will present itself to you.

An Angelic Reflection: The day I am too old for toys is the day I am too old.

SPIRITUAL WARRIOR

An Angel Reminder: The territory of spiritual warriors is the soul; their weapons are love and understanding; their goal is to unite with the inner nature.

The principles of spiritual warriorship are the complete opposite of the popular concept of military fighting. The spiritual warrior's quest involves not domination but surrender, not hating but understanding, not killing but giving birth. Each of us is a spiritual warrior, doing battle with ourselves. But since we cannot be our own enemies and survive, our goal is not self-annihilation but self-realization. As spiritual warriors, we seek to conquer the mystery of our earthly journeys, to become one with our purposes, and to live lives of spiritual, moral, mental, and physical congruence. Accomplishing this requires equal amounts of patience, perseverance, awareness, humility, integrity, confidence, and trust.

The most important principle of spiritual warriorship is connecting to one's basic goodness, for, in the words of Tibetan master Chögyam Trungpa, "Unless we can discover that basic ground of goodness in our own lives, we cannot hope to improve the lives of others." Try to connect to your basic goodness, and ask the angels to help you.

An Angelic Reflection: As I begin to love and appreciate the goodness that I see in me, I begin to see the goodness in others.

SUN

An Angel Reminder: "As both a physical and a spiritual source of power, the sun provides an example of the way that the effective outpouring of essential light and life is followed not by exhaustion but by perpetual and abundant renewal."

Geoffrey Hodson

The sun sustains all life here on earth, and everything revolves around it. This is why the sun is often the symbol for God, the omnipresent life force of our universe. It brings warmth, nourishment, and light to the earth; like God, whose light of truth dispels the darkness, the sun illuminates all, bringing us, every morning, from darkness into light. Unlike the moon, which symbolizes the principles of receptivity, passivity, and intuition, the sun embodies the active energy of the universe. So in the morning, if we rise and greet the sun in homage, absorbing its revitalizing rays and thanking it for giving us a new day and new start, we may discover that all of our relationships are suddenly infused with warmth, light, and new life.

Face east and greet the sun in the morning. Allow the golden rays of love to penetrate your being, and allow a moment of gratitude for the sun's energy to fill your soul. Imagine that the sun's rays are ushering a host of angels to earth to illuminate your day.

An Angelic Reflection: At daybreak I allow the sun to illuminate my life with love; at sunset I keep the lovelight burning bright within my heart.

$\mathcal{L}$AUGHTER

An Angel Reminder: We never laugh alone; the angels always join us in divine laughter.

Laughter is a universal language. We share the gift of laughter with all of humanity. We also share this gift with the angels and with God. Laughter tickles our souls and massages our hearts. Laughter frees emotional channels, cleaning them out when we laugh so hard that we cry. Laughter creates true magic when we merge with the divine intelligence that pervades the cosmos and understand that no matter how absurd life gets, we still have the capacity to laugh. Often when the angels are near, a person will hear faint giggling and joyful laughter. When this happens to you, join in with a good belly laugh and feel your heart opening up.

It isn't always easy to laugh. We need to stay conscious of the importance of laughing. The best thing about laughing is we never know when something is going to strike us funny. It can happen anywhere, anytime, and sometimes where you would least expect it. Sometimes the angels tickle our funny bones at a serious moment and we just can't help but laugh. This changes everything, and we realize we have the choice to laugh instead of lament. Stay aware of the importance of laughter, and the angels will see to it that you laugh often.

An Angel Reflection: I laugh, therefore I am.

Co-operate

An Angel Reminder: "Let's co-operate and cheat the devil."

Manly P. Hall

To co-operate means to operate with others in a helpful and functional way toward a common end. To co-operate with one's own life means to be helpful to oneself and to look toward a functional and spiritual way to live. We can do this best by co-operating first with the angels and their message from God. The message the angels give us about co-operation is that people must not seek power over others or try to control a situation so that it turns out best for them at the expense of others. We often hear of companies with spiritual aims and goals that have run into trouble because they could not find others to co-operate with. Too many companies are seeking to control, not co-operate. And too many controllers are far worse than too many chefs in the kitchen. The human need to control is eating away at the infrastructure of life's operations.

Think about your habits in regard to co-operation. Do you co-operate with others? Do you notice when others are not co-operative? Ask yourself if you could be a more co-operative person in a particular situation. Quite often co-operating means taking less than we think we deserve. Co-operating is one of our only hopes for the future of humanity. We must co-operate with one another, with heaven, and with nature, if the prognosis for human life is going to be positive.

An Angelic Reflection: I will learn to allow the good of the group to prevail. I will respect and co-operate with the angels' message to love one another.

$\mathcal{D}$RAWN

An Angel Reminder: The angels are drawing you closer to heaven.

To be drawn means to be pulled in a given direction. When we are drawn to something we are attracted to it; it has enticed our interest. We can ask ourselves if we are drawn or driven by life. If we are driven we want to be in the driver's seat and go straight ahead by ourselves. On the other hand, if we are drawn to life we allow a higher power and the angels to pull us in a certain direction, trusting that it is the right way and enjoying the byways.

Think about drawing, as in drawing a picture. How does this relate to being drawn to life? How can you draw out the qualities you want from life, like artists draw out the beauty of what they see? Explore the possibility of becoming a life artist and drawing what you truly want from life.

An Angelic Reflection: I am ready to let the angels draw me in the direction of heaven.

SOMETHING SPECIAL

An Angel Reminder: We don't need to be something special; we are something special by being born a human being.

Now that the angel consciousness movement is well under way, many people think that they have been called by the angels to do amazing things. This is true in part. Each of us is called upon to do something truly amazing, and that is to be ourselves and to live out the life that we choose. Sometimes life seems so ordinary and the cards we have been dealt seem to be the very cards we didn't want. At these times it is tempting to fantasize that we are very different and special, not like those ordinary everyday people around us. When we realize that the ordinary things about us are actually quite extraordinary, we will be able to take our special places in the universe and do something great.

Fantasize about the great role you have to play here on earth. Think about how the angels have picked you, the most special and interesting human they have found, to talk to and help them guide the world. Imagine that your life is more important than the common people whom the angels only guard and guide, but rarely talk to. Now, if you want to really go to extremes, imagine that one of the archangels has come to you and has told you that you are to do something important. By now you probably see how absurd it is to go overboard with our importance. The angels see us all as special. Life is short; keep it in perspective.

An Angelic Reflection: I will not get caught up in an illusion of uniqueness that takes me away from the experience of being human.

*S*TRESS ADDICTION

An Angel Reminder: Stress is a distraction from our true selves.

Like anything else, stress can become an addiction if we become used to it. Stress addicts don't seem to know, or remember, how to live without a high level of tension to keep them feeling alive. While they often complain about the treadmill of their lives, they seem to continually create more stress for themselves in the form of worka-holism, constant deadlines, damaging relation-ships, financial pressures, and just generally severe overextension of energy and time. When stress becomes more and more of a fixture in our lives, the angels suggest that we stop and take a long, hard look at why we are creating unhappiness for ourselves, what we may be running from, and whether or not we re-ally want to live in turmoil instead of peace.

If you are under a lot of stress, are you willing to look at how you might be creating it? What purpose does it serve? What would you have to face if all the stress suddenly left your life?

An Angelic Reflection: I study the example of the angels, who are the essence of serenity, not stress.

Cosmic Jokers

An Angel Reminder: It is in being able to laugh at our powerlessness that we discover our power.

The cosmic jokers are an important part of the mythology of many cultures. They are the clowns, the tricksters, and the disrupters, whose function is to remind us that nothing is so serious, including ourselves, that it can't be instantly deflated by the well-aimed arrow of divine realism. The jokes of the cosmos can come in the form of humor, humiliation, or pain; their severity is proportional to the degree to which we are attached to the illusion of our own self-importance. When we find ourselves feeling overburdened by life, overfond of our own opinions, or overcome by the desire to control everyone and everything around us, we should probably put on steel underwear. For a cosmic kick in the pants is surely coming to send us flying into the arms of our infinitely patient, infinitely loving angels, who will happily remind us that laughter is freedom.

Has the cosmos played any jokes, practical or impractical, on you lately? If so, what were you being told, and how did you respond?

An Angelic Reflection: I expect the unexpected and am never disappointed.

$\mathcal{R}$AIN

An Angel Reminder: "Isn't it a lovely day to be caught in the rain?"

Fred Astaire and Ginger Rogers, Top Hat

The rain is one of those marvelous events of nature that calls to our wild side. Hollywood movies, after all, are full of scenes like the one in which Fred Astaire and Ginger Rogers fall in love in a downpour or Gene Kelly goes singin' in the rain, letting the whole world know he is in love while getting happily drenched to the bone. In our younger and more daring days, perhaps, we were not afraid of the rain. But as we grow older and less adventurous, we tend to venture out into life armed with the swords and shields of umbrellas and slickers. Have we forgotten how liberating and invigorating it can be to strip off the layers of the years and dance with the rain— to do, every once in a while, something thoroughly crazy, to stand unafraid to reveal our true selves before the world, accepting all of its moods with complete, unfettered jubilation?

When was the last time you gave vent to your wild side? The next time it rains, do something out of the ordinary. An example: one sixty-five-year-old man we know ran out into the rain in his underwear to cut his wife a rose from the backyard. Whatever you do, remain in the rain long enough to step out of the routineness of life but not long enough, of course, to catch pneumonia!

An Angelic Reflection: I have a strong sense of wonder and adventure.

Mystic Testimony

An Angel Reminder: "What people need now—more than oxygen—is real mystic testimony."

Andrew Harvey

Finding the hidden stories of our lives and connecting with our own mystical selves is fun and exciting. When we uncover something that is spiritually symbolic to us, we begin to find our spiritual roots. Each of us has a treasure chest of our own mysteries—like the mystery of why we are attracted to certain people, places, and things. To understand our own mysteries we must look at our obsessions, tendencies, tastes, and the fragments of dream pictures that stay in our minds and examine them for clues that may lend insight to the deeper parts of who we are. When we begin the process of discovering our spiritual roots, our lives will be full of mystical experiences. A testimony is evidence in support of something; our mystical experiences provide us with testimony in support of our connection to the Divine.

Be mysterious. Be unfinished. Be surprising to yourself and others. Allow mystical experiences to be a regular part of your life. Ask the angels to help you gain insight into your inner life. Have fun with your own mystery, and remember that the story never ends.

An Angelic Reflection: My life is full of mystical testimony.

SPACE

An Angel Reminder: "And let the winds of heaven dance between you. . . ."

Kahlil Gibran, The Prophet

We all need our space. And we all need to remember that others need theirs. But sometimes we are afraid of space, confusing it with isolation, loneliness, and distance rather than welcoming it as an opportunity for reflection and regeneration. The angels regard space—the freedom to be where and who we want to be—as essential to our growth, our happiness, and our sanity. While it may sometimes seem a luxury in today's hectic, crowded, overcommitted world, space is actually a necessity, something we have to put our effort into creating and allowing if we want to be healthy and balanced. Whenever we feel the effects of extreme pressure and stress, it's time to call upon the angels to help us create both physical and mental space for ourselves and to help us use that space to reconnect with our calm centers. Kahlil Gibran symbolized the space between lovers as the winds of heaven, for it is within the infinite space of heaven that we unite with the Divine.

If you have trouble allowing yourself and others space, or if you fear space as an exercise in loneliness and aimlessness, ask the angels to help you visualize a protective bubble of light around you. Let this bubble be your space, your place to be free of all the worries and expectations of the outside world. Relax inside this warm, comforting bubble; let your mind slow down, let your thoughts flow freely, knowing that you may enter or exit the bubble at any time.

An Angelic Reflection: I welcome the calming freedom of space in my life.

OBVIOUS

An Angel Reminder: It is obvious that common sense is not so common.

When something is obvious, it is easily understood, recognized quickly, and very visible. No matter how obvious some things are, we miss them, even when they are right in front of our eyes. We like to complicate things. If the answers we are looking for are obvious and uncomplicated, we ignore them in search of a deeper meaning. What we need is a deeper sense of what is obvious. If you feel hurt, something has hurt you. If you are feeling tired, you need rest. If you want to have a friend, you must be a friend. If you want the angels in your life, you must invite them in.

Go back to basic common sense whenever you are feeling confused, and look for the obvious. Don't disregard feelings. You don't have to overreact to something, but if you feel a certain way, there is most likely an obvious reason why. If you sense trouble, look in the obvious places for a troublemaker. Ask the angels to help you see and accept the obvious.

An Angelic Reflection: I will look first at what is obvious for answers, then go beyond the obvious for more questioning.

RAGEDY

An Angel Reminder: "Prepare, then, for opportunity disguised as loss."

Ralph Blum, The Book of Runes

It is said that once when a woman went to the Buddha sobbing over the loss of her child, demanding to know why she should be visited with such misfortune, the Buddha replied, "Go to every house in your village and find me one that has not been touched by death." Of course the woman could not; death—loss—is an inevitable part of life. When discussing angels, the question of tragedy always comes up. Why would the angels help some people and not others? Why would one person's guardian angel rescue him or her from danger, while another person dies or loses someone dear? The answer lies in the Buddha's reply: sooner or later, everyone must encounter loss. It is *how* one copes with that loss that determines one's happiness or misery. The angels cannot prevent tragedy from occurring if it is time for us to encounter it on our own soul's path. But they can help us to see that, if viewed as "opportunity disguised as loss," tragedy, no matter how devastating, can always lead to new life.

Think of the losses you've experienced in your life. What are the good—the growth-producing—things that came from them? If you are now going through a loss of some sort, allow yourself to grieve. At the same time, try to accept the fact that this loss is necessary for your soul's growth, and know that with the angels as your loving companions, you will emerge from the difficulty renewed in some way.

An Angelic Reflection: I know that loss is part of life. I will accept it, learn from it, and continue to grow.

*M*ENTAL SANCTITY

An Angel Reminder: The mind is the universal place of worship.

Imagine a sacred room where God lives. Let's say this room is in your house, and it is up to you to decide who gets to go in and be with God. Our minds are such sacred chambers. A mind is like a force field surrounding the soul, spirit, and body. Because we encounter God and the angels within this force field, it is important for us to keep sacred space available in which to welcome our divine friends. We must always remember that our minds are inviolable and protected by the angels. Our thoughts are private until we share them. Not everyone will understand your innermost spiritual thoughts and feelings, so often the right thing to do is keep them to yourself and to your angels, and to create enough privacy in your life to have the time and space to reflect upon and nourish them. In this way, our sacred room of the mind becomes our haven of spiritual resource and sustenance.

Do you have your sacred room ready and available for your use any time you need it? Is God comfortable there? This room is your inner place where you can try out new ideas, heal yourself, relax, communicate with the angels, and open your soul to divine inspiration.

An Angelic Reflection: My mind is a private sanctuary, a place of refuge against the storms of negativity, and a meeting place for God and the angels.

*T*HE OTHER PERSON'S ANGEL

An Angel Reminder: When the door to the mind closes, we can always climb through the open window of the soul.

When we are having trouble communicating with some-one, it can be extremely helpful to talk to that person's angel instead. What we can't accomplish through words or reason can often be achieved through communicating with the other's spiritual rather than physical self. In her book *A Gift of Love,* metapsychiatrist Ann Linthorst tells a story about a father who couldn't seem to get through to his drug-addicted son. "The father began, as he put it, to have 'long talks with the boy's angel,' and eventually the boy was healed and he was able to talk directly to him." How we choose to see the other person's angel is up to us; we may envision an actual guardian angel, or we may simply communicate with the pure spiritual self of the other. Either way, the angels assure us that our love and concern will be heard and processed at the deeper level, the level where true change takes place.

If communication with someone in your life seems blocked, try having a conversation with that person's angel. What are your needs? Your concerns? What would you most like this person to know? Communicate everything to the other's angel, making sure you are coming from a place of loving concern rather than anger and frustration. Talk to that per-son's angel whenever you feel you need to, and trust that the message will get through in its own time, in its own way.

An Angelic Reflection: I know that the angels are divine messengers in every sense of the term.

*S*PIRITUAL INDIVIDUALIST

An Angel Reminder: Never become too comfortable with answers or affiliations.

Spiritual individualists keep their minds fresh and their interest in the big picture of life keen by having more questions than answers at any given time. Spiritual individualists are freethinkers; they do not rely on any one religion or philosophy to tell them what is right or wrong. Instead, they perceive that there are deeper truths in all human situations, truths that go beyond right or wrong. Spiritual individualists would never try to change beliefs, sway thinking, or deprive people of their right to reach their own conclusions. They seek mutual respect in this arena, and they move on quickly if they feel the heat of extreme dogma. After all, dogma is meant to be accepted as true without question, and spiritual individualists seek questions, not answers.

The spiritual individualist wants to know God, not just be told about God. Do you want to really experience God in your own life, in your own ways? If the answer is yes, get to know the voice of the Divine God Within. You can learn to connect with the God Within for your own answers and for interesting new questions. Ask the angels to help you get to know God and to enjoy knowing God as they do. How can you really trust God if you don't know God for yourself?

An Angelic Reflection: I am a freethinker who wants to know God in my own true way.

MARRIAGE

An Angel Reminder: "The fault, dear Brutus, lies not in our stars but in ourselves."

Shakespeare, Julius Caesar

Marriage is a state to which many of us aspire without really knowing why. Perhaps we're seeking companionship, love, or passion. Or we may want a family, a home, and financial security. But too often we look to marriage as a way to fulfill our emotional and physical needs without fully understanding that the union of two people carries with it a spiritual duty—to the self, to each other, and to those new souls it may bring into the world. To the angels, marriage is not a legal contract, not a legitimized sexual union, not a house and kids, but a shared quest for spiritual truth and a shared commitment to spiritual growth. It involves taking responsibility for our own happiness or unhappiness; allowing a spouse the same right; and cherishing, not condemning, the other for being who she or he is. When we encounter problems, we recognize that the fault, as well as the solution to our problems, lies not in the other person but in ourselves—our beliefs, attitudes, and willingness or unwillingness to replace recrimination with understanding.

What are your attitudes toward marriage? If you are married, are you happy? If not, how would you like things to change? If you are divorced, what did you learn about marriage? If you would like to be or are planning on getting married, what are you expecting to get from marriage? What are you expecting to give?

An Angelic Reflection: I know that marriage calls for spiritual growth and understanding.

SEED

An Angel Reminder: "In this small grain of wheat are contained all the laws of the universe and the forces of nature."

Zoroaster

A seed will not grow if we try to plant it in a carpet or a hardwood floor. A seed planted in the earth, where it belongs, in contact with the soil, the rain, the air, the sunshine, and the light of the moon, will grow into a useful plant. Like the seed, we too need to get out of our artificial environments and go into the garden, close to the forces of nature, to learn and expand our knowledge of the universe. The seed grows into a plant, and the plant offers an abundance of seeds to continue the great process of life. Like the seed, if we are planted in a natural way to promote growth, we too will offer many seeds of light to help continue the great process, the indestructible power of life.

Do you get out of your artificial environment often enough to learn from nature? Buy a seed and plant it. While it grows, gain insight from the process. Ask the angels and nature spirits to watch over your seed with you and help you become part of the process of growth. The larger our spirits grow the more room they need to expand, so if needed get out into the open air and bloom.

An Angelic Reflection: I am a seed of light.

$\mathcal{A}$NGELIC

An Angel Reminder: Our true selves are angelic.

What does *angelic* really mean? Many times we confuse being angelic with being nice, which usually means doing just what everyone is comfortable with. Niceness can be an angelic quality, but it can also be a substitute for honesty, a way of avoiding confrontation, an attempt to please others in order to receive approval. The angels are not "nice"; they are loving but honest. They will never lead us down a primrose path; they will keep us apprised of the truth, regardless of how troublesome we perceive it to be. Being angelic means, above all, being true to ourselves and willing to be truthful with others. Our true selves know the situations we really want to be in and those that we don't. Being angelic is not always easy. Sometimes it means facing uncomfortable situations and having the courage and discipline to live in personal integrity, no matter how difficult that may become. But the reward is well worth the effort, for we will experience, through our angelic selves, the joy of knowing—and allowing others to know and value—who we really are.

Are you expecting the angels to be nice to you all the time? Are you wanting them to act according to your own set of rules instead of the Creator's? Are there people in your life who make you angry because they're not "nice"—although they may be honest? Are you nice when you should be more truthful? How might your life change the more true to yourself you become?

An Angelic Reflection: As I grow in personal truth, I allow my truly angelic self to emerge.

$\mathcal{E}$VERY FACE

An Angel Reminder: One moon shows in every pool. In every pool the one moon.

Zen saying

Just as the one moon shows in every pool, the one God shows in every face. All religions that worship God worship the same God. Does God have a different face in each religion? No, but humans interpret God in their own ways, which may make it seem that some religions are worshiping a different God. Most of the world's religions are based on moral teachings designed to uplift the soul, and most include a belief in angels. With all the supposed differences among religious beliefs, the experiences of God are very similar, and God remains the same.

How much do you know about the world's great religions? It is easy to pick up bits and pieces of information these days about Eastern religions, and many people strive to be eclectic in their spiritual readings and teachings. Explore the many teachings for insight into the religions of humankind, and you will find that although our beliefs may differ greatly, the God we all worship is the same.

An Angelic Reflection: I know if I look beyond the name of religion, I will see the same God in every face.

$\mathcal{T}$IME

An Angel Reminder: If we had no clocks, what time would it be?

We take the twenty-four-hour day for granted. But did you know that the Black Plague was instrumental in giving us a sense of time as we now know it? Before the plague, time was considered the domain of God. People did not live by the clock but rather thought of time in terms of day and night, the seasons, life and death, eternity. But when the worst episode of the plague struck Europe in the fourteenth century, attitudes toward time changed. As workforces were decimated, work hours were extended into the night. Suddenly clocks and bells began to signal the hours, and people began to live their lives not by God's time but by merchants' time, the measure we still use today. Time, then, is an arbitrary concept, which we can create or uncreate. While we may have to live in *physical* time, we can increase our awareness and experience of *psychic* time. Those who have had mystical experiences know that time can be suspended. A dream may seem to span several hours but may actually last only two minutes. The angels invite us to explore above and beyond traditional boundaries of time and space so as to appreciate the nonlinear, truly infinite nature of God's time.

Try noticing how time passes in your life. When do you forget about time? When do the hours seem to drag? Have you experienced timeless moments? Keep a journal, and you will begin to see how you can actually contract and expand time.

An Angelic Reflection: I know that time is infinite and that many different realities can exist in the same space at the same moment.

SUCCESS

An Angel Reminder: We can fail only if we fail to try.

In our society success is synonymous with two things: money and power. But the angels measure success by entirely different standards. First of all, to the angels money and power have no value in and of themselves. If money and power are employed for the good of all, then the person who has them could be deemed successful—not for having them but for the accompanying sense of gratitude, compassion, and generosity. Second, to the angels there is no such thing as failure, because everything we do is part of the discovery process. We can fail in life—fall short of our soul's mark—only if we fail to try, to explore, to risk. If we live according to our values, do what we love and are inspired to do, and are not afraid to experiment with life, we are automatic successes, no matter how much money we make or how high a position we have attained.

Do you feel successful? If so, why? Do you think the angels would view you as successful for the same reasons? Start to think of success in terms of your own values. Do you enjoy what you do and feel you are making a contribution to the world in some way? If you haven't yet achieved your goals, work at learning from your experience while enjoying the process.

An Angelic Reflection: I explore, I risk, I learn, I succeed.

$\mathcal{F}$EARS

An Angel Reminder: Life is not so much a matter of what we have done as what we have not done.

In the movie *Defending Your Life,* Albert Brooks's character has died and finds himself in the position of defending his life in court. In this court he has to account for the times when he allowed his fears to keep him from taking risks that would have brought him success and happiness. The court administers no punishment. If the defendant is found to have too many fears, she or he simply has to go back to earth and try again. Since fears rarely feature common sense as their primary attribute, the only purpose they serve in our lives is to challenge us to move beyond them. How are you doing so far? Are you an adventurer, an explorer, a discoverer of life? Or would you have a lot to explain if the angels held court and asked you about the times you wouldn't take that risk and break free from the shackles of your little fears?

Think of a fear you have and ask yourself if it has kept you from doing what your heart may be leading you to do. Maybe a fear of flying has kept you from the adventure and education of travel. A fear of success may be holding you back from doing your best. Or a fear of letting people know who you really are might keep you from developing deep friendships or finding a love relationship. Whatever your fears may be, think of what your life could be like without them. Now begin to let them go.

An Angelic Reflection: I am not a prisoner of my fears. They challenge me to live fully, and I accept their challenge.

OSMOSIS

An Angel Reminder: Assimilate the positive.

Osmosis is a process of assimilation or absorption that happens gradually and naturally. When we assimilate information by osmosis it can involve simply being in the presence of a teacher we want to learn from. Osmosis starts with intention. If we intend to learn something, we begin to pick up information on many different levels. Supposedly our unconscious minds are always awake and learning, picking up signals and processing information that translates into the way we carry ourselves and the signals we give out. Osmosis is a two-way street; while we are absorbing information and nuances from others, they are doing the same with us.

It is wise to be aware of the subtle power of osmosis; then we will be more aware of who we are around and what we may absorb without being completely conscious of it. If we keep the angels present around us, by our intent to live in angel consciousness, then by osmosis we will be learning many things from the angels at all times.

An Angelic Reflection: I will assimilate and absorb the divine impulses of the angels, and I will give out angel energy through the power of osmosis for those in my presence.

*E*XPLANATIONS

An Angel Reminder: "Who can explain it? Who can tell you why? Fools give you reasons; wise men never try."

Rodgers and Hammerstein, South Pacific

Do you sometimes feel that the more you try to explain yourself, the less you are understood? Or, do you often try to explain something about life that you don't understand, hoping that it may lose its power over you? For example, when tragedy strikes, we may try desperately to come up with some explanation for it. But how could we really explain tragedy? And why do we need to? We think that if we explain the unknown, we will have nothing to fear. But the angels understand that some things are unknown to us for a reason and that only by accepting the mystery as it is do we free ourselves to move past fear. In time we will know all that is to be known, but for now angel wisdom tells us to accept the seemingly inexplicable and proceed forward in our quest for enlightenment.

Accept the fact that sometimes, maybe often, you are not going to be understood. Accept the fact that here on earth there are some things you may never understand. Ask the angels to guide you past explanations and into moment-to-moment living.

An Angelic Reflection: Through reflecting upon and accepting what I don't yet understand, I grow closer to the true meaning of life.

Anger and Hatred

An Angel Reminder: "Anger and hatred are the materials from which hell is made."

Thich Nhat Hanh

Anger is an energy that can be either defused or rechanneled into positive action. Hatred is anger that has been allowed to get out of control. Have you ever watched someone in the throes of hatred? Have you noticed how that person's face distorts, his or her voice intensifies, and others present start to squirm? We all have reasons to be angry; there are many injustices in the world and in our lives. But when we indulge in hatred, we have lost our power to reason with our anger and our chance to transform it into a constructive force. The angels ask us not to let the sun go down upon our anger. They urge us to avoid the deadly trap of hatred by reflecting upon our anger and taking action to either defuse it or express it productively or creatively.

If anger is taking up more space in your consciousness than peace and acceptance, it's time to stop and think about why you are holding onto it. Look in a mirror to see what anger does to your features and how it appears to others. Then talk to your anger; ask it why it remains in your life, what purpose it serves. Finally, ask the angels for the most appropriate and useful way to release your anger and move on to a more centered and compassionate state of being.

An Angelic Reflection: I work with my anger, transforming it into constructive energy.

$\mathcal{W}$ATER SPIRITS

An Angel Reminder: "All water spirits can teach us about our inner feelings. In learning to connect with them, we can gain many benefits."

Ted Andrews

We begin life in water. Water is the primary element that keeps our bodies running. Water represents purification, emotions, and mystery. Most humans feel best when they live near a natural source of water. The water spirits are the guardian angels of natural sources of water, and they can be seen by some dancing in waterfalls and riding the waves of the ocean. Water spirits have many names, and many different myths surround them. Water spirits include the undines, water sprites, water faeries, nymphs, and of course the mermaids. In order to see them it is important to know them. You may not be able to see them with your eyes, but you will see them in your imagination's eye and feel their spirits once you are ready to acknowledge their presence.

In his book Enchantment of the Faerie Realm, *Ted Andrews suggests many creative ways to contact the water spirits. One particularly beautiful way is to go to a pond at dawn or dusk and toss flower blossoms into it, then watch ripples form around the flowers as the water sprites gather around to enjoy the flower. Find a pond, lake, or stream near where you live and go spend some quiet time just sitting near the water. Write down any thoughts or feelings that come to you as you attune to the realm of the water spirits.*

An Angelic Reflection: I attune my mind and heart to the essence of life-giving water and the many guardian spirits that preserve its mystery.

SPIRITUAL OIL CHANGE

An Angel Reminder: Don't forget to change your oil before taking any spiritual trips.

Sometimes we hesitate to make one change in our lives because we think it will lead to too many more. But think of how many changes you make in your car before buying a new one. You change the oil when it gets dirty, for motor oil keeps things running smoothly, and keeping the oil clean extends the life of the car. After you change the oil in a car you can go the same places with your car; you don't have to change its behavior or get a new car! Keep your own spiritual oil fresh and change it often. In this way, you can keep your life running smoothly without trading it in for a new one.

Maybe it is time to change the oil in your life. Changing the oil could represent eating differently, ceasing to do something you know is not productive, using creative energy to dispel depression, bringing angel consciousness into all you do, or discovering a new spiritual thought system to explore. Making positive changes in your life does not have to mean radically changing your behavior.

An Angelic Reflection: I will keep my mind running smoothly by changing my spiritual oil.

*A*NGEL MEDICINE

An Angel Reminder: The angels carry the medicine of Divine Creation.

Angel medicine is anything that improves our mental peace and brings harmony to our souls and spirit, strengthening our connection to the Divine Creator. Angel medicine is not dispensed in pills or liquid, and it will never be studied or developed in a scientific laboratory. Instead, it is personal to us—our own unique prescription for relief from self-doubt, frustration, and other forms of unhappiness. When we take our angel medicine, we receive understanding and personal power. In certain Native American thought systems, each creature is said to carry its own medicine. Through distinctive patterns of behavior, for instance, each animal can send us messages to help us achieve clarity. Just as we can call upon the medicine of a certain animal, we can also call upon the medicine of a certain angel for help and understanding. Remember that there are angels representing each divine quality and that they are only too happy to bring that quality into your life.

Design your own angel medicine cabinet. What would you find within? What do you need to stock up on? What should you get rid of because it has expired? Create an angel medicine bag. Get a little pouch and fill it with items symbolizing your own angel medicine. Some ideas for things to include in your pouch: beautiful rocks or stones, a feather, a heart, small pictures, a saying, a prayer request, ancestral artifacts, religious medals, flowers, or whatever is meaningful to you.

An Angelic Reflection: The medicine of the angels touches my soul and heals my spirit.

*C*LEANING 'HOUSE

An Angel Reminder: Housework is an inner as well as an outer activity.

Many of us spend a good deal of time ordering and straightening our physical environments while forgetting to do the same for our mental/emotional living spaces. We need to go regularly into the closets and storage spaces of our lives to clear out the old and make room for the new. Do we have old debts that need to be taken care of? People whom we need to confront, reconnect with, or let go of? Projects that either need to be completed or released? Beliefs that are no longer relevant to our current situation? The angels know that the more clutter we accumulate in our lives, the more overwhelmed we feel and the more difficult it becomes to sort things out. But when we take the time to clean house and free ourselves from old burdens, we can experience the lightness of being that allows us to move, effortlessly and joyously like the angels, on to new goals and experiences.

Is it time to do some inner housecleaning? Make a list of all the old junk you've been meaning to get around to dealing with someday. What can be kept? What needs to be completed? What needs to be thrown out? Invite the angels in as your cleaning crew, and ask them to give you suggestions for how best to put things in order.

An Angelic Reflection: As I continue to confront and complete things, I experience a wonderful sense of satisfaction and freedom.

*A*NGEL CONFERENCES

An Angel Reminder: The angels are our most valued consultants.

In the workplace, conferences are essential events, designed to disseminate information, generate new ideas, offer support, and keep everybody on course. The angels approve of conferences and like to be invited to them. We can hold an angel conference any time we like, for any purpose. Angel conferences are useful in helping us plan our goals and discover the actions we need to take to reach them. Or we can call a conference with the angels if we're having problems with people or issues. The angels act as our staff and consultants; we can count on them for advice, and we can also assign them tasks that we can't handle. There is no set way to hold an angel conference; the only rule is to let your imagination run wild and *have fun with the process*. After all, you wouldn't want to risk boring the angels.

Hold an angel conference. Ask anybody you choose, from God as the chair to saints, archangels, famous people past or present whom you admire—there's no restriction. Have fun; be creative. You can then invite specific angels who have expertise in the areas in which you need help. Ask them to give you suggestions and inspirations as to appropriate actions to take. Don't be shy; the angels love to work for you. Keep the conference full of light, beauty, gratitude, and positive energy. Write down any insights or ideas you receive, and remember to thank the angels for their time and effort.

An Angelic Reflection: The angels are always available to assist me in attaining clarity, purpose, and power in my life.

CRAFTSMANSHIP

An Angel Reminder: True craftsmanship understands that no one thing exists apart from another.

In the early years of the century, the Craftsman movement in architecture and design took those two disciplines to new heights of grace and symmetry. Craftsman architects believed that a house existed not apart from but in conjunction with the total environment. So they aspired to perfection in both form and function. Working closely with the wealthy owners of the home to be, the craftsman architect was planner, interior designer, landscaper; he would often extend a subtle design theme from the structure of the house through the interior decor and into the yard and gardens to create an effect of harmony and balance in which even the minutest objects played an integral part. The mere placement of a lamp, for instance—its shape and the light and shadows it cast in a room—was as important as the structural planning of the home itself. As a result, when a Craftsman home was sold and the new owner brought in new furnishings, the magnificence of the house seemed to mysteriously disappear, for without the splendid synthesis of object and space, structure and surroundings, it lost its soul.

Can you imagine what the world would be like if everyone adopted the Craftsman attitude toward life? How can you bring a little of the Craftsman philosophy into your life?

An Angelic Reflection: I strive for harmony and wholeness in all that I do.

$\mathcal{P}$OISE

An Angel Reminder: Poise is a natural effect of living in angel consciousness.

Poise is the quality to cultivate if you want to have more stability and confidence in your everyday life. A poised manner exudes dignity and promotes peace. Contrary to popular belief, poise is not something that is learned in acting or charm school. Rather, genuine poise is the natural outgrowth of a balanced inner nature. When our inner nature is balanced, we never lose our composure. Instead, we remain calm in mind and manner, no matter what the situation. Poise also has another meaning: to be suspended in a state of readiness for action. When we are poised, we are balanced both mentally and physically, at peace with but completely aware of our surroundings, able to reason and respond with thoughtfulness, clarity, and quickness of mind and body.

Wake up in the morning and decide that you will remain poised throughout your day. Write a declaration stating that regardless of the insanity around you in the world, regardless of the unhappiness, anger, and instability of the outside illusions, you will remain calm and centered and never lose your poise. Ask the angels to help remind you that each time your poise is threatened you must go back to your center of calmness and breathe deeply. Any action taken when we are calm, poised, and conscious of the angels will be the right action.

An Angelic Reflection: I will practice the art of poise in my everyday life, knowing that a calm center keeps the angels close to my heart.

SCOPE

An Angel Reminder: "Ah, but a man's reach should exceed his grasp, or what's a heaven for?"

Robert Browning

If it seems the world is closing in on you, then it may be a perfect time to widen your scope. Your scope is the range of your perceptions, thoughts, and actions. When you broaden your scope, your breadth of opportunity expands. Some of us think that we have a broad view of things because we have adopted a spiritual outlook, but unless we make the effort to see new things and adjust to new information each moment, our broad views will quickly narrow. Widening one's scope means making the choice to grow, to accept changes, and to find hidden information. The angels are master teachers when it comes to widening the range of your perceptions.

A scope is an instrument for observing or looking closer at something. For example, a microscope allows you to see tiny details up close, and a telescope allows you to see far away. Give yourself an angelscope. If you need insight into something that is difficult to understand, put it under your angelscope for a lighter, brighter, and grander view.

An Angelic Reflection: I will improve my view of life by widening my scope.

$\mathcal{I}$NNOCENCE

An Angel Reminder: Innocence is always just a breath away.

Our souls remain in a pure state of innocence. Why? Because innocence allows us freedom from rigid beliefs and stale ways of being, all of which inhibit the soul's growth. Because it is so often confused with naïveté, or even stupidity, innocence is often not rewarded in a society that puts a high value on criticism and opinion. True innocence, however, is the opposite of naïveté; one must be extremely conscious and at peace with oneself in order to risk being free of preconception, judgment, and other dogmatic behaviors that we so often use to define and secure our identity. What prevents us from allowing ourselves to become innocent? Fear of looking foolish, of acting like a child rather than an adult? Worries that weigh us down so heavily that we feel guilty about setting our minds free simply to enjoy life for a moment, a day, or the rest of our lives? When we wish to rediscover our natural innocence, all we need to do is call upon the angels, for innocence is their natural state as well.

Imagine the angels giving your soul a bath, washing it in innocence. Take a deep breath and allow a moment of innocence to fill your being.

An Angelic Reflection: My soul and spirit are innocent and free.

$\mathcal{T}$EACHERS

An Angel Reminder: The angels are your spiritual helpers, and it is important to use their help regardless of what spiritual teaching you are investigating.

A Zen master was once asked by his students to explain the moon. Without saying a word he pointed his finger at the moon. His students were amazed and said, "Ah, the moon is a finger!" Most of us are prone to making the same mistake concerning the angels. The angels point to God; they don't want us to focus on them but rather on the nature of God. Many spiritual teachers and teachings also point to the Divine, and it is important not to confuse the teachers with the message. Some teachers may want you to confuse them with the Divine, so use discernment. There are teachers for each level of awareness we reach. All teachings can be of value, when you look beyond the teacher and search for information.

A passive student will rarely question and is quite happy to be told what to do and how to learn. An active student will look beyond the information and find new facets of learning. The angels want us to be more active in learning about life and to remember that we are all teachers for one another. And teachers too have to keep learning, for "the unfed mind devours itself."

An Angelic Reflection: I will seek to understand the nature of things and find the essence of spiritual teachings.

$\mathcal{T}$REES

An Angel Reminder: A tree gives freely and generously.

Trees are magical and spiritual symbols. The tree of life and the tree of knowledge are bridges between heaven and earth with the branches reaching high to the heavens and the roots traveling deep within the earth. Without trees, life on earth would be barren and uninhabitable. Trees filter our air; the roots secure the topsoil we grow our food in; we use trees to build our homes; trees shade us from the hot sun and provide windbreaks; we burn trees for fuel to cook with and keep us warm; and many foods, medicines, and countless other useful items that we take for granted come from trees. Have you ever noticed how children are naturally drawn to play in and around trees? Did you have a favorite tree as a child? Make a point of appreciating trees; it will truly enrich your life.

Trees have guardian spirits, and we can learn many things from sitting quietly near a tree and communicating with its energy. Tree spirits can have their favorite human, just as we can choose our favorite tree. Find a tree that you are free to enjoy, and get to know it. To greet your tree, stand back so that it is in full view and take your eyes to the top of the tree, admiring the space where heaven meets earth. Then look at the details of your tree, the beauty of its branches, the strength of its roots. Trees can teach us about strength, dignity, peace, and giving.

An Angelic Reflection: I will honor the trees and thank them for the strength and peace that they bring to human life.

$\mathcal{B}$OURGEOIS

An Angel Reminder: "Too many people spend money they haven't earned, to buy things they don't want, to impress people they don't like."

Will Rogers

Some people make slaves out of themselves by joining the bourgeoisie. What happens is that they become overly concerned with possessions, and they demand respectability for being conventional—being the same as someone else and fitting in. Slaves work for someone else's good. Bourgeois slaves are working to impress someone else or keep up with what others are doing so that they are not free to be themselves and do what they really want. Joining the bourgeoisie is a sidetrack to avoid living your own life. Some people don't even realize they've fallen into the trap of convention. It takes so much time and energy to run around a treadmill, they forget that they can choose to get out and go forward.

Don't be a slave to convention or to the way you think things should be. Stop trying to fit into an illu-sion. The angels welcome diversity and individuality. Free yourself from any hint of bourgeois entrapment by buying what you want—not to impress anyone else—and spending money you do have.

An Angelic Reflection: The angels honor my individuality, and I will honor the angels by living true to my means and being grateful for the chance to be me.

𝒜NXIETY

An Angel Reminder: We have everything we need to control everything we need to control.

Anxiety is really only an alarm bell, urging us to slow down, let go, and call on the angels. We experience anxiety only when we feel out of control. But when we realize that, with the exception of our own actions and responses, we can or need to control very little else in life, we have taken our first step toward inner peace. The angels are anxiety busters; we can call on them whenever we need them, even for the smallest requests and especially for the smallest fears. So when you start to feel out of control and panicked, don't just ignore the problem and put on a stiff upper lip. Instead, admit that you're feeling anxious and then surrender to the angels, knowing that they will restore your inner balance. All you have to do is trust them when they tell you that *everything is going to be all right!*

If you feel that anxiety is getting the best of you, immediately take time out from what you are doing. Lie down if you can or sit comfortably, and begin to breathe deeply (preferably through the nose), allowing the air to glide gently into your abdomen. As you breathe, imagine that the angels are bathing you in a restful golden light. Continue to breathe and feel the warmth of this light permeate your being. Start to repeat in your mind: "Everything is going to be all right." Keep repeating this, and allow yourself to feel calmed by the protective embrace of the angels.

An Angelic Reflection: Next time I start to panic I will surrender to the angels, allowing myself to be protected by their love and guided by their wisdom.

ILTER

An Angel Reminder: We stay in good working order when we balance our lives.

Kilter means good working order, and *out of kilter* means not working properly. We have many lessons to learn about balance. Balance in our minds, bodies, and spirits will keep us in good working and playing order, and we attain balance by knowing how to establish boundaries. This is not easy, but it is important. There is only one way another person can truly hurt and bother us, and that is by crossing our boundaries, physically or mentally, without being invited.

Do you establish boundaries easily, or do you find yourself eventually uncomfortable in certain relationships without knowing why? The discomfort comes when we forget to recognize our own boundaries and fail to stop a person from traipsing across them. Setting boundaries isn't easy for people who will do anything to avoid a conflict. Maybe you think that setting boundaries is unkind. Establishing your boundaries is actually the kindest thing you can do for yourself and for others.

An Angelic Reflection: I respect my own boundaries and the boundaries of others; I live with the beauty of inner peace.

$\mathcal{B}$ODY

An Angel Reminder: We are the holy trinity of body, mind, and spirit.

In our search for spiritual truth, we often find ourselves living in a mental rather than a physical realm. As a result, we may begin to neglect our physical selves. While we may perceive the goal of a spiritual quest to be the transcendence of the physical dimension, and while we know that the body is ultimately no more than a piece of clothing that we shed when we leave the earth, we cannot be in genuine alignment with heaven until we are in alignment with ourselves. If we are in poor health, fatigued, or overstressed, we cannot be pure channels for higher consciousness. The angels want us to take care of our bodies as well as our spirits, for it is through the physical that we contact our higher selves. When we nurture our bodies correctly and lovingly, we increase our physical and mental energy, which in turn fuels our creative power and our capacity for enthusiasm and joy, opening us up to all the wonders of the angelic realm.

How do you relate to your body? Do you treat it lovingly, or do you neglect it? Are you proud or ashamed of it? Start looking in the mirror and seeing yourself as the angels see you, with complete love, appreciation, and respect. Then translate this love, appreciation, and respect into everyday actions that you can take to honor your body and make yourself feel comfortable as a physical being.

An Angelic Reflection: As I absorb the loving and freeing energy of the angels, I become more loving, accepting, and caring toward my body.

DIVERGENT THINKING

An Angel Reminder: Never be afraid to diverge from the norm.

Two types of thinking can be used in problem solving. Convergent thinking looks for the one right answer. Divergent thinking, by contrast, looks for many answers and possibilities. Both types of thinking have their rightful places. Convergent thinking is important if you are following specific instructions, such as starting a car or using an electrical appliance. However, most human problems are way too complex to be handled with convergent thinking. Divergent thinking sends us in any direction we want, allowing us to come up with new questions to ask ourselves. We find new and exciting ways to do things by thinking in a divergent manner.

Divergent thinking has not been valued in many classrooms, because many people are comfortable only with questions that have one right answer. Convergent thinking limits the ways in which people use resources. Divergent thinking leads to cleverness and resourcefulness. The angels will help you think in a more divergent way, because they encourage creativity and they love to help you come up with possibilities. Next time you encounter a problem, use your resources and think divergently.

An Angelic Reflection: I will allow my thinking to venture down the roads less traveled.

$\mathcal{F}$LATTERY

An Angel Reminder: "The more we love our friends, the less we flatter them."

Molière

Because all of us want to feel accepted and appreciated, we can easily succumb to the temptation of flattery. But there is a great difference between flattery and compliments. Flattery is, ultimately, insincere praise, an attempt on the part of the flatterer to gain something from the object of adulation. A compliment, however, is a genuine expression of admiration or appreciation that flows naturally out of the giver's heart and perceptions. The angels are not the least bit impressed by flattery. They remind us that as long as we feel good about ourselves and work at living in integrity, we will be able to tell the difference between flattery and compliments and we will not feel the need to flatter others in order to fish for approval or material gain. Neither will we be susceptible to the envy and jealousy that prevent us from giving compliments, for honest self-love naturally generates love and appreciation for others.

If you have trouble telling the difference between flattery and compliments, note how you physically react to each. When we are being flattered, we can often sense a disturbance in the solar plexus, an instinctive tightening of the area that makes us slightly uncomfortable. When we are being complimented, we tend to feel a warmth in the same area, a rush of pleasant energy. Become aware of the motivations behind flattery, and act accordingly.

An Angelic Reflection: I can feel worthy and accepted without either giving or receiving flattery.

MATURITY

An Angel Reminder: We are all designed to improve with age.

Through maturity we learn to use our minds and come to our sensibilities, but maturity has a stern connotation. It brings to one's mind a picture of adults acting sensibly and not having any fun. Maturing is actually a wonderful and natural process by which we develop intelligence, reasoning capabilities, and an open mind. With angel consciousness, maturity does not mean we have to leave our childlike natures behind us. Rather, we add wisdom to the inner child and learn to integrate childlike wonder into our adult minds. The angels teach us to appreciate the paradox of life, enjoy metaphors and irony, and above all find the humor in all of it.

If you have been taking maturity too seriously lately, lighten up and have some fun. Being sensible does not mean being a fuddy-duddy. The natural way to mature is to allow your mind to be more open. The unnatural way is to become more rigid and set in your ways. Which way are you maturing? Ask the angels to help you mature the natural way. They'll help you add a little zest to your life.

An Angelic Reflection: I will allow a natural sense of maturity to open my mind and bring me to my senses.

𝒥UDGES

An Angel Reminder: "Do not judge lest you be judged yourselves. For in the way you judge, you will be judged; and by your standard of measure, it shall be measured to you."

Matthew 7:1, 2 (New American Standard Bible)

Each little judge here on the earth has her or his own set of ideas and opinions by which to measure the progress of the rest of the world. This is, of course, an exercise in futility; the world couldn't possibly measure up to any one particular judge's standards because then it wouldn't be fair to the other judges, each of whom has a different formula for perfection. The angels know that right and wrong are anything but black-and-white issues. What if something is right in one person's heart that seems wrong to another? Who is right? Who is wrong? Judgmental people are never really happy because they need to feel superior to others in order to feel worthwhile. The angels are not judges; they are spiritual helpers. They do not sit on a bench all day, deciding whether or not someone deserves their help. They simply act from the highest place, regardless of what has happened in a person's life.

Whenever you find yourself passing judgment on someone else, start to see differences and variations instead of black and white, right and wrong. Let go of the ideals you use for judging, and respect other people's right to their viewpoints. Or, if others just seem to be acting stupidly, don't judge—let them go through their own process in their own time.

An Angelic Reflection: I allow myself and others the right to be who and where we are at this point in our life paths.

CHASING

**An Angel Reminder: Whatever we chase,
we drive into flight.**

Cats are great examples of the futility of chasing. When
we try to force cats to sit on our laps, they struggle to get
free. When we want them to come into the house, they
play hard to get. But if we sit down and occupy ourselves
with something that does not involve them, they scratch
on the door to get in and beg to sit on our laps. Just so
with the angels. If we chase them and demand that they
appear to us, they watch us from a distance. When we
begin to use our energy to live our lives instead of chasing things that are out of reach,
the angels will appear to us all the time, and
we will be so involved in living that we will
consider them a natural part of the scenery.

*If we catch the thing we are chasing, it has not
come to us freely. Sometimes we chase without recognizing it. For example, we may chase our mates around
trying to change their behavior, and the more we chase
and try to change them, the more pronounced the behavior becomes. Look into a frustrating aspect in your
life. Are you chasing something? If so, give up the chase
and get involved with something else. The results will
amaze you.*

**An Angelic Reflection: I will extend an open invitation
to those I love to come to me when they choose.**

$\mathcal{A}$VAILABLE

An Angel Reminder: To be available to the angels, all we need is an open mind and a trusting heart.

Many things that are freely available to us can bring us a sense of inner peace. A smile is always available to us; although we may not always feel like smiling, when we do our minds get a signal that something positive is happening. Our imaginations are available to us twenty-four hours a day. Space is always available for us to stop what we are doing, close our eyes, and take in a deep, cleansing breath. A sense of humor is always available to us to put things in perspective and give our immune systems a boost. And, of course, the angels are always available to us for spiritual sustenance. For good things to be available to us, however, we must also make ourselves available to receive them. If you want to see the sunrise, you need to get up early and position yourself in the right place to view it. If we harbor rigid preconceptions about the way things have to be before we can be satisfied with our lives, we may not be available to the things we yearn for should they present themselves to us in other guises. To be truly available means to let go of all our preconceptions of what constitutes happiness and let the angels write the definitions. Then we just might find joy in the most unexpected places.

What have you been available for lately? What do you feel is available to you? What are some things you could do that would make you more available to the angels?

An Angelic Reflection: When I am available, my inner door is always open to receive the guests of the spirit, who bear the gifts I am seeking.

$\mathcal{P}$RACTICE

An Angel Reminder: "Tell me, I'll forget. Show me, I may remember. But involve me and I'll understand."

Chinese proverb

Anything worth doing is worth practicing. If you want to enjoy doing what you love, you will want to take the time to practice it. Practice is great for freeing yourself to explore new ways of doing things. If you are practicing it means you give yourself the chance to play at something until you get it right, whatever that means to you. We learn best by getting involved in something, knowing it inside and out. When we practice our art, we become comfortable with our talents and we put more energy into doing than into thinking about doing. Practice allows us to be one with the Divine and involved with life.

A spiritual practice is something we incorporate into our lives on a regular basis to help us live mindfully of the Divine. When we choose to learn something, we cannot expect to master it overnight. When we choose to use our free will for the goodwill of the Divine, we can't expect an instant change. It takes effort to do good, and the more we practice, the more effortless and natural living a good life will be.

An Angelic Reflection: I will practice getting involved in life, love, and laughter.

ATTACHMENT

An Angel Reminder: When we are too attached to the things of the earth, we are not free to soar with the angels.

In virtually every spiritual philosophy, attachment is synonymous with suffering. When we are attached to something or someone, we inevitably experience pain because, sooner or later, we are going to have to relinquish all of our earthly possessions. They were only on loan to us anyway. People leave us, either through death or moving on. Material acquisitions wear out or are lost, stolen, destroyed, or left behind when we pass on. As long as we cling to relationships and things, we risk being imprisoned by either deception or apprehension. We either believe, mistakenly, that they are ours forever, or we live in the shadow of the fear that we will lose them. The opposite of attachment, then, is not only detachment, but freedom. When we can appreciate the gifts that have been loaned to us on earth and also let go of them when their time is up, we experience the freedom of spirit that enables us to recognize and receive the next gift that is in store for us. For when something is removed from our lives, it is only to make room for something better to replace it.

Is there anything—object or relationship—in your life that you feel you can't live without? Practice letting go of those things that are dearest to you. Imagine that they have left your life. What might come in to take their places?

An Angelic Reflection: As I am grateful for the summer of fulfillment, so I am equally grateful for the winter of rebirth.

GRACIOUS OFFERINGS

An Angel Reminder: Life offers us the opportunity to love deeply. Let us offer life something back in return.

Making an offering when you receive something is a way of showing gratitude. Offerings of money are traditional in religious gatherings, and certain Native American cultures offer tobacco to the land if they need to take something from it. For example, if they cut down a tree they offer tobacco to honor the spirit of the tree that will provide them wood. When we consciously offer something back, we appreciate what we receive. We never own the land; we borrow it and it provides for us. We don't own spiritual teachings; we borrow them and gain much from spiritual sustenance. Offerings are not meant to be ostentatious; the act of offering is a quiet ritual no one needs to know about except you and the angels.

You can make offerings to the angels by keeping beauty around you and acting beautiful. If you have a shrine or spiritual focus place, offer flowers to the Divine. Offerings are not sacrifices meant to attract something into your life. An offering is simply a thank-you note to the universe. Stop before you take something from nature, and make a ritual of offering something back. Be creative and have fun with your offerings.

An Angelic Reflection: I am grateful for the bountiful harvest of goodness the universe provides for me. I will offer my appreciation for what I receive.

$\mathcal{N}$ATURE

An Angel Reminder:

> "Tree at my window, window tree
> My sash is lowered when night comes on;
> But let there never be curtain drawn
> Between you and me."

Robert Frost

We have become far removed from our ancestors, not only in time and space but also in consciousness, for unlike them we neither understand nor respect nature and its many powers. But the angels know that in separating ourselves from nature, we have denied our very source. Neglecting our physical, emotional, and spiritual health as we try desperately to keep pace with a world that consistently outruns us, we have found ourselves at the mercy of the technology we created to serve us. When we reconnect to nature, however, we become conscious of our true source of strength and peace. The earth that nourishes us, the air that rejuvenates us, the water that cleanses us, the stillness that calms us—all of this is what we have forgotten, and what the angels want us to remember if we are to experience wholeness and balance in our lives.

Take more time to reconnect with nature in your life. When you go for a walk, fine-tune all of your senses to the sights, sounds, scents, and textures around you. Feel the solid strength of the trees, the richness of the earth, the softness of the grass, the freshness of the air. See everything in nature with reverent eyes, and feel yourself becoming more alive.

An Angelic Reflection: I feel and rejoice in my connection to the universal life force.

$\mathcal{D}$EFECTS

An Angel Reminder: We are not machines; we are spirit and light.

We use the strangest words to describe human nature. For example, we call our shortcomings or imperfections *defects*. A defect is a lack of something necessary or desirable. Humans are not defective; we are not machines where a necessary part or desirable option, such as air conditioning or power steering, was left out. We are exactly the way we need to be for the lives that we are living. Our so-called defects and faults really provide the ingredients for being interesting. What we refer to as personality defects most likely foster our growth and self-awareness. If we are lacking something necessary, we can probably find it hiding somewhere in our psyches. If we recognize something or desire it, it is available to us. The questions to ask are: Do we want it? Will it help us?

We need to stop labeling all our problems as faults or defects. When we label something we alienate ourselves from it, and we stop analyzing it for further understanding. Are you defective? If you answer yes, stop and really think about why you feel this way. Look for something positive about your so-called defects, and know that with the angels in your life, imperfect means "just right."

An Angelic Reflection: I am entirely ready to turn my defects into spiritual fuel.

ATTENTION

An Angelic Reminder: The quality of attention you attract depends on the quality that you give out.

We all have a basic need for attention, be it positive or negative. Some people seek attention by trying to control those around them; others seek it by allowing themselves to be controlled. Some people seek attention by trying to shock or agitate the world into noticing them. Often we seek attention through public works or office or through recognition for our talents and gifts. However we go after attention, one fact remains: when we let our egos control our higher selves, we feel separated from the angels. The angels don't reward the earthly accomplishments for which the ego craves recognition. Yet when our hearts lead us to feel gratitude or to give love to the world unconditionally, the angels will shower us with attention.

An old joke tells of a stingy woman who was so miserly that she wouldn't send her children to school when she heard that they had to "pay" attention. How generous are you in paying attention to the needs of others? Do you hoard attention for yourself? Do you feel that the world pays you enough attention? The next time you feel that you need some attention, try giving some to others free of charge, with joy and genuine interest. You will begin to act like a magnet, attracting positive attention to yourself.

An Angelic Reflection: When I pay close attention to the pursuit of a high quality life, I am aware of the angels paying close attention to me.

$\mathcal{T}$OUCH

An Angel Reminder: All humans need to be touched; no one is above it and no one is exempt.

Touch is a way we communicate warmth with our bodies. During the nineteenth century, it was discovered that children could die from a disease called *marasmus*, a Greek word meaning "wasting away." This finally stopped when Dr. Henry Chapin noticed that the babies who died had been kept in sterile environments, ruling out germs as the cause of death, but that they had never been picked up and held. He found a simple solution. He brought in women to hold the babies, talk to them, and stroke them, and the mortality rate for *marasmus* rapidly vanished. We often fantasize that the angels envy humans at times, for one advantage we have over the angels is that we can physically touch and hug our loved ones.

It is important that we find ways of communicating warmth with our bodies. Of course we cannot go around touching everyone we meet, but we do need to find a way to touch and be touched. Think about your own life and ask yourself if you need more bodily warmth on an everyday basis. If you find yourself alone and unable to reach out to another human, try getting a kitten or a puppy and showing it lots of love and attention through petting and stroking.

An Angelic Reflection: I know that the most special aspect of being human is my ability to reach out and touch someone.

Wake-up call

An Angel Reminder: "You have slept for millions and millions of years. Why not wake up this morning?"

Kabir, The Kabir Book

According to a number of spiritual philosophies, reality as we perceive it is an illusion. Although we may think we're awake, humans are essentially asleep, dreaming the dream that is life. When we are awake, we have attained consciousness—or, in this context, enlightenment. Once awake, we forgo our sense of separateness, our dependence on our egos, for the joyful realization that we are one with the universe and God. We understand that our souls are part of the infinite, that our earthly attachments are but fragments of the life dream, that the more we allow ourselves to commune with God through prayer and meditation, the more we will transcend suffering and fear of death. The angels want us to become enlightened—filled with the light of higher consciousness. They want us to wake up to the Creator's unconditional love that flows through us, nourishing the lives of our fellow human beings who, also being part of the Creator, are part of us.

When you wake up tomorrow morning, spend at least ten minutes breathing deeply and meditating on the feeling of being loved solely and completely for who you are. Then spend another few minutes meditating on the image of this love flowing out of you in a current to everyone and everything around you.

An Angelic Reflection: I am awake to the power I have as an instrument of unconditional love to transform my environment and my life.

$\mathcal{F}$REE SPIRIT

An Angel Reminder: To be a free spirit, free spirit.

We think of free spirits as those rare individuals who
have somehow managed to live by their own, not society's, rules. Free spirits are often perceived as blithely
uninhibited, bordering on crazy. They make
wonderful characters in novels and movies
because they dare to go where most of us only
dream of going—into the dangerous, entic-
ing realms of excitement, passion, and re-
bellion. Actually, however, free spirits
are simply people who have allowed
their spirits the freedom to explore life. The angels
encourage us to give our spirits a Declaration of Independence—from fear, unhappiness, criticism, and
the expectations of others. After all, like all of us,
our spirits have the right to life, liberty, and the pursuit of happiness. When we honor the spirit—the
breath of life—within us, we are honoring the true, and
therefore divine, self.

*How have you treated your spirit? Have you confined it in a
prison of fear or allowed it to be broken by sadness and despair? Or have you allowed it to soar, exploring and exulting
in life's many joys and possibilities?*

An Angelic Reflection: My spirit is free; my path is light.

$\mathcal{V}$ISION

An Angel Reminder: From high above the angels always see the big picture.

Vision has several different meanings. One is sight itself. Another is a goal, a dream, a picture of how you want things to be. And yet a third involves a mystical experience, a sighting of something beyond the ordinary senses. The angels' definition of vision incorporates all of these meanings into one big expansion of perception. When we acquire angelic vision, we see clearly—into and beyond the present confines of time and space. We open what the mystics refer to as the third eye, the eye of all-seeingness. We perceive many different levels of reality, and we use the information to create what is not yet but what can and will be. The angels want to help us improve our vision. They want us to be open, not closed, to all possibilities and to hold a vision of what we desire to accomplish deep in our consciousness, allowing that vision to grow and develop at its own pace, in its own way. We can then see the big picture instead of getting stuck in one of the pieces of the puzzle.

Do you have a vision, a dream, of something you want to create or achieve? If not, write down a list of interferences—worries or doubts—that might be holding you back from seeing the big picture. Become flexible about your personal big picture, and imagine that you are looking at it as the angels do, from above. How have past actions and experiences contributed to present circumstances? What do you see in your future?

An Angelic Reflection: I always hold on to my vision, but I never restrain it.

ANGEL COMMUNITY

An Angel Reminder: Support your local angel community and the angels will support you.

By definition a community is a group of people with common interests, fellowship, or origins, living in the same locality under the same government. We often hear people lament that they miss a sense of community and fellowship in these hurried days. The angels say, "If you miss a sense of community, then create your own angel community." An angel community is a group of people living in angel consciousness and supporting one another under the divine government of the angels. Remember that an angel community is a state of mind, and the people who belong don't need to be recruited, only silently supported.

Find people and places in your local community that give you a sense of welcome, and support them. If at a certain gas station the people are friendly, helpful, and give you a kind word when you leave, designate this as your angel community gas station. Seek grocery stores, bookstores, and other establishments that promote goodwill, and designate them part of your community. Get to know the people who work there and show an interest in them. If their prices are a little higher, spend the extra pennies. The return from the angels is worth what you pay for.

An Angelic Reflection: I will go the extra mile for the angels and those people in my community who promote goodwill.

MAGNETIZING

An Angel Reminder: We are far more powerful than we think.

We might often feel the victims of circumstance or the beneficiaries of luck, but in reality things don't just happen to us. We bring events into our lives. Although we may not be aware of it, we are magnets, drawing people and situations to us through the powerful energy force of our thoughts and belief systems. So when we desire something, our thoughts and beliefs about it will literally set things in motion. If we believe that we can have something and that it is in our best interests and the interests of others for us to have it, our higher selves—the parts of our psyches that are in communication with the angels— will begin to create it for us. We will send out an energy that connects with a corresponding energy in the universe, drawing back to us the people, circumstances, and opportunities that will help us attain our goals.

Think about something that you want. If you think that it is appropriate for you and that no one else will be harmed by your having it, practice a little magnetization. Get in a relaxed state, close your eyes, and see yourself as a powerful magnet, sending out strong beams of positive magnetic energy. Adopt an attitude of relaxed optimism. Visualize what you want, believe that you can have it, and trust that it will come to you. See the magnetic energy going out into the universe, connecting with the thing that you want, and drawing it back to you. Do this exercise once or twice a day, and see what happens.

An Angelic Reflection: I am a magnet of positive energy, drawing the things that are best for me into my life.

$\mathcal{T}$HEORY

An Angel Reminder: The angels have a theory about humans—that they are good at heart.

A theory is a way to explain something that hasn't been tested or can't really be tested. Having your own theories about things can be fun and helpful, as long as you don't get too attached to them. There are many mysteries in life that we cannot explain, but we can formulate our own theories about them. We can take pieces of information we find in books and from teachings and examine the theories that make sense to us. Theories are allowed to be abstract, meaning you don't need to base them on concrete existence. With all this in mind, have fun with your theories and go forth to explore the mysteries of life.

Some of your theories may help others understand things in the same way they help you. Before you can share your theories with others, you first have to formulate them. One theory to keep in mind is that we are all free to have our own theories. Theories are personal yet fun to share, especially if you keep your mind open. Don't get upset if someone doesn't buy your theories or if someone wants to add to or change them. Theories are always subject to change.

An Angelic Reflection: I have a theory that the angels are with us now to help keep hope, love, light, and peace thriving on the earth, through the beauty of humanity.

$\mathcal{L}$ET IT BE

An Angel Reminder: "In times of trouble . . . Mother Mary comes to me / Speaking words of wisdom, 'Let it be, let it be.'"

Paul McCartney, "Let It Be"

When you encounter a frustration about which you can, for the present, do nothing, can you be patient and trusting? Or do you fret and worry the situation to death? It is easy to "let it be" only when we have complete trust in our own integrity and in the integrity of the universe. When we trust our own integrity, we can do exactly what feels right to us without being attached to what others think. When we trust the integrity of the universe, we can relinquish our need to control the outcome of every situation and can wait calmly for insight and guidance. There is a wonderful tale about a Zen master who was wrongfully accused of impregnating a young girl. His only response was, "Is that so?" He was banished from the village in shame. Some time later the villagers came to the master in apology, telling him that the girl had confessed her lie. The master smiled and replied, "Is that so?"

If someone is thinking or saying negative things about you, remember that the less attention you give the problem, the less energy it will have. Don't try to defend yourself; let the angels defend you and simply let it be, knowing that we are giving the angels the room to engineer the best outcome.

An Angelic Reflection: Sometimes patience and trust are my best defenses.

SOCIAL COMPETENCE

An Angel Reminder: Those we admire possess admirable traits.

Believe it or not, job security depends more on people's degree of social competence than on their technical knowledge, job skills, or efficiency. Studies have revealed that even for jobs in industry and engineering, social incompetence accounts for 60 to 80 percent of terminations, compared to 20 to 40 percent for technical incompetence. A good personality and the ability to lead others with warmth and respect are the top ingredients for a success story. We are not born with perfect social skill; it is learned behavior, and our personalities are refined as we mature. If you find that you could use a refresher course in social competence, it is never too late to learn a better way of interacting with people.

What makes for a socially competent, angel-conscious person? Generosity of spirit, truly caring about those around you, being genuinely interested in and fascinated with others, being a good listener, practicing kindness, and above all truly wanting to get along with others and make them happy. If you truly want something you will figure out how to have it. So if your personality needs a little help and angelic refinement, ask the angels for guidance. They are true social geniuses.

An Angelic Reflection: I know that showing warmth and respect for others will always take me farther than technical knowledge and efficiency.

STIRRINGS

An Angel Reminder: Listen to the stirrings, for life begins as a stirring within.

Sometimes destiny announces its presence within us in the form of a stirring—a tiny fluttering, like the distant flapping of angels' wings, that beckons to us to follow wherever it will lead. We may from time to time feel a slight tugging at our hearts to change careers, go back to school, embark on a spiritual search, or just try something we've always dreamed—or never dared to dream—of doing. For a moment we may listen to these small whisperings, with excitement building inside of us. But we usually allow them to be drowned out by the booming voice of common sense, which will generally inform us, in no uncertain terms, that we're being foolish and impractical. Yet if we have the courage to let these tiny seeds of possibility grow and take root within us, to explore them just a bit, we might at least discover their purpose. They may just be fantasies—or they may be the signposts pointing us in the direction we're supposed to be going. The angels want us to pay more attention to that which stirs within us, for it could be the beginning of a new life.

Whenever you feel a stirring to move in a certain direction, stop and listen to it. What does it feel like inside of you? What sensations of excitement or yearning does it awaken? Keep a journal or file of these inner signals and notice which ones feel strongest and most persistent.

An Angelic Reflection: I take the time to turn toward the direction in which my heart is stirring.

ATTRACTIVENESS

An Angel Reminder: The most beautiful people of all are those who see beauty in others.

Too often we yearn for attractiveness without realizing that it is already there, inside of us, waiting patiently for us to let it out. Attractiveness is an angelic gift that comes to us with no strings attached at the moment of our entrance into the world. Everyone gets this gift, regardless of size or shape or color. Attractiveness is too often confused, in our culture, with sexual allure. But true attractiveness, say the angels, has nothing to do with one's physical appearance. It is rather a state of mind, an attitude, a be-attitude that all of us can adopt, anytime, anywhere. Those who are truly attractive have a sparkle about them, a love of life that is infectious. And both people and angels instinctively gravitate to life lovers. So as long as we radiate warmth, joy, humor, and hope, we will always be attractive. We will never cease to draw people to us, to warm their souls by our inner fire.

Who do you know that embodies, to you, the true spirit of attractiveness? What are your most attractive qualities? How would becoming more in touch with your own attractiveness change your life?

An Angelic Reflection: As long as I am able to feel joy, to make myself and others laugh, and to radiate genuine caring, I will always be a magnet of love.

*M*ODUS OPERANDI

An Angel Reminder: We each have an operating system through which we process our experiences of the angels.

Humans have different processing systems, and it is helpful to be aware of differences so we can respect them, both in ourselves and in others. Some people process information in a mostly visual manner; a visual person wants to see and explore by having a look. Other people have an audible way of receiving life; they hear things others may miss and are very sensitive to noise. Touch can be the deciding factor in learning for some people; if they can touch something it becomes real to them. You will understand the angels best if you are aware of your own modus operandi.

Get to know the way you receive information best and then explore your other senses. Visually, the angels often appear as flashes of light or bright balls of light. Audibly, you may hear the angels singing, giggling, or sending you quiet little messages of inspiration. By touch, the angels may give you a tingling sensation when near, or you may feel a gentle and loving hand on your shoulder. The scents the angels emit when they are near is like a heavenly version of rose or jasmine. It is important that we use each of our senses to expand our relationships to the angels.

An Angelic Reflection: I will begin to realize my sense of the angels.

$\mathcal{H}$IGH OPINIONS

An Angel Reminder: Defending high opinions uses up valuable energy.

Having high opinions about yourself and your abilities can get you into trouble. For example, if you are too sure about your talents, you may forget to stretch and expand yourself to reach new heights. High opinions of yourself may keep you from enjoying someone else's talents and gifts or from learning what each person has to offer. An opinion is an evaluation or judgment. There is no reason you cannot like what you do and evaluate it as excellent, but if you get attached to your evaluation you may shortchange yourself and get stuck with pride. Pride is a trap, and the only way out is humility. You will gain high esteem when you let go of haughty opinions.

Opinions can be dangerous, especially when they are preceded by a high or low judgment. It is good to realize just exactly what opinions are and strive to be free from them regarding ourselves and others. Stale opinions stink. Open the windows and let the opinions out and the freshness of new insight in.

An Angelic Reflection: My true estimate of myself has nothing to do with opinions, only with inner truth.

$\mathcal{D}$EBTS

An Angel Reminder: Debts are our chance to realize our true power.

How do we handle our debts? Do we pay them immediately? Do we put them off? Do we ignore them? Do we live in fear of them? The angels remind us that any debt we have created in our lives needs to be repaid—not in the shadow of fear, however, but in the spirit of thankfulness. In order to deal effectively with debt, we must first acknowledge that the debt exists and that it won't go away if we close our eyes. Next we must disassociate ourselves from the debt, realizing that we and the money we owe are not one and the same and that we are still good and worthy despite our debts. Finally, we must adopt the spirit of thankfulness. Giving thanks for the debt may seem impossible, but it is actually the most crucial step: When we begin to repay, on a regular basis, everyone to whom we owe something, *while thanking them for their generosity,* we will dissolve our debts peacefully and joyfully, no matter how much or how little we are able to pay at any one time.

If you are in debt, write down what you owe and to whom. Now, regardless of how difficult or ridiculous it seems, thank the universe for these debts and your creditors for their goodness. Say aloud, "I am now repaying all of my debts in calmness, gratefulness, and good faith," and ask the angels to guide you in accomplishing this worthy task.

An Angelic Reflection: As soon as I greet my debts with joy, they are already in the process of being dissolved.

A WE

An Angel Reminder: The angels are truly awesome!

Awe is a combination of wonder, reverence, dread, and fear. It is sometimes a paradoxical feeling; the wonder draws us near to the source of our awe, but the reverence and fear cause us to step back from it. Awe is an emotion long associated with the angels. In ancient times the angels were thought of as heavenly soldiers who would defend nations, deliver powerful messages such as Gabriel's announcement to Mary, and administer, at times, the necessary harshness in demanding that divine, not human, will be done. Although this aspect of angels has not changed, current angel interest endows angels with a kinder and gentler approach in their dealings with humans. While the angels certainly don't want to cause us fear, they do want us to step back and honor their incredible power. We need to continue to be in awe of them in order to maintain the proper, respectful balance between earth and heaven.

Reflect on what makes the angels so interesting and awesome. They are often depicted as very large beings; they have incredible power that could stop the force of any human invention; they are otherworldly; and they practice divine indifference to humans. It is fine to personalize the angels as our friends and helpers, but they never want us to lose respect and awe for their ultimate mission: that God's will be done.

An Angelic Reflection: I am in awe of the angels' complete devotion to God.

$\mathcal{F}$LOWERS

An Angel Reminder: Flowers are the art projects angels make for the divine gallery of God.

If you want to have a ready-made angel experience, learn to fully appreciate flowers. Flowers are the closest thing to heaven on earth, except perhaps a newborn child. You won't understand how heavenly flowers are unless you experience them with the angels in mind. Flowers are divine creations; their value extends beyond just their incredible beauty. The fragrance of certain flowers can restore balance in our beings, and each type of flower has its own energy imprint, which speaks to our souls. Flowers strike a sense of gratitude in our hearts. Witnessing a field of flowers or a colorful flower garden will lift our spirits to heavenly heights.

Learning to fully appreciate flowers is simple. Plant some in your yard. Buy cut flowers to brighten your home. Find a flower garden, single out the flower of your choice, then look at it for at least two or three minutes. While you are out appreciating flowers, remember that the angels are with you to deepen your experience.

An Angelic Reflection: I am grateful for the message of love that lives within each flower.

EAUTY

An Angel Reminder: Beauty is the reflection of God.

One of the most valuable gifts the angels give us is the ability to perceive beauty with heightened awareness so that it becomes a vitamin for our souls. With this gift of angelic perception, looking at a flower becomes an event of the first magnitude. We not only see the beauty of its colors; we feel the beauty in our hearts, and we rejoice in the gratitude that rushes through our souls. When we allow the angels into our lives, beauty becomes a true "high." The deepest resonances of beautiful music become part of us. Masterpieces of art or literature speak to us on the level of both appreciation and inspiration. There is also a practical side to the importance of beauty. People behave better when they are in beautiful surroundings. A neighborhood where the occupants take the time to plant flowers and keep their homes radiating beauty acquires more value, both monetarily and spiritually. Beauty is both a curative and a restorative; where there is beauty, there is healing, and where there is healing, there is renewed life. All of us can respond to beauty, but it is even better when we create it. It is then that we are acting as true angelic messengers on earth, sowing the seeds of higher consciousness.

With your last pennies, would you buy bread for your body or hyacinths for your soul? Begin noticing things of beauty around you, and keep a daily record of what you see and experience.

An Angelic Reflection: Beauty is the mother's milk through which the Divine feeds my soul. And as my soul is nourished, so will my other needs be met.

Optimystic

An Angel Reminder: The bright side is where the angels are.

Optimism is taking a positive, hopeful view of a situation. Mysticism involves a contemplative quest for union with the Divine. Put the two together and you have "optimysticism." An optimystic is a person who searches for enlightenment with an attitude of joyous expectation, creating a positive environment on earth in which the Divine can flourish. The angels encourage us to become optimystics—to adopt an attitude of hope, humor, trust, and lighthearted expectation in transcending the ordinary and making the extraordinary a natural part of our lives. The optimystic invites God and the angels into everyday life on every level. Because he or she believes in the best of both worlds, the optimystic will see the best and experience the best that both heaven and earth have to offer.

If you'd like to become an optimystic, believe in the power of wishing and hope; interpret everything as an instance of luck; acknowledge but do not dwell on suffering; accept and be open to mystical experiences; banish superstition; and remember to infuse your spiritual journey with plenty of fun, play, and humor.

An Angelic Reflection: I look on the bright side, not in naïveté but in gratitude, expectation, and trust.

WORLD WITHOUT END

An Angel Reminder: The world, according to the angels, will never end as long as there are human souls who love.

Are we, citizens of this beautiful planet, experiencing the end of the world? It all depends on which world you are talking about. If it is the world of greed, hatred, doubt, sorrow, and ugliness, that world has done nothing but end ever since it began. Each time a civilization has chosen to allow negative and greedy aspects to flourish, destruction has come to put an end to the imbalance. Look at what has survived from past civilizations; think of what was salvaged from the rubble. Art, philosophy, music, beauty, love—all the enlightening aspects survive and are still a thriving part of the world without end, the world the angels help to govern. Light cannot be destroyed. Light will remain, and if we decide to be a part of the light we will remain, as keepers of the light, forever and for always.

Carlos Santana, when asked if he thought that the world is getting really bad, said, "I really feel that things are bad for people who believe that without them the world cannot go on. For them, the world is ending. I think that for people who wake up in the morning and can hardly wait to do something for someone else—for them the world is just beginning." Ask yourself what world you want to be a part of.

An Angelic Reflection: I know that no matter how dark the earthly world seems to get, the beautiful light of the angels' world is always shining in my heart.

Sweetness

An Angel Reminder: "How sweet it is!"

Some people dismiss the angels, thinking they are all sweetness and light. Maybe the angels *are* all sweetness and light, maybe they add a little sweetener to our lives. What exactly is sweetness? Some of the definitions of *sweet* are: pleasing to the senses, fragrant, melodious, fresh, lovable, and not bitter tasting. Anything sweet requires balance. We say that something too sweet is sickeningly sweet. Artificial sweetness leaves a bad taste in our mouths, just as sweet talk hits a sour note in our minds. Natural sweetness is the best, and the angels are naturally sweet.

Are you naturally sweet? Do you feel naturally loving and sweet toward people? In order to be naturally sweet you must get rid of your bitterness, which results from resentment, and resentment results from depending on others for too many things. If you need a little natural sweetener in your life, ask the angels to come and bless you with their sweetness and light.

An Angelic Reflection: I am a naturally sweet ingredient in the process of life.

CREATIVE STATE

An Angel Reminder: "Where it comes from, who knows? My paintings paint themselves. I don't remember thinking much inside where I'm going next."

Jimmy Cagney

A popular myth says that the world is divided into two types of people, creative and uncreative. But to those of us who wistfully say, "I wish I were a creative person," the angels reply, "You are!" Anyone can get into the creative state, which is simply an increased level of energy that comes from doing what we truly enjoy. As Jimmy Cagney observed, the creative state is definitely not one of thinking or planning. In order to get into it, one doesn't have to do anything except let go. As we become absorbed in the thing that absorbs us, we are conscious only of the moment. We forget to worry, to judge; instead, we focus all our energy on the activity that is giving us joy. The angels encourage us to get into the creative state as often as we can, because it is there that we are most receptive to their guidance and inspiration.

If you have trouble envisioning yourself as a creative person, think about something you really enjoy doing and how it feels when you're really into it. Connect to the high energy flow that you experience; feel yourself soaring, perhaps entering an entirely new realm of consciousness. Realize that this is the creative state and that it is available to you at any time.

An Angelic Reflection: The creative state is my natural state.

SELF-TREATMENT

An Angel Reminder: Treat yourself to a wonderful life.

How we treat ourselves indicates how we treat others. Creating healthy boundaries in our relationships is good for our well-being, and if we do it ourselves, we will appreciate it when others do the same. However, if we do not create healthy boundaries, we will resent it when others do. If we see others taking care of their souls' evolution when we are not, we will think that they are self-centered instead of centered in themselves. If we treat ourselves with kindness and compassion, then we will treat others that way too. It is all very simple, yet very important. We are on the earth to take care of ourselves first; only then will we be able to truly care about another's well-being.

Is it easy for you to be kind to yourself and to others? Do you like to see others setting their own healthy boundaries? Do you treat your friends differently from the way you treat your family? Start to think about all the ways you treat yourself and others. Think about the way you treat the angels and how the angels treat you.

An Angelic Reflection: I will treat myself with kindness and then I can care for others.

$\mathcal{B}$ANISHING FEAR

An Angel Reminder: Fear belongs to the future; we belong to the present.

Fear is probably the biggest challenge to growth we encounter, for it is the single most effective barrier to our living in the state of peace and joy that is natural to our souls. Fortunately, since fear belongs to the realm of the mind and not the soul, it can be overcome through a change in our thoughts and perceptions. The primary thing to remember is that fear is almost always projection, not reality. It involves something that might happen or might not happen but that hasn't happened yet. We can then ask the angels to protect us by keeping us centered in the moment and grounded in reality. They will help us replace fear with faith in God's ever-present love and in our own inner resources, and then we will have the strength to cope with the worst and the ingenuity to create the best.

Is something you're afraid of weighing heavily on you or perhaps even dominating your life? If so, play the fear out in your imagination. What's the worst thing that can happen to you if your fears materialize? Be creative; pull out all the stops and play it out to the hilt. Experience your most terrible terror. Then take a deep breath and, on the exhale, release all the fear. Visualize the fear leaving your body and your life, and know that whatever happens you are protected by divine love.

An Angelic Reflection: I don't expect to live without fear, but I strive to learn how to live with it.

CREATING CHANGE

An Angel Reminder: Change always carries with it at least one reward—growth.

Why do we get stuck in old, unproductive patterns? Usually it's because they are familiar and therefore comfortable to us. In other words, we may have gotten comfortable with our discomfort. When we feel like we're in a rut, it isn't just time for a change, it's time for us to create that change. We need to look at the behaviors that got us where we are and are holding us back from going where we'd like to go. We need to be honest with ourselves: *are* we comfortable with our discomfort? Are we afraid of the risks that always accompany change? We need to clearly envision the lives we'd like to create for ourselves, and we need to believe that we can have and are entitled to those lives. At this point the angels can give us a push out of the rut of comfortable discomfort and onto the road to true joy.

If you feel like you're in a rut in some area of your life, why do you continue to spin your wheels? Is it easier for you to settle for the familiar instead of venturing into the unknown? What's the worst thing that could happen to you if you got out of the rut? The best?

An Angelic Reflection: I create necessary change in my life with confidence and enthusiasm.

*M*AGNANIMOUS

**An Angel Reminder: Only the contented are
magnanimous.**

Chinese wisdom

A magnanimous person is noble in conduct, never petty,
above revenge, high-minded, largehearted, forgiving,
and deeply contented. When we are contented we are not
bothered by ourselves, and this leaves us time to be concerned about others in a positive, magnanimous way. So
if we want to be more magnanimous in our lives, we
must be more content within our souls. If we truly wish
to practice high-minded, exalted thinking, we only need
to make an appointment with our soul physicians, the angels, who are naturally and thoroughly magnanimous.
They will help us to release bitterness and disappointment so that we can shift our concentration from revenge
to forgiveness. When we allow contentment to flourish in
our lives, the angels happily step in to instruct us in the
art of magnanimous living.

*Tell the angels you are ready to practice the art of living mag-
nanimously. Then heed their warning signals every time you
allow your mind to wander into the low corridors of petty
grievances. You may hear a little voice asking if you really
want to be ruled by negative thoughts. Since you will no
longer be able to answer yes, you will begin to discover ways
to release feelings of anger, resentment, and discontent, and
you will be on your way to magnanimous living.*

**An Angelic Reflection: I will allow the angels to bring
me contentment and open my heart to the spirit of
magnanimity.**

$\mathcal{A}$RT

An Angel Reminder: Art is a journey to the center of one's being.

Art is a lot like God: the more one seeks to define it, the more elusive it becomes. The angels do not seek to define art; neither do they adhere to the belief that in order to produce art, one must be an artist. To the angels, art is not a discipline but an experience, not a commodity but an essence, not an end but a means. It is an attempt to understand and interpret life, to connect us with our own souls, and our own souls with divine intelligence. As such, art is above all an interactive process; a work of art comes to life only when it is seen, heard, and felt, which means that all of us are cocreators in the artistic process. And in the same way, when we create something purely out of love for the process, not the ego, we are all artists, reveling in the transcendent joy of creation. Perhaps Franz Kafka put it best: "To hammer a table together in such a way that this hammering is one's all and at the same time a nothing. . . . This indeed is what art is about. And life."

Do you consider yourself an artist? Have you ever wanted to be one? Make up your own definition of art as it applies and relates to you. Begin to see yourself as an artist in whatever you do that is meaningful to you.

An Angelic Reflection: Art is an inclusive, not an exclusive, experience that continually enriches my life.

$\mathcal{Y}$EARNING FOR LIFE

An Angel Reminder: Never assume that people want to die. Rather, assume that they may not know how to live.

In his attempt to explain self-destructive human behaviors, Sigmund Freud developed the theory that most people have a death wish. Had he been of a more spiritual than intellectual persuasion, he might have observed that what people really have is a deep yearning for a life full of meaning, spirituality, and love. But when we don't recognize our instinctual need for love and meaning, our natural yearnings often turn toward a wish to extinguish all feelings, because feelings have become painful and lacking. Therefore many of us seek comfort from other sources, some of which drain spiritual energy rather than replenish it. Some people may excuse a life-defeating addiction, such as cigarette smoking, by saying that it is just their natural death instinct. This so confuses and depresses them that they give up in despair, continuing destructive behaviors with the mistaken belief that the behaviors are natural, when in truth what is natural to us is to seek happiness, light, and truth. To believe in and choose not to change a death instinct makes the angels work overtime. They would much rather play than work—with humans who are guided by their instinct for life.

Do you have any behaviors that fall into the category of an unconscious death wish? How could the angels help you alter your behavior?

An Angelic Reflection: I will accept my yearning for life.

$\mathcal{M}$EMORY

An Angel Reminder: Remember who you are.

Most functions of our mind depend on memory. Feelings, reason, perceptions, judgments, and awareness of self are all related to memory. Memory is more permanent than matter. A cell's memory outlives the cell itself, which is why habits can be so hard to change; our cells remember what life was like before. Memory comes from the Latin word *memorari,* "to be mindful of." Our memory banks are where we store information that we have perceived as important. It is said that the memory of all our lives (past and present) is stored in our unconscious minds. If we are mindful enough, we may remember our earlier experiences with the angels when the veils were more transparent, or earlier still when we remained in heaven.

Do you have any memories that haunt you? If so, ask the angels to help you sort them out and reach a deeper understanding. Is there something you would like to remember but find fading fast each time you try? If so, go into a deeper state of consciousness and meditate on the memory. Become more mindful of the power of memory in all that you do.

An Angelic Reflection: I remember love.

$\mathcal{G}$OOD DAY

An Angel Reminder: In order to create the perfect day, we must plan not only our schedules but also our attitudes.

At the end of the day, we usually reflect upon the kind of day we had. But how many of us reflect in advance upon what kind of day we will have? With the angels as our aides, we can virtually assure that every day will be a good day—in the sense that we perceive it as such. The night before, we can mentally map out the following day, seeing ourselves rising in joy and confidence, feeling healthy and energetic, dealing with our duties calmly and efficiently. When we awake, we can take some deep breaths, greet the day in thanks, welcome the new experiences that are in store, whatever they may be, and immediately begin to put out the relaxed and joyous energy that will make the next twenty-four hours a positive experience.

Before you go to sleep, ask the angels to send you the perfect energy for your perfect day. Then take a piece of paper and write about the coming day as if it already happened. Your angel day planner might look something like this: "I woke up at 6:30 feeling wonderful, grateful to be alive, and excited about the new day. I showered, greeted the sun, and ate an energizing, relaxed breakfast. I had a great drive to work, allowing myself plenty of time to take a fifteen-minute walk before going to the office. . . . My projects went beautifully and my meeting with _____ was even better than I expected. . . ." Be creative and enjoy the next twenty-four hours.

An Angelic Reflection: I am in complete control of the quality of my day.

$\mathcal{M}$OODS

An Angel Reminder: Our moods are like the wind—one minute blowing fiercely, the next breathing gently, but always moving on.

Our moods can be one of our greatest resources, for they reveal to us the many interesting facets of our personalities. Thanks to our moods, we are spared the embarrassment of being totally boring and predictable. We may even surprise ourselves by the various shades and colors our emotions acquire in response to different stimuli. The angels encourage us to work with our moods while at the same time detaching from them. Because they are a powerful form of energy, our moods can fuel our creativity. But we must not become their victims, for they are ultimately only passing phases of our personalities, not enduring aspects of our essential natures.

Become aware of your different moods and how and why you respond to different situations. Use your moods creatively. Whether you're in a "good" mood or a "bad" mood, try to express yourself through your current emotion and see if you come to greater peace and clarity as a result.

An Angelic Reflection: I allow my emotions to teach me about myself without engulfing myself in them.

*T*HE SENSITIVES

An Angel Reminder: Sensitives have the power to endure if they take good care of themselves.

To be sensitive means to be capable of receiving impressions and perceiving nuances quickly. A sensitive person is responsive and aware of the feelings of others. Humans come in degrees of sensitivity, and those with a great deal of it we call *sensitives*. E. M. Forster describes an "aristocracy of the sensitive" in *Two Cheers for Democracy*: "Members are to be found in all nations and classes, and all through the ages, and there is a secret understanding between them when they meet. They represent the true human tradition, the one permanent victory of our queer race over cruelty and chaos. . . . They are sensitive for others as well as for themselves, they are considerate without being fussy, their pluck is not swankiness but the power to endure, and they can take a joke."

Being sensitive has its cost. The loudness and offensiveness of life can cause a sensitive to become too touchy, quick to take offense, easily irritated, and made to feel that life is a series of bombardments. If you are a sensitive, you must take care of yourself. First, align yourself fully with the angels, then do everyday things to keep yourself mentally healthy: get enough sleep, stay away from loud and coarse people, take long walks in the park, and take some quiet time each day to enjoy your sensitivity and your sensitive friends.

An Angelic Reflection: I will become a part of the permanent victory over cruelty and chaos by taking good care of my sensitive nature.

$\mathcal{L}$OOKS GOOD ON PAPER

An Angel Reminder: Stop chasing paper.

Some people look great on paper. They have impressive degrees, sought-after awards, and smart investments, but it all exists on a piece of paper and never really gives them a sense of inner self-worth. Accomplishments and degrees are great and to be admired, but what is all this paper really worth if you don't get along with people and benefit from the rich rewards of loving, meaningful relationships? Each human has worth way beyond any impressive papers. If you feel deprived because you don't have any paper that states your credentials, you could always go visit the Wizard of Oz.

Think about your life's true worth, the worth that you carry in your heart. If you find that you feel lacking, ask the angels to help guide you in the direction of accomplishments that give you a sense of worth. Seek investments that have a lasting value beyond paper. Think about how you would feel if you had to witness the angels burning all your valuable papers and asking you to carry on without them.

An Angelic Reflection: The sense of love and accomplishment that I carry in my heart will last longer than anything said on paper.

MANDALA

An Angel Reminder: Everything in heaven and earth is a unity.

The Hindu word *mandala* means "magic circle." The circle represents God, "the One." Within it are diagrams illustrating the unity of heaven and earth. A typical Chinese mandala features the circle surrounding the yin/yang—male/female—heaven/earth symbol of two conjoined fish. Another familiar mandalic design is the circle around the intersecting triangles of the six-pointed star, the Christian symbol of the incarnation. Mandalas have traditionally been seen as pictures of inner reality, and when used in contemplation or meditation, they can help to reveal deeper dimensions of the psyche. The mandala is not confined to Eastern mysticism, however; it has been an important symbol in every culture. Carl Jung devoted much of his life to the study of the mandala and its unique healing powers. We can create our own mandalas and in so doing can discover a powerful tool for opening the unconscious, restoring inner balance, and enhancing psychic perception.

Draw a circle, and inside of it designate four main points, which represent the four directions, four seasons, or four elements. Now choose an image or symbol that represents you at this moment, and place that image in the center of the circle. Make your mandala a daily companion. Contemplate it, meditate upon it, reflect upon it, and draw creative and spiritual energy from it.

An Angelic Reflection: I am part of the magic circle of life.

$\mathcal{Y}$OUR PRINCE HAS COME

An Angel Reminder: Happiness will not arrive on a white horse at some vague future date to rescue us from our illusions.

A great cartoon appeared some years back. It showed a woman sitting on a rock daydreaming about Mr. Right. "Someday my prince will come," she muses happily. A man on a white horse rides up behind her and announces, "I'm here."

"And he'll be tall and handsome and charming," she continues, oblivious to her visitor.

"Ma'am?" the prince repeats. "It's me. Prince Charming."

"And he'll have a great sense of humor and he'll be a great lover. . . ."

"Listen to me!" Prince Charming pleads. "I'm already here!"

"And he'll pick me up and carry me off and we'll live happily ever after. . . ."

At which point the prince shrugs his shoulders in defeat and turns and rides off. In the final frame of the cartoon, the woman is still staring off into space, sighing, "Yes, someday my prince will come. . . ."

Are you too busy living in the future to notice the happiness and opportunities that already exist in the present?

An Angelic Reflection: Because I possess the mental and spiritual tools to create future happiness, I already have everything I need to create happiness in the present.

*F*OCUS

An Angel Reminder: A life, like a camera, cannot produce clear results without focus.

We all go through periods in which we can't seem to accomplish anything meaningful. At these frustrating times we need to develop the very quality that we seem to lack the most—a sense of focus. When we are focused, we have a goal, and we do not allow ourselves to become distracted by activities or people who get in the way of our reaching it. We have properly prioritized our time and energy, and no matter what obstacles or discouragements we may encounter, our goal remains in focus. How does one become focused? The angels suggest that we begin with the little things. When we can successfully focus on setting small daily goals and completing them, we can then turn our attention to the larger projects and activities that give our lives meaning and purpose and excite our interests and passions. Because the angels love to see us court life with the ardor of the lover for the beloved, they can help us pursue what gives us joy and enhances our lives and the lives of others.

On a sheet of paper, make two columns. If there are areas in your life in which you would like to be more focused—for instance, career, personal relationships, getting in shape—write them down in the left-hand column. In the right-hand column write down any actions you can think of that might help you to develop focus. Now ask the angels to give you the concentration and clarity of vision you need to reach your goals.

An Angelic Reflection: I am focused on my bliss and my purpose.

Summer

An Angel Reminder: "In the midst of winter I finally learned that there was in me an invincible summer."
Albert Camus

Summer is a time of ripening, of coming to fruition. All the energies of the universe now favor abundance: the days are long and warm, the nights rich with all the fragrances of the earth. The seed that was planted in the spring comes to term in the summer; the heat of the sun alternates with the softness of the rain to bring the earth to its apex of fulfillment. Summer is also a time of relaxation and appreciation; it is the traditional vacation season, when we put aside our duties and cares to make room for rest and rejuvenation. At the end of the summer we taste the satisfaction of the fruits of our labors, as what we have put our energy and faith into can now be realized.

If anything in your life has entered the season of summer, make sure that you allow yourself to fully savor it, and know that you have earned it. If you are still waiting for something important to come to fruition, the angels encourage you to be patient, take heart, and remember that one season always gives way to the next.

An Angelic Reflection: I allow myself to rejoice in the season of plenty.

$\mathcal{U}$PSIDE-DOWN WORLD

An Angel Reminder: The world may not be sane, but there is an order to the disorder.

A certain nineteenth-century eccentric, having decided that the world was upside down, stipulated in his will that he be buried on his head, so that in death he would have the satisfaction of at last being right side up. While most of us would not go quite as far as this man to make a point, we probably secretly applaud his audacity, for who among us hasn't found the world to be, on more than one occasion, a Mad Hatter's tea party? There is too much that doesn't make sense, too many injustices, too many acts of random violence, too many laxative commercials, and too many freeways to let us believe for one moment that this is the way it's supposed to be. The angels know that while the world is no Garden of Eden, we don't all have to walk around on our heads in order to be right side up. We can still maintain our serenity, our spirituality, and our sanity by remembering that for every act of madness there is always a corresponding act of beauty. In fact, as long as we're consigned to earthly duty, that's our job—to be anchors of sensibility, oases of joy, guideposts of hope in an imperfect paradise.

When the world's madness becomes too bewildering for you, it may be time for an adventure in antiseriousness. Abstain from watching or reading all news for a day and realize that, for this particular moment, the only antidote to the insanity is to devote yourself to the pursuit of happiness and fun.

An Angelic Reflection: I make the most of the world as it is.

*M*ONEY

An Angel Reminder: Money is our helper, not our master.

Myths about money directly affect how we perceive and deal with it. Here are a few that you may recognize: Money doesn't grow on trees. Money can't buy happiness or love. Money is evil. But the truth of the matter is that money, in and of itself, is nothing but paper. If you want to prove this, simply throw a thousand-dollar bill to a couple of kittens and see how long it takes for them to kill it and eat it. The angels caution us to remember that the only power money has is the power we ourselves give it. When we understand that we are the power source behind money; that we create how much of it we have and direct its flow in our lives; that we determine whether or not it is to be used for happiness or selfish gain, then money loses its power over us.

Take some time out to reflect upon your perceptions and beliefs about money. Are you afraid of it? Obsessed by it? Envious of those who have it? Indifferent to it? If you'd like to have more money flow into your life, begin to see it as a tool for happiness, growth, and satisfaction. Welcome it with love, do not attach any power to it, and ask the angels to generate the energy necessary to draw more of it to you.

An Angelic Reflection: When it comes to money, I always have the exact amount that I believe I can have and am entitled to.

CRITICISM

An Angel Reminder: "Works of art are of an infinite solitude, and no means of approach is so useless as criticism. Only love can touch and hold them and be fair to them."

Rainer Maria Rilke, Letters to a Young Poet *(Stephen Mitchell)*

Critics are accorded a high place in our society. We pay professional critics a great deal of money to give us their opinions, and we often pay the nonprofessional critics in our lives far too much attention. How often have we allowed our self-esteem or ambition to be crushed by criticism? How often have we listened to the critics instead of our hearts? And how often have we criticized others in an effort, either conscious or not, to boost our own sense of superiority? Although criticism may seem, like law enforcement, to be a necessary occupation that keeps the forces of mediocrity and egomania in check, it is too often used to inflate the ego of the critic at the expense of the object of criticism. There is a great distinction between opinion and truth. The angels, after all, are not critics; they are guides, who show us, *through* our mistakes, how to be the best that we can be.

How does criticism generally affect you? If you find that you tend to be overcritical; if you are too easily influenced or hurt by criticism; or if you are overly resistant to it, try reassessing the meaning of criticism in your life—the role it played in your past, the feelings it plugs into now.

An Angelic Reflection: I try whenever possible to replace criticism with concern and judgment with love in my dealings with others.

COMMUNICATION

An Angel Reminder: In communication, the goal is not to speak but to understand and be understood.

We tend to confuse communication with talking. But real communication is actually perfecting the art of listening. When we communicate with nature or God or the angels, we listen to the feelings, thoughts, and ideas we receive through meditation, contemplation, and silent interaction with the nonverbal forces of the universe. We should use more of these reflective skills in our communication with others. When people are talking to us, instead of hearing what we want to hear or immediately responding to what we think we hear, we should listen closely to what they are really telling us. As we listen, we can check in with them, repeating what they have said and asking if we have understood them correctly. We should also watch for important nonverbal cues, like tone of voice, eye movements, and body language. In developing our listening skills, we learn true understanding.

Observe your patterns of communication. Do you allow yourself to really hear what someone else is saying, or do you talk a lot instead of listen? Do you anticipate another's response, or are you quick on the defense? Try communicating the way the angels do—with awareness, compassion, love, and understanding—and see how your relationships begin to change.

An Angelic Reflection: I speak from the heart and listen for the soul.

$\mathcal{B}$ONDING

An Angel Reminder: Allow your bonds to be held with the glue of love, not the cement of dependence.

A bond is a special link uniting us with another human in a deep and meaningful way. We often hear about the bonding process that happens between a mother, father, and child. Friendship is a bonding process where two people unite themselves in a supportive relationship. Lasting, loving bonds are what make life interesting. It is important that we keep our bonding free from the stickiness of dependence. We can do this only when we feel good about who we are and are willing to let others feel good about who they are. We are only as great as we are whole. In our bonds we must remain whole and unique and allow plenty of room for the angels to help keep us free from losing a part of ourselves in another.

Think about the common bonds in your relationships. Are they based on love, freedom, and respect? If you are a parent, are you happy to let your children be who they want to be? Are you comfortable with letting your life-mate be who he or she is and have his or her own set of friends? What is your link with groups? If you need help in bonding, bond first with the angels to find your true link with the Divine. Then you will know what is right and true in each relationship you develop.

An Angelic Reflection: The angels provide the missing link that bonds me in truth and beauty to other souls of the same light.

Words

An Angel Reminder: Words are the building blocks of thoughts.

Words are powerful tools that we use in many different and interesting ways. This book is a collection of words arranged to put forth information on living in angel consciousness. However, we cannot tell you how to live with words, since living involves action and experience. Words can direct our experiences, for they can program our minds in a certain way. That is why it is important to be conscious of what we declare. For example, many people throw around phrases like, "That makes me sick" or "This is killing me." Do you think they want to be sick or die over something stupid? Probably not, so it is best not to repeat declarations that could program an outcome we don't want.

Be more conscious of the words you choose. When you slip and say something you recognize as a negative program, say "cancel" or "delete" right away. It never hurts to take a day off, or even an hour away, from words. Don't read anything, don't listen to the radio or watch the TV, don't answer your phone, and ask the angels for the ears to hear and the eyes to see what you are creating with the power of words.

An Angelic Reflection: I will not let the power of words program my mind for unnecessary trouble; I will affirm that life is worth living.

MANTRA

An Angel Reminder: "I continued to worship Him daily by means of the Gayatri mantra. . . . And now He dwells within my soul and inspires all my thoughts."

Maharishi Devendranath Tagore

A mantra is a centering device. It can be a sacred sentence or some form of sound that tunes us in to our inner vibrations—that pure frequency through which we commune with divine energy. Mantras have long been an integral part of Eastern meditation. Their primary function is to provide a focal point for the mind and body so that the breathing and consciousness are directed to a fixed center and do not become distracted. Religious traditions place great emphasis on the meaning of the mantra, which can be anything from a single word, such as the well-known *Om* ("the hidden name of God") to an entire prayer. In Christian contemplation, the Jesus Prayer has been used as a mantra. When a mantra is used in this way, it becomes embedded in the psyche and the soul through repetition, and eventually it becomes a living prayer—an active part of our being.

Take a meaningful concept, such as love, or a short prayer and sit in meditation, repeating it as you breathe deeply and rhythmically. If you wish to become more serious about using a mantra as a profound spiritual tool, talk to some experienced individuals and read about mantras. The appropriate mantra and teacher will present themselves to you.

An Angelic Reflection: I lift my consciousness to join in song with the pure tones of heaven.

CREATING AN ATTITUDE

An Angel Reminder: We can alter what we see by altering how we see it.

Sometimes, if a situation is causing us frustration or unhappiness, we need to revise our perceptions about it. The angels are available in times like these to help us create an attitude. Creating an attitude inevitably changes the situation by changing the way we see it. Creating an attitude can be an enjoyable process; the angels suggest, for instance, that we make it into a game that we can play with ourselves at any time, anywhere. The object of the game is to replace a negative attitude with an angelic one, and then watch how our experiences change accordingly. The major negative attitudes that hinder our happiness and progress are worry, fear, hatred, despair, selfishness, ingratitude, and humorlessness. When we adopt instead the angelic equivalents of trust, peace, love, hope, generosity, thankfulness, and lightheartedness, the angels guarantee that we will find ourselves less and less able to be unhappy in the face of all the joy we've created.

If something is getting you down, create the appropriate angelic attitude to counteract the negative effects. Instead of hating your obnoxious co-worker, for instance, you can choose an attitude of thankfulness for not having to be this person!

An Angelic Reflection: I create the attitudes that give me the freedom of self-empowerment.

COMETS

An Angel Reminder: Here today, gone tomorrow, never forgotten.

Some people are like comets. They streak through our lives in a flash of excitement, love, and awe. Then they are gone, never to be seen again, although we think of them often. Cometlike people cannot be held onto or controlled. They need to keep moving, lighting up yet another sky. Sadly, some comet types die too young, and we miss them and grieve deeply in their absence. But the angels know that each comet person who has left the earth at a young age exits in a burst of light that remains for the good of those left behind. A comet would never want us to mourn its disappearance. So comet people want us to remember the joy they left behind and to allow the love we had for them to continue to grow, blessing others in its path.

Have you ever been touched by cometlike people in your life? Did you allow them to leave freely with light and love, or did you mourn and suffer their loss for too long? Comet people teach us the highest form of unconditional love and acceptance. Next time you think of your comet people, cry a little if you need to. Then smile and send them a blast of love. This will give them a little extra fuel to shine a bit brighter wherever they are, and they will reflect the light back into your heart.

An Angelic Reflection: I know in my heart that love continues to grow across the barriers of time and space.

*D*AWN

An Angel Reminder: A new day is always dawning.

Dawn is the first light of day, a time when we welcome the gradual rising of the sun. A dawning is a new beginning, a chance to start over with a new flood of light. At dawn the world begins to grow lighter. With the angels in our lives we have made a decision, at some level of our consciousness, to grow lighter in our lives and therefore offer more light for the planet. Let the angels dawn on you. Begin to grow lighter, and you will shine as bright as the first light of day.

The next time you have a problem, sleep on it and ask the angels for a new look at it in the morning. Let your answers dawn on you, by giving up and letting go. Grow light.

An Angelic Reflection: I know that no matter what happens in my little world, the sun will always come up tomorrow.

REAMS

An Angel Reminder: Dreams have little to do with logic and everything to do with inner happiness.

We use the term *dream* to describe both the pictures and images that come to us when we are asleep, as well as our deepest desires and hopes. In a way this implies that if we have a dream, it is unreal and only useful to the part of us that is sleeping. But the angels know that dreams—both waking and sleeping—are not unreal, only the *unrealized* aspects of ourselves. The dreams we have when we are asleep are avenues through which the angels may send us messages that give us insights into our waking lives. The dreams we have for our lives are also means by which the angels speak to our souls, encouraging us to dare to envision and pursue our highest aspirations. The dream state is a state of complete openness to information that cannot be processed through the intellect. It is a magical, mystical, miraculous state in which thoughts may become ideas and ideas solutions. Never be afraid to dream, for it is through dreams that we awaken to our inner—and most important—reality.

Think back to when you were young and make a list of all the dreams you can remember having. Have any of them come true? If you are one of the fortunate souls who stayed with their dream and are living it, ask the angels to continually send you ideas to help expand and renew your dream. If you have a dream that you have not yet realized, be open to angelic suggestion and inspiration and know that if your desire is strong enough, you will attain your dream.

An Angelic Reflection: I honor my dreams and pursue my aspirations.

$\mathcal{P}$REPARATION

An Angel Reminder: Be prepared for the best of all outcomes.

Preparation is an activity we do each day. We prepare dinner, we prepare ourselves to go out of the house, and we prepare ourselves to handle situations. To prepare means to make ourselves ready and willing to go forth. Preparation can be both positive and negative. For example, if you are told a major storm is coming your way, and you prepare yourself to be afraid and anxious, then you create fear. When you prepare yourself to handle the storm with courage and the proper supplies, then you have a better chance of surviving the storm victorious and fearless. The angels are always available to help us prepare for the very best in life.

Positive affirmations are helpful in the process of preparation. Ask the angels to help you come up with affirmations that prepare you for all the situations you encounter. An affirmation is a statement that declares the truth, so declare the truth that you want to happen, and you will be better prepared to face life.

An Angelic Reflection: I am prepared for the best and ready for the adventure.

$\mathcal{H}$APPINESS

An Angel Reminder: Happiness without reason is the ultimate freedom.

Contrary to how it may sometimes seem, our circumstances do not determine our happiness. We alone control our ability to be happy or unhappy, through our reactions to and attitudes toward our circumstances. Those who are truly happy are not corks at the mercy of the waves of circumstance; they are the captains of their own ships. If we are in unhappy situations, we can strive to find ways to release ourselves from them. Or, if the present situations can't be changed, we can learn to accept them and be happy anyway. If we want certain things that we know will fulfill us, such as a loving partner or good health or a creative job or career, we can work toward them, making and visualizing goals and exploring the steps we need to take to make them a reality. But even as we are in the process of reaching those goals, we can be happy, by choosing to respond to life with humor instead of worry, curiosity instead of hesitation, love instead of fear, hopefulness instead of despair.

The angels are happiness trainers, with a workout program that is the essence of pleasure, not pain. If you want to sign up for their happiness workout, all you have to do is be willing to (1) live in the now and be awake to new experiences; (2) see events as interesting and instructive instead of good or bad; (3) accept people as they are, with no expectations; (4) give up suffering and worrying; and (5) be generous with your love.

An Angelic Reflection: Happiness is not just within my reach; it is already in my grasp.

$\mathcal{A}$LIVE

An Angel Reminder: The state of being alive is far more than breathing in and out.

When was the last time many of us really felt alive? Not only do a lot of our activities dull our senses, they can actually cause us to forget what aliveness is. To the angels aliveness is connectedness—to our bodies, our souls, our spirits, to nature, to others, to the divine mystery that is alive in every breath we take. Aliveness is like a buzzing current of electricity that keeps us running on full power. It is such a powerful sensation, in fact, that sometimes we are threatened by it. If we are too immersed in routine, if we are unhappy or depressed in our career or relationships, if we are under a great deal of tension, we tend to pull the plug and disconnect from our aliveness, engaging in activities that will help us to escape from the restless, cornered energy within. The angels urge us to do the things we need to do to reconnect to our aliveness so that we can create the kinds of lives for ourselves that we are meant to have.

Recall some times in the past that you have felt most alive. What were the circumstances? How did aliveness actually feel? If you need to start aliveness up again in your life, make a list of all the activities that make you feel happy, enthusiastic, energized, and excited to be alive, and begin doing them as often as you can.

An Angelic Reflection: I welcome aliveness into my life.

$\mathcal{H}$OME

An Angel Reminder: No matter what you do or how far away you go, you can always come home.

A true home is a place of acceptance, a place where you know the light is always on to greet you. Some of us were fortunate enough to have grown up in such a place; others of us have never known a true home. But regardless of whether or not we have a physical place that we can call home, the angels' home is always open to us. It is ours to take refuge in from the cares of the world and to return to regardless of how far we may stray. Just as the prodigal son was welcomed back after his waywardness, we are always welcomed back to the angels' loving hearth, and the welcoming is always a little sweeter when we return after one of our own reckless adventures, wiser through our mistakes and more ready for love. So, as we journey, we know that the angels are always there, both to support our need for risk, exploration, and new experiences, and to provide a resting place for our hearts and souls.

Whenever you feel far from home, take time out to do a meditation. Get in a completely relaxed position, close your eyes, breathe deeply, and envision, as clearly as you can, the angels welcoming you into their—and your—home. See all the details of this home, interior and exterior. Create the ideal home for yourself, see the angels in it, and know that it is yours to return to, in meditation, whenever you need guidance, comfort, or rest.

An Angelic Reflection: At the angels' home, the doors are never locked and the light of love is always left on for me.

SELLING

An Angel Reminder: You can't sell yourself, because you are priceless.

We hear a lot in the material age about the importance of "selling yourself." We're told to go out there and conquer, to toot our own horns, to win promotions and people by awesome displays of confidence and assertiveness. There is much to be said for appreciating oneself and making the most of one's abilities. But selling oneself is another story. We are not commodities to be purchased; we do not have to convince anyone—least of all the angels—of our value. All we have to do is be ourselves, to the best of our abilities.

Do you feel, in your job or relationships, that you have to sell yourself in order to make people notice and appreciate you? If so, have some fun with this concept. On a piece of paper or cardboard, make a "For Sale" sign and put a picture of yourself on it. List all of your outstanding qualities, and don't be bashful. "Must see to believe! Dream person! Sharp, funny, compassionate, full of love! High energy, low mainte-nance. . . . Body needs a little work, but ba-sically in great condition. . . ." You get the idea. Now put a price on yourself, put the sign up on the refrigerator, and appreciate the ridiculousness of the whole thing!

An Angelic Reflection: I do not have to sell myself in order to know and honor my own value.

$\mathcal{V}$ISION QUEST

An Angel Reminder: "I had to entirely disengage myself from the physical. I needed no people, no food, no interruptions. I needed positive proof of my purpose in life. I needed a Vision Quest."

Mary Summer Rain, Spirit Song

The Native American vision quest is a particularly potent ritual through which one gains insight into one's destiny through self-sacrifice. The vision quest is the journey of ultimate aloneness. The one who quests first purifies body and mind through sweat baths and then goes off to an isolated place, remaining for days and nights, like Jesus in the desert, fasting, encountering good and evil spirits, and receiving instruction from the appropriate animal emissaries of the supernatural through dreams and visions. Should we so choose, we too can commune with divine intelligence in order to become clearer about our purpose. While we do not necessarily have to undergo the arduous rituals of the traditional vision quest, we do need to set aside time to go off by ourselves, become one with the rhythms and sounds of nature, and allow the great mystery to reveal itself to us in whatever form it chooses.

If you feel you would like to learn more about your earthly purpose, you may want to read more about the concept and practice of the vision quest. Then design your own personal vision quest and, if you like, invoke the angels as your guides and messengers.

An Angelic Reflection: I stand before heaven, totally vulnerable and totally at peace, ready to receive the gift of my purpose.

$\mathcal{W}$HY NOT?

An Angel Reminder: Every success begins with a "why not?"

Of all the ideas and dreams we conceive, how many of them do we carry to term? Nine, or maybe ten, times out of ten we cancel out our inspirations with all the reasons they won't work in reality. The angels want us to dispense with the excuses that abort the creative process and to replace them with one simple question: "Why not?" Then nine, or maybe ten, times out of ten we will find that nothing is really keeping us from at least exploring our dreams and desires. Then we can realistically assess which ones are not only possible but appropriate for us to pursue.

What would you like to do that you think you can't? What are your reasons for not being able to realize your desire? Try to differentiate between reasons and excuses—objections that seem realistic, and objections that may be coming from fear of rejection or failure or success. If you would like to follow up on an inspiration, take just one action a day toward exploring it further.

An Angelic Reflection: I take a realistic attitude toward my ideas and am not afraid to explore the ones that ignite the spirit of creativity within me.

$\mathcal{P}$ILGRIMAGE

An Angel Reminder: "When you go on a pilgrimage, you set out from where you happen to be and start walking toward a place of great sanctity in the hope of returning from it renewed, enriched and sanctified."

Frederick Franck, Art as a Way

The pilgrimages of old involved a radical departure from everyday life. A pilgrim—in the strictest sense of the term—was that courageous soul who was willing to forsake all familiar worldly things for a spiritual journey that was both perilous and liberating. In fact, the more perilous the way, the more freeing it is, for it is in the throes of true peril that we are usually forced to let go of our attachments to what once seemed important in order to discover what is truly important. But we don't have to travel beyond our own selves, our own turf, to go on a pilgrimage. Since life itself is a pilgrimage toward death—which can mean either the cessation or the transcendence of our physical selves—the angels consider us all pilgrims. Our inner journeys—our searches for meaning, place, purpose, peace—are our pilgrimages, and our paths are the form of expression our lives take.

If you were a pilgrim, where would you be going? Think about your spiritual and creative goals, and visualize your life as a path toward them. What do you need to take with you on your pilgrimage? What do you need to leave behind? What things might distract you from your goal?

An Angelic Reflection: My daily actions and reflections keep me centered on, not distracted from, my spiritual goals.

ARMTH

An Angel Reminder: A warm heart is a compassionate heart.

You know what it is like to have warm feelings toward someone. It feels good and natural, because we are warm-blooded creatures. When we feel warmth we are smiling inside. Warmth is a signal that we are for, not against, another. Warmth is often a gut feeling, meaning we feel it for some and not for others, and we don't always have a logical explanation why. When we radiate warmth, we send out a signal that we are friendly and kind. A warm feeling that is not attached to an action or condition is the beginning of true compassion.

Is there anyone you could warm up to? Any feelings you could hold over the fire to burn away the chill? Imagine someone to whom you have a cold response, and bring a peaceful feeling into your being. Then allow your feelings and image of this person to warm up slowly but surely. Feel the warmth radiating from your heart to the other person's heart. Leave words alone, and feel the warmth.

An Angelic Reflection: I am a warm-blooded creature who radiates warmth and kindness, without effort, straight from my heart.

ESISTANCE

An Angel Reminder:

> "Water on the mountain
> The image of OBSTRUCTION
> Thus the superior man turns his attention to
> himself
> And molds his character."

The I Ching

When we encounter resistance in our lives, it may be a sign that we're not on the right path. If we feel like we're trying too hard to make something work, this can be a signal to stop, take a deep breath, and release our attachment to the outcome. The angels want us to be aware that when something is right for us, when it is meant to be, things tend to fall into place and go smoothly of their own accord. This doesn't mean that we shouldn't work toward things, that we don't have to put out effort. The key is to be able to differentiate between effort and strain, energy use and energy drain. In the latter situation, the angels encourage us to let go and go inward, countering resistance not with more effort, but with introspection and understanding.

If something that you want isn't coming to you, no matter how much effort you're putting out or how many clever strategies you've developed, ask yourself why you're knocking your head against a wall. What will happen if you let go, concentrate on what is working in your life, and allow things to come to you in their own time?

An Angelic Reflection: When things aren't going my way, I trust in the timing of the universe.

RELEASING THE PAST

An Angel Reminder: We cannot change the past, but we can change its effect on the present.

Although we may intellectually believe that the past is past, for many of us it is all too present. We may be clinging to childhood beliefs or experiences that are no longer relevant to our lives or our destinies. We may have old wounds, old fears that inhibit our ability to move forward, holding us back from living joyfully and adventurously. The result is that we act from an unconscious rather than a conscious place, perpetuating old patterns that are no longer beneficial to our growth—if indeed they ever were. The angels remind us that we are not prisoners of our pasts, slaves of our memories. We are free at any time to become aware of our behavior patterns and belief systems, retaining those that contribute to our sense of vitality and fulfillment and discarding those that belong to another place and time.

Are any experiences from your past impeding your progress now? If so, become aware of how these memories are affecting you, and understand that you are in control of them, not the other way around.

An Angelic Reflection: I know that as a human being I am not a fixed conclusion but an everchanging response to life.

Doing What You Love

An Angel Reminder: Those who do what they love are in tune with their purposes on earth.

Too many of us have been brought up to believe that work is not meant to be enjoyed, let alone loved. Work is meant to give us a paycheck, not excite, energize, or fulfill us. The angels, however, know that the opposite is true. Not only can we earn a living doing what we love; we owe it to ourselves to pursue that end. When we find ourselves in jobs we dislike, that frustrate, sadden, or otherwise enervate us, our souls are telling us that we just aren't in the right place. When we are doing what we love, by contrast, we feel and radiate joy and enthusiasm, improving not only our own lives but also our environments. The angels want us to know that our loving can be our living, and they will instantly answer our requests for help and guidance in aligning our souls with our sources of income.

Do you believe that you can make a living doing what you love? If you would like to believe this, make a list of the jobs you have enjoyed and the ones you haven't. Try to find the distinguishing features within each category. When you have discovered what jobs made you happy and why, fashion the perfect job for yourself, using all the positive elements you've listed. Now visualize yourself in this job, believe that you will have it, and ask the angels to send you the energy and opportunities you need to create it.

An Angelic Reflection: When I do what I love, I create the kind of environment in which abundance flourishes.

CURIOSITY

An Angel Reminder: Curiosity may have killed the cat. On the other hand, it may have gotten the cat a great meal.

As children, we are motivated almost entirely by curiosity. Our wonder at the world, our desire to know the whys and hows of everything around us, fuels our search for knowledge, our ability to dream and imagine, and our excitement for life. As we grow older, however, many of us lose our connection to our natural curiosity. We seek security in the known; we define ourselves by our beliefs and opinions; we grow stale in the familiar. The angels know that curiosity is the breath of life, that it can actually keep us alive. Many scientists and artists, for instance, live far longer than the average life span and are active and productive into their eighties and nineties simply because they continue to be curious about the whys and hows of life and to find new mysteries to explore.

How curious are you about life? Do you enjoy exploring new places, new ideas? Do you tend to accept things as they are or try to find out why and how they came to be? Think about what excites your curiosity, and try to bring more of it into your life.

An Angelic Reflection: The more curious I am, the more alive I become.

MEANING

An Angel Reminder: "You can't take it with you" is a saying that refers only to material wealth and acquisitions. You can and will take with you all the gifts of the spirit.

Above all, most of us are seeking meaning in our lives. Sometimes, however, we don't even realize that we are searching for meaning; we only know that somewhere deep inside of us is a gnawing void, an empty space that is yearning to be filled with something to warm our hearts and give our lives a sense of joyful purpose. The angels gently remind us that the only way for us to truly fill the void is by developing personal spiritual values. When we ask the angels for something in particular, they may not bring the something we think we want. But they will bring us something meaningful. Love, peace, joy, happiness, creativity, and humor are gifts the angels give freely to bring meaning into our lives. With such gifts, we are also given a new power of perception to help us detect what isn't meaningful to our growth and awareness.

Pretend that your house is on fire and you only have time to save the five things in it that are most meaningful to you. What would those five things be? Why did you choose them? Think of some of the things you do that are not particularly good for you. Ask yourself if the motive underlying your actions is a need to find meaning in your life, to satisfy an empty space in your soul.

An Angelic Reflection: The angels know that the only lasting gifts are those of the human spirit. As long as I have love, joy, light, and inner peace, my life will be full of meaning.

GUILT

An Angel Reminder: Guilt inhibits growth.

When we experience feelings of guilt, the angels want us to "Just say no!" Why? Because guilt inhibits growth. Guilt is like a well of mud; as soon as we step in we start sinking. Regretting what we have or haven't done only makes us feel that much more despairing and that much less capable of feeling joy and spreading joy to others. All right—so we're not perfect. We've made mistakes, hurt others. But instead of feeling guilty, which leads only to severe self-paralysis, the angels ask us gently to become aware: of our actions and motivations, of what we can learn from the experience, and of how we can move beyond guilt into self-acceptance so that we can once again begin to live.

Make a list of everything you feel guilty about. Ask yourself how guilt has made you a stronger, happier, more productive, or better person. If you can't come up with a reply, resolve to release, right now, all guilt from your life and to replace it with self-love and self-awareness.

An Angelic Reflection:
Awareness, not guilt, helps me
to grow.

$\mathcal{P}$ROSPERITY

An Angel Reminder: Prosperity is not money.

Too often we confuse prosperity with money. Money is a tool; prosperity, however, is a state of consciousness. Someone with a great deal of money may not feel prosperous, while someone else with far less money may consider himself or herself quite prosperous. *Prosperity* actually means "good fortune," "flourishing," and "success," none of which require money—in the angels' dictionary, anyway—in order to be attained. To the angels, true prosperity is the satisfaction of feeling secure, fulfilled, and loved. These three basic needs are always at the core of our desires for money. In reality, however, they are totally independent of our finances. Regardless of how much money we think we need in order to have what we desire, we can always discover areas in our lives in which we already feel secure, fulfilled, and loved. This is not to say that money may not help us to feel even more prosperous. But it is only when we already have the feeling of prosperity within us that we will be able to generate and use money for its higher purpose—in our lives and the lives of others.

Do a prosperity check on yourself. What are the deeper needs that are behind your desire for money? Now think of some areas in your life in which you already feel powerful, secure, and worthy. Think of fun activities that you are already able to do, even without all the money you dream of. Connect to the feeling of prosperity that's already within you, and begin radiating it outward.

An Angelic Reflection: I do not need more money in order to feel prosperous.

SERENITY

An Angel Reminder: "In the same way that a single match illuminates darkness, a glimpse of serenity changes how we see every aspect of our existence."

Joseph V. Bailey

Serenity is a mixture of acceptance, gratitude, willingness, deep peace, and tranquillity. It comes from deep inside us once we have given up the idea that we have control over life. Serenity has always been with us, even when we are ruffled by life's turmoil. Our souls are waiting in calmness and tranquillity, sending signals to our minds that we do not need to be disturbed. We don't always receive the signals very clearly, because often we are too busy trying to fix a situation or change it. Serenity's signals become very clear when we take the time to calm down and listen to the wise inner voice.

When we are tranquil and serene we learn how to truly live by wisdom. To learn how to have serenity in our lives, we must practice constantly by calming the storm in our minds. We can do this by meditating regularly and by simply paying attention to the places where others have found serenity. Think of things that you can do that will bring you serenity, and get in the habit of doing them regularly.

An Angelic Reflection: My life is floating in a sea of tranquillity; my body is the boat, my mind the sail, and my soul the water.

*C*OLOR ATTRACTION

An Angel Reminder: The angels often express themselves through color.

Colors are vibrations of light, broken down into different wavelengths. At the refined vibratory level of the angelic realm, color becomes like music, expressing many dimensions of thought and feeling in an infinite combination of tones. As beings of light, the angels are also beings of color, and they may reach us through different colors that spark something in our unconscious. Certain colors, for instance, are traditionally associated with emotions and spiritual qualities: red symbolizes passion and the life force; pink, unconditional love; blue, peace and healing; violet, intuition and inner knowing; yellow, faith, intelligence, and joy; green, nature and spiritual restoration; and so on. The angels suggest that we become more aware of whenever we find ourselves inexplicably attracted to a certain color or when specific colors seem to bring out our beauty and vibrancy, for these colors relay important messages to our minds about emotions we need to connect with and qualities we need to develop.

Make a list of some of your favorite colors and how they make you feel. What are "your" colors—the shades that complement your natural coloring and cause your face to light up when you wear them? Study the meanings associated with those colors, and reflect upon their possible relationship to your life and your specific quests.

An Angelic Reflection: I am attracted to colors that enhance my inner beauty and reflect my spiritual goals.

*M*AGIC WORDS

An Angel Reminder: No problem.

Magic words are words that make things all better. For example, if a child spills milk all over the table, the magic words to say are, "That's okay." Then the child knows immediately that he or she didn't do anything wrong and that the situation is manageable. We can use the magic words *that's okay* in our lives when we encounter an accidental event. Proclaiming these words will begin to lighten the situation. Other magic words to use in annoying situations are "No problem" and "I can handle that." If you want to have fun with a situation the magic words are: "How interesting."

Next time you encounter a situation that begins to try your patience, say the magic words over and over until you feel lightness and humor blanket your reaction. Imagine the angels saying magic words to you when you need to hear them. When you go to sleep at night, ask the angels to whisper in your ear, "It's okay, there is no problem, all is well and you are loved."

An Angelic Reflection: I will accept that all is well and that life is interesting, to say the least.

*I*NSPIRATION/BREATH

An Angel Reminder: As we learn to breathe, we become inspired.

The word *inspiration* has an interesting triple meaning. While it is most commonly defined as a moment of creative or spiritual illumination, its Latin origin means "to draw in breath." And *to inspire* also means to uplift others. There is, then, a physical as well as a mental and spiritual component to inspiration. When we practice deep breathing, we are "inspiring"—drawing breath into the deepest spaces, training it to flow throughout the body, from the diaphragm to the belly to the lungs, and out through our nostrils. As our bodies are cleansed, our blood recharged, our beings both calmed and invigorated, mental blocks begin to dissolve and our chakras—the different energy centers in our bodies—open up, allowing us better access to the divine energy that illuminates our creative and spiritual selves. And, as we are so inspired, we radiate that breath of life to others. As the Yoga master Paramahansa Yogananda observed, "When you attune yourself to the Infinite Mind during meditation, inspiration, creative power and energy flow into you and divine bliss extends from you to all beings."

Notice how you breathe, and take the time to do some deep-breathing meditation each day. Notice how your mental and physical energy begin to change as more oxygen flows through your body. Keep track of corresponding inspirations and creative breakthroughs.

An Angelic Reflection: The breath of divine love and inspiration courses through me.

$\mathcal{H}$IDDEN BLESSINGS

An Angel Reminder: A blessing is a special favor granted by God.

Angels are most often unseen presences in our lives, and therefore we may never actually know the many ways they interact with our destiny. We are always free to speculate, and looking for the signs of their presence is a fun way to keep angel consciousness alive and flowing. Next time you find yourself impatient over something, like getting stuck behind a slow car in traffic, imagine that the angels are saving you from danger up ahead. Keep in mind that you are in the right place at the right time when the angels are in your life. Always keep your eyes, ears, and your heart open to spot the angels' hidden blessings.

Blessings from the angels are not only a means of saving us from danger. Blessings are also a way the angels promote happiness in our lives and contribute to our well-being. Make an effort to count your hidden blessings and express gratitude when you find one. Keep a sense of wonder about you, and don't be afraid to acknowledge any signs that the angels are near. If you are worried that others may not believe you, then don't tell them about it. A hidden blessing for you may be a problem for someone else.

An Angelic Reflection: I will count my hidden blessings and be grateful for the many ways the angels contribute to my life.

$\mathcal{N}$ATURAL

An Angel Reminder: We each have a natural way of being that flows with the course of nature.

When we are acting from our natural state of being we are without affectations. An affectation is a behavior that is put on for display, for pretense. It does not come from a genuine place and is not necessary in our lives, although we may think it is. When we cultivate affectations, it is usually because we are afraid to be who we really are. We feel unsure of our inner value, and we believe that we must present a face other than our own to the world in order to be accepted. There is nothing artificial about the angels. They are a human's most valuable natural resource, for they promote the sacred qualities of love, compassion, truth, and genuineness that bring us into accord with the Creator. It is natural for us to receive these qualities and cultivate them in our lives. It is natural for us to be happy and satisfied with our true selves. Too often we take unnatural courses through life and the beautiful qualities the angels promote seem to elude us. But when we become aware of what is truly natural for us, we can allow the angels to help us live naturally. The angels are a natural ingredient in our lives when we are at peace in body, mind, and soul.

Think of an affectation or artificial additive you may have picked up on your travels through life. When you feel ready to present yourself to the world without affectations, call upon the angels to help you discover and delight in your true nature—the naturally wonderful way to be.

An Angelic Reflection: I allow the natural qualities of heaven to prevail in my life.

KNOWING

An Angel Reminder: The angels know us without having to believe in our existence.

Do you believe in angels? The angels would rather that you *know* them and not waste your time trying to believe in them. Belief closes the door; knowing leaves it open, allowing change and more knowledge to freely step in. The other side of belief is doubt; belief cannot exist without it. But when we know something in our hearts, we trust, and that is the antidote to doubt. When we know the angels in our hearts, we transcend human belief systems. You do not need to prove your knowledge to anyone; it is yours to keep and cherish. And when that knowledge involves the angels, your life will be proof in favor of heaven.

Think about any belief you have and ask yourself where it came from. What information keeps you glued to the belief? Start to take your beliefs less seriously and enjoy the lightness of knowing something in your heart.

An Angelic Reflection: My heart peacefully rests in knowing the angels from the deepest and most secure part of my being.

SABBATH

An Angel Reminder: Activity is self-defeating if we are too busy for God and the angels.

In the Jewish tradition the Sabbath, the seventh day, was meant to be spent doing nothing but delighting in creation. No work—not even cooking—was allowed. But today the Sabbath is either ignored as an outmoded tradition that no longer fits in with high-speed twentieth-century existence or is confused with going to church for a few hours of required religion. To the angels, however, the Sabbath is a restorative measure that can benefit anyone and everyone, regardless of religious beliefs. A weekly sabbatical from our regular routines is a far better tension reliever than an extra-strength painkiller. A day of genuine spiritual rest can work wonders for our health and centeredness. We reflect upon the real reason we are here, which is not simply to work or to distract ourselves, but to constantly rejoice in the mystery of creation.

Try to set aside one day solely for the purpose of rest and contemplation. If you have a spouse and/or children, invite them to participate. The day is up to you; it does not have to be Saturday or Sunday. Make a pact with yourself to forgo all work, cooking, answering phones, TV watching, moviegoing, and any other distractions. Use this valuable time to draw closer to the angels and bring peace into your private world. Then note its effect upon you when you resume your regular routine.

An Angelic Reflection: I make spiritual rest a regular part of my life.

*I*F ONLY

An Angel Reminder: If your grandmother had wheels she'd be a bus.

"If only" is a state of mind we get into when we believe that we're living in deprivation instead of abundance. "If only" I had a million dollars, a great relationship, the perfect job. "If only" I had a gorgeous body, a huge house, parents who understood me. "If only" world peace would come, health care were free, the IRS would disappear, *then* my life would be perfect. Well, to that the angels reply, "If only" you understood that what you do have is perfect for where you are at the present moment, you would then be able to create even more abundance. For we make our lives perfect not by bemoaning what doesn't exist, but by valuing, learning from, and working with what does.

What are some of your "if onlys"? Does wishing turn them into reality? For each "if only," think of a resource you already possess that could help you get to where you want to be.

An Angelic Reflection: I am not a victim of the fates but the codesigner, with the angels, of my destiny.

*B*ELIEF SYSTEMS

An Angel Reminder: "If you think there is a solution, you are part of the problem."

George Carlin

A belief is something we accept as true and readily place our confidence in. We all have a system for our beliefs. Some of us share the belief system of a particular religion, and some of us march out on our own. Belief systems come with rules and principles meant to keep beliefs intact. Belief systems are full of problems, because the vast range of human experiences does not fit neatly into categories. Conflicts arise when our beliefs do not fit our experiences. When this happens we may strike out at others or look for someone to blame. We need to let go of our strict beliefs and accept new information without fear. Beliefs are like rules; they are meant to be adjusted and changed.

It is wisest to concern ourselves with developing and understanding God in our own lives rather than going after the devil in others. We all at times try to change others' beliefs. For example, if we are vegetarians, we want the whole world to stop eating meat. Those who eat animals become targets for change, and we end up spending too much time concerned with what others are doing. The important lesson is: live your life as you see best for you, and if it works and you are admirable and true, others will be interested in your system of beliefs.

An Angelic Reflection: I will not fear change, I will allow my beliefs room to grow, and I will let go of rigid thinking.

THE RIGHT STUFF

An Angel Reminder: The right stuff is what the universe gives at the right time.

How do we know whether we should try to manifest a desire? The angelic rule of thumb is that we can have everything in life that will contribute to our growth and happiness without harming others or interfering with their rights or their happiness. Of course, we sometimes desperately want what is not right for us, to the point where we can easily convince ourselves that we are entitled to it. But because we are then working against our own good, if we succeed in our misguided quest, we will either encounter insurmountable obstacles or will eventually experience pain, dissatisfaction, and disillusionment. If there's something we really want, we need to be clear about our motivations, and we need to think carefully about what effect getting it will have on our lives and the lives of others. If something that we want isn't appropriate, we need to be honest with ourselves and release our desires to the angels, knowing that they will bring whatever is right for us into our lives at exactly the right time.

What are some of the things you've wanted in the past that you're now glad you never got? What are some of the things you want right now? Why do you want them? Ask the angels to guide you always toward those things that will fulfill the needs of your highest self.

An Angelic Reflection: I allow the universe to show me what's right for me.

*T*HE SACRED GARDEN

An Angel Reminder: The most beautiful gardens are those that are planted with the seeds of hope, tended with love, watered with joy, and cultivated with gratitude.

Our lives are like gardens. Some are overflowing with beauty, color, and creativity. Others are useful, productive, and nourishing. Many seem like they are afraid to grow, for fear of appearing too magnificent. And some remain unkempt and untended, the grass dry and lifeless, the plants choked by weeds and withering from neglect. Fortunately, because a garden is a living, changing entity, we can always resuscitate it, dislodging any undesirable elements and replacing them with new growth. We can do that with our lives too. If things feel drab, we can add a touch of color. If we haven't yet bloomed, we can learn new ways to express ourselves. If we feel frustrated, we can weed out the things that seem to be choking us and impeding our progress. The angels can plant the seeds of hope, mirth, ambition, and faith within us and water them until they blossom into a life rich with joy, wisdom, and vitality.

Picture your life as a garden. Draw it on paper if you like. Is it radiant and thriving? Or do you need to do some weeding? What kinds of flowers and plants would you like it to have? Which new items would you select from the angels' seed catalogue?

An Angelic Reflection: My life is full of color, beauty, and healthful attitudes that provide joy and nourishment for those who come into my sacred garden.

$\mathcal{V}$ACATION

An Angel Reminder: The best vacation provides us freedom from ordinary reality.

Are you so serious about life that you are often bewildered by others' ability to have fun or to content themselves with a seemingly trite existence? Do you ever ask, "Why me, God?" when things don't go your way? Do you spend too much time analyzing unimportant aspects of yourself and others? Is it difficult for you to ignore the negative side of life? If you answered yes to any of the above questions, you are on the list for a wonderful vacation package only offered by the angels—a vacation from yourself. A vacation from yourself will give you a completely new take on life, as you begin to see your usual worries in heavenly perspective. You may even find yourself laughing about them! Or at least you may smile a little at how amusing our human fretfulness must sometimes seem to the cosmic joy keepers.

Even if you cannot take real time off from your usual daily routine, the angels can still give you a wonderful vacation. Begin by making a conscious effort to be aware of when you become self-absorbed. Ask the angels to gently remind you when it is time to shift your focus to the world outside yourself. Allow yourself and others to have fun for absolutely no reason at all.

An Angelic Reflection: I can go on the vacation that humor provides anytime, anywhere.

ꝓLACE OF FREEDOM

An Angel Reminder: Heaven is a free state.

Just the word *freedom* strikes a chord in each of our minds, because freedom is a powerful predilection for humans. Deep inside our souls, each of us longs to be free in mind, body, and spirit. It is important that we find our place of freedom. It can be a journal to write our free thoughts in; a place to go where we are freely accepted; a special room in the mind, decorated just the way we like, to go and fantasize with freedom; or some art supplies, such as a canvas or bag of clay, to create with freely. The angels are free from many of the issues that hamper our freedom of spirit. They can help us see beyond the material confines. Ultimately we will discover that human beliefs blocking freedom are illusions, since we have always been free. You are free now.

To find out how free you feel now, ask yourself the following questions: Do you have free time—time to do whatever you want in the moment? Do you allow your mind freedom to roam the galaxies of thought? Or are you always plotting your escape, believing that someday you will be free?

An Angelic Reflection: I am a free soul.

AITING

An Angel Reminder: "The rain will come in its own time. We cannot make it happen; we have to wait for it."

The I Ching

How difficult it is sometimes to wait for life to unfold, to restrain ourselves from trying to hurry it along or make things happen before their time. In our eagerness for results, however, we forget that waiting is as important a part of life as doing. There is a purpose to waiting; as Richard Wilhelm observes in his translation of the *I Ching,* the Chinese *Book of Changes,* "Waiting is not mere empty hoping. It has the inner certainty of reaching the goal." It is interesting to note that the hexagram entitled "Waiting" in the *I Ching* is also referred to as "Nourishment." The period of waiting is a valuable time, during which we can strengthen our inner resources. If there is nothing we can do about a situation except wait, we can use that opportunity to plan, relax, research, reflect—all highly useful activities that invariably lead in the direction of illumination. As the Norse equivalent of the *I Ching,* the *Runes,* suggests, "When fishermen can't go to sea, they repair nets."

If you are currently in a position of waiting, how can you use the time productively? What do you think the purpose of the waiting is in your life? Instead of becoming frustrated or despairing, try thanking the waiting for providing a breather in your life, a chance to nourish yourself physically, emotionally, and spiritually as you gain a new perspective on the situation.

An Angelic Reflection: Like any other opportunity, waiting can be used to my advantage.

ADAPTABILITY

An Angel Reminder: The angels are adaptability agents; they take us through changes gracefully.

A positive side effect from spending time on personal and spiritual growth is that we become adaptable. Being adaptable means we adjust easily to new situations; we accept change instead of resisting change. An adaptable person relishes new challenges and learns to remain comfortable under pressure. Adaptability gives us the chance to keep our minds open to change, and this keeps us young at heart. It takes work and practice to become adaptable, and it is well worth the effort. A truly adaptable person worries very little, is flexible with people, tolerates others' viewpoints, easily stays true to her or his own values, and reserves time to enjoy life.

Are you adaptable and open to change? Are you easygoing most of the time, rarely letting others' moods and behavior bother you? Think of new ways you can be adaptable. Avoid letting others who are less adaptable push you to your limit or try to control you. People with good dispositions, who are exceptionally adaptable, are sometimes mistaken for pushovers. However, true adaptability allows your open mind to see this before it becomes a problem. The angels will protect you, if you protect yourself by establishing good boundaries.

An Angelic Reflection: I am adaptable and open to change. I will accept change and adjust my thoughts to fit my experiences.

SINS

An Angel Reminder: A sin is a choice we make to remove ourselves from higher consciousness.

Mahatma Gandhi wrote that there are seven sins in the world:

(1) Wealth without work, (2) pleasure without conscience, (3) knowledge without character, (4) commerce without morality, (5) science without humanity, (6) worship without sacrifice, (7) politics without principle.

A sin can be thought of as an imbalancing action that favors our own egos and pleasure at the expense of the highest good of all. To Gandhi, the most damaging aspect of sin is not the action itself, but the emptiness of an existence that has rejected higher consciousness. Thus wealth is meaningless without the satisfaction and joy of having earned it. Without conscience, pleasure is nothing more than addiction. Knowledge without character is useless; worship without sacrifice is hypocrisy. Because we as human beings were given the gifts of intelligence, conscience, and free will, we have a responsibility to the universe. We are expected to act not blindly or selfishly, but with a higher consciousness built upon a secure moral and spiritual foundation.

For several days, try keeping a journal of all of your actions. Record the actions themselves in one column and the motivations behind them in another. At the end of three days, sit down with your journal and reflect upon its revelations. You will have a new awareness of how consciously or unconsciously you are living your life.

An Angelic Reflection: I choose to make full use of my capacity for conscious and compassionate behavior.

𝒫LENTIFUL

An Angel Reminder: The angels provide a plentiful supply of heavenly love.

Plentiful means there is more than enough. When God and the angels give to us they give us more than we ask for. Realize that you have plenty. Plenty of beauty, love, happiness, and joy is available to you at all times in endless supply. There is plenty of creative energy for you to use to make your life interesting. Exciting new adventures are in plentiful supply for you to experience. Money is plentiful; you only need to know how to "make it." Plenty of friends are waiting all around the world to meet you someday. And you could never run out of angels to help make your life full of meaning and blessings.

What do you need in your life right now that is in plentiful supply on the planet but in meager quantity in your life? If it exists, you can have it. If you need something, ask God and the angels to help you cocreate it. They will always make sure you have more than enough, if you are willing to accept it.

An Angelic Reflection: I've got plenty.

SELF-IMAGE

An Angel Reminder: There is no need to preserve a self-image; let it go and be part of the whole.

Your self-image can get you into a lot of trouble, if you place too much importance on your past experiences and let them define who you are. For example, if you were ever heavily in debt you may still identify yourself as an indebted person. If you have been in business, you may identify yourself by your successes while climbing the ladder of material possessions. We all need to develop good self-images, but we don't need to let them keep us from new experiences. One of the most freeing experiences we can have is to let go of our self-images and become one with the unity of life. Then we will no longer see ourselves as little containers filled with a rigid personality, a set of beliefs, and a bank account.

Have you ever felt like you were in a timeless space and didn't know where the external world began or you ended? If so, you merged with the unity of life, with the true life force that does not concern itself with images or bank accounts. What could you do to loosen the tight belt of your own self-image? Some ideas: change your hairstyle, take up an unusual hobby, wear something "inappropriate" to your next social function, and, most important, pay attention to your connection to life.

An Angelic Reflection: I am not an image of my past; I am a bright reflection of the moment.

PERSONAL SPACE

An Angel Reminder: God respects your privacy.

The right to privacy is losing value. In a world where phones can be easily tapped and information conned out of us in cunning and dangerous ways, we may feel like there is nowhere to run to have a private thought or moment with ourselves. We may be led to believe that privacy is not our right, but it is and it is respected in heaven. Don't be afraid to have private thoughts. Even if you don't like their content, allow yourself to explore thoughts privately without judging yourself. Privacy is a blessing, a grace from God, and it is up to us to protect our own privacy. The angels are good at helping us protect our privacy. We can let them in on our secrets, and they will keep the privacy invaders busy doing something else so we can enjoy our sacred personal space.

One problem with being a private person is that it captures the curiosity of meddling people. Some people see a private sign as an invitation. Think about your own issues of privacy and learn ways to protect yours. Next time you need some private time, ask the angels to help you create a sacred space, and visualize reflecting shields around you that will turn people in a different direction if they start to come after you.

An Angelic Reflection: My personal space is mine alone. I can think, dream, be, fantasize, and do whatever I want, and I value and cherish my right to privacy.

$\mathcal{F}$REELANCE

An Angel Reminder: Create your own circumstances.

We hear the term *freelance* often these days. We have freelance writers, freelance artists, and freelance inventors and consultants. The term *freelance* comes from the time of knights in shining armor. A "free lance" was an independent knight, free from the rule of any lord, who roamed the country looking for adventure with his lance. Today a freelance is someone who is independent of bosses and influences from groups. Freelancers live by their own principles. Becoming a freelance is a wonderful way to free your life if you have the courage to deal with the risks involved.

Be a freelance for God. This way you are not under the rule of any other human, but you take your cues from the highest power in the universe. The angels will help you establish yourself as a freelance. You only have to make the decision to stick to your values, do the work involved in a fun and fresh way, and have the determination to stay true to your higher purpose.

An Angelic Reflection: I am free to choose my own way through life and my own life's work.

$\mathcal{B}$EHIND YOU

An Angel Reminder: It is good to know what is behind you.

The best way to find out what is behind us is to take a good look. Our shadows are behind us. Our shadows follow us around wherever we go; they are a natural part of our being in the flesh. The shadow can cause us problems when we decide that it is bad and we are good—in other words, when we try to split off from our shadow self. We all want to assure ourselves that we are really and truly good and would never think of causing harm to another. Yet the possibility of causing harm to another is ever present in each human, and when we recognize it and accept it, then we are able to choose not to act it out.

Know what is behind you. Imagine that your guardian angel is always behind you to guide you with full awareness in each situation you encounter. Put the past behind you, but don't deny it. Accept your shadow and let it follow you.

An Angelic Reflection: With the angels as my guides, I can face what is behind me.

*M*OTHER EARTH

An Angel Reminder: As above, so below.

Many of us are very worried about Mother Earth. Could our pollution and manipulations of the forces of nature really mean the end of our planet? Or do we give ourselves too much credit and power, as if we could control the destiny of an entire planet? The angels have a secret for us: they know that Mother Earth could evict us all at any time if she wanted to. Can it be that deep down we understand this and are perhaps more worried about what will happen to us, rather than what will happen to Mother Earth? In shopping for Mother Earth's tombstone, we waste whatever valuable energy we have for improving her life. We get caught up in the doomsday game instead of honoring and beautifying our own lives and respecting the lives with which we come in contact. Respect the fact that natural resources have to be replenished and not misused. Be wise in your actions concerning her, love her beauty—much of which is born out of destruction—and strive for inner peace, a specialty of the angels. This will do more to save Mother Earth than all the bumper stickers you could buy.

How could you join forces with the angels to save the humans? Begin concentrating on bringing the consciousness of peace and harmony into your daily life and actions, and let God take care of Mother Earth's ultimate destiny.

An Angelic Reflection: I know that developing inner peace is the first and most important step toward achieving peace on earth.

CHARISMA

An Angel Reminder: Charisma is a natural trait.

The word *charisma* comes from the Greek word *kharisma*, which means divine gift. When we refer to someone as having charisma, we notice that they draw loving attention from others. They can master a group with exceptional ability and secure devotion in people. You may think that only certain people are fortunate enough to be born with charisma, but charisma is inherent in all of us. Each of us has a divine gift, and charisma comes naturally when we share our divine gifts with love in our hearts. Charisma means that we inspire enthusiasm in others, and this can happen only when we truly love what we are doing.

Have you identified your own divine gifts? If not, now is a perfect time with the angels in your consciousness. Have you ever enjoyed a time of attracting positive attention and admiration from others? Think about why and how it happened. Like any good thing, charisma requires balance in body, mind, and spirit, so be careful with your divine gifts; use discernment in where and how you give them. Define what you are willing to give freely.

An Angelic Reflection: I know that my soul is charismatic. My life will shine with love when I share my divine gifts with the world.

$\mathcal{W}$ALK AWAY

An Angel Reminder: Don't walk away mad. Just walk away.

One of the most difficult tests in life concerns people in whose personal dramas we suddenly find ourselves on stage, playing a role for which we didn't audition. If they are chronic complainers, we become the sympathizers or advice givers. If they attack us, we try to fight back. Whatever the game, we end up wasting our valuable time and energy on frustration and anger. The angels have a simple solution for people on whom reason seems to have no effect. Walk away from them—not in anger or fear, but in neutrality. If you feel afraid or guilty about walking away, remember that by nonjudgmentally refusing to let these people drain your energy or suck you into the black hole of their lives, you are exhibiting not cowardice, avoidance, or hard-heartedness, but courage, wisdom, and compassion.

If someone in your life is causing you unnecessary frustration, do not try to fight or reason. Simply remove yourself from that person's negative force field. If you have to be in the same room at home or at work, you can still put up a psychic shield. Either smile and say nothing at all or state, quietly and firmly, "I don't believe I can be of help to you at this time." Then calmly resume your activities. The person may not like the message, but he or she will *get it.*

An Angelic Reflection: I do not have to be influenced or intimidated by negativity. I can always walk away.

SINGING

An Angel Reminder: "Learn to sing, learn to see your life and work as a song by the universe."

Brian Swimme

You don't have to be a professional singer or have perfect pitch to enjoy singing. Singing was once an important part of any human gathering. Even a simple town meeting would include a song. Our chances to sing with a group are not as numerous as they used to be, but that doesn't mean we have to stop singing. The angels sing all day long, praising God with their beautiful songs. Our lives can be beautiful songs that we sing with the angels to praise God. It is natural for us to want to sing. If we suppress a natural urge we will feel like something is missing from our lives. Don't miss the chance to sing your song!

Sing your heart out. Sing your worries. Invent your own lyrics to go with instrumental music about what is going on in your life. Sing while you work and play. Sing, and the angels will sing with you. Whistle along to a song, and soon you will be giggling with joy. It is hard to whistle when you feel the urge to laugh; let it go!

An Angelic Reflection: I will sing my song with joy, and I will connect with the universal song of love.

$\mathcal{P}$ERMISSION

An Angel Reminder: Give yourself permission to be interesting.

God gives permission; God has allowed humans free will. We too must give our loved ones permission to stumble and fall if that is what they need to do to grow and expand their knowledge. The kindest thing we can do for others is to allow them to make their own mistakes and learn from them, then be there when they need our love. Of course, this takes careful thought and pure awareness, because sometimes we are called upon to step in and help those who are not able to help themselves. For example, you would never walk by a child being abused without doing your part to stop it. Free will is a confusing concept for us, but it is truly the most valuable gift we are given as humans. When we make the choice to use our free will to learn from our mistakes, choosing to value all of life as a learning experience designed to help us understand God, then we will accomplish what we came here for. Let's give one another permission to grow.

Can you give people permission to be who they are and not try to change them and their destinies? Is it easy for you to allow people who do things differently than you or people you don't fully understand to do what they want to do? Have permission to be yourself, and allow the process of life to unfold in its own beautiful way.

An Angelic Reflection: I give the world permission to unfold, and I give myself and my loved ones permission to use our own free will.

QUEEN OF ANGELS

An Angel Reminder: Mary is the Divine Mother of mercy. She is the symbol of true compassion and unconditional motherly love.

Mary, the mother of Christ, is often referred to as the Queen of Angels. Mary is touching the lives of those involved in angel consciousness in a deep way. The important part of Mary's message is its universality. In Medjugorje she speaks of a peace and conversion that come from the heart and from daily prayer. She says faith cannot exist without prayer. The issue is not whether or not to believe Mary is appearing to humans, but rather, the timely message. Profound changes are happening on the earth. We need to restore the divine qualities of compassion and mercy, and that is why Mary is touching our hearts and why the angels are so prevalent now.

Kuan Yin is the Chinese bodhisattva of compassion and mercy. Her name means "she who hearkens to the cries of the world." Most of the world's cultures have a Mother Mary or a Kuan Yin archetype. Next time you find yourself in need of comfort or mercy, ask the Divine Mother archetype to make herself known in your life. She is especially helpful with emergency situations that seem impossible and overwhelming. Learn to ask for divine help and pray daily, and you will be all right.

An Angelic Reflection: I know that no matter how difficult a situation I encounter, there is a divine energy waiting to restore hope in my heart.

$\mathcal{L}$EARNING

An Angel Reminder: In the act of learning, the mind and the heart must be equal participants.

Society traditionally looks at learning as acquiring knowledge of facts and ideas. But while knowledge of the mind is undeniably important, it is of little ultimate value without corresponding knowledge of the heart. The angels view learning as acquiring understanding of ourselves and others. As we learn about our patterns of behavior, the reasons we do the things that we do, and as we become more willing to try to understand why others act the way they do, we become more in control of our lives. We graduate from being creatures of habit to mature individuals for whom all experiences become a source of learning and an impetus for change. In so doing, our mistakes become our successes and we acquire true wisdom—knowledge born of compassion, strengthened through awareness, and applied for growth.

If a particular difficulty in your life has caused you to turn to this meditation, what can you learn from this difficulty? How could you learn more from it? View the difficulty as a gift from the angels, an ideal chance to learn more about yourself, why you are in the situation, and how you may be able to solve your problem through understanding and altering key behavior patterns.

An Angelic Reflection: All experiences that are given to me are valuable opportunities for learning and change.

STOP CARING

**An Angel Reminder: Stop caring about
the things you cannot change.**

If you are constantly bothered by the way others treat
you, or if you find that things
they do perturb you, the best
way to have a peaceful life is to
stop caring. This doesn't mean that
you stop caring about the people themselves and
their highest good; it means that you stop caring
and investing your time in the things that they do. If
we focus too heavily on the things we don't get back from
the people we care about, all our attention will be on issues of lack. Give to yourself by taking a break from caring about what people do.

*Investigate what you care about and why. Ask yourself the
real reason why you care about how someone acts or behaves
in a certain situation. What do you have invested in the way
others behave? If the answers are your own self-worth, your
dignity, or your meal ticket, it is time to rethink and recare
about the real things that bring you self-worth. Each time a
thought of someone else's negative behavior starts to repeat itself in your mind, stop it by saying to yourself: I choose not to
care about this; it has nothing to do with me or my overall life
plan.*

**An Angelic Reflection: I will care more about the beauty of
life, and less about people's behavior patterns.**

*E*NERGY

An Angel Reminder: Every moment of our lives is a response to and a generation of some form of energy.

We constantly broadcast and receive energy, not only verbally but also nonverbally through our thoughts, emotions, and body language. The angels encourage us to become aware of the effect we have on others and the similar effect they have on us through this often unconscious transmittal of energy waves. We will then be less vulnerable to outside influences and more in touch with our own choices. We can tune the energy that constantly pulsates in and around us to a higher, purer vibration that can change our environments and our lives. By becoming more conscious of the thoughts and feelings that we are sending out into the world, and by trusting our inner guidance and intuition, we will better be able to sense and interpret existing energy and to send and receive the kind of energy we desire.

Start sensing the energy around you. Note your energy level when you get up in the morning, and how it changes throughout the day. Become aware of how your energy changes around others. Do some people seem to give you energy, while others seem to take it away? Pay attention to how your nonverbal energy broadcasts seem to affect others, and begin to send out the kind of energy you'd like to receive.

An Angelic Reflection: My unspoken thoughts and feelings have a powerful effect on my life and the lives of those around me.

$\mathcal{A}$PPROVAL

An Angel Reminder: You do not need to be approved; you are sanctioned by heaven.

What is your approval rating? If you know, then you are in trouble. How could we have an approval rating when it is no one else's business to approve what we do? Seeking approval gets us into all kinds of trouble. We agree to do things we don't want to do out of the fear that the person asking may disapprove of us if we say no. Approval causes some people to lie about themselves. It is natural to want approval—to want to be regarded favorably by people— but the trouble comes in seeking others' approval before we approve of who we are. The whole issue of approval is foreign to the angels. It is just another way humans give away their freedom of being.

Next time you feel uncomfortable about an agreement you made, ask yourself if it was made because you were seeking approval. Stop looking for approval in all the wrong places by not seeking it in the first place. Ask the angels to help you stay conscious of entering agreements that you really want to make, not ones designed for the illusion of approval. The joke is, others don't really approve of us anyway; they are too busy seeking their own approval.

An Angelic Reflection: I am endorsed by heaven; I am sanctioned by the angels. I will look beyond approval and live an honest life.

OETRY

An Angel Reminder: We are all poems in search of a voice.

"A poem," said Robert Frost, "begins in delight and ends in wisdom." So does life, if it is lived as the angels would like us to live it. And poetry is, after all, life transformed into verse—the surging, exhilarating, untamed current of human thought, feeling, and experience. We do not have to be able to write poetry to experience it, for poetry is everywhere, within us and without. Have you ever watched the lyrical movement of trees in the breeze, the rhythmic soaring of birds overhead, the measured emergence of the stars as they become visible in the evening sky? Have you ever listened to your inner poetry—your thoughts, your dreams, the song of your own soul? The angels have given you many poems, waiting like the stars to come out and illuminate the heaven that is within. And they believe that the poet is the embodiment of courage, for he or she dares to give a voice to the yearnings that too often lie buried in human hearts. Unearth your yearnings; give them a voice. It is then that your life can begin again in delight and end in wisdom.

What are the poems of your soul? See if you can write a poem about one of them. If you have difficulty getting started, try reading some poetry every day. Coming into contact with the poetry of others will help to awaken the poetry within you.

Angelic Reflection: I recognize and activate the poems of my soul.

LABOR PAINS

An Angel Reminder: Nothing comes from nothing.

When you give birth to something, whether it is a child, a creative project, a new business, or a new aspect of yourself, you will experience labor—birthing pains. Labor is effort, hard work, but if we don't go through labor we won't give birth to anything new. If labor is so difficult and painful, why would we sign up to birth something new? Because the rewards and the blessings we receive are worth every second of the pain. We have the ability to forget pain after it has gone, and we can also choose to be creative with our pain. The angels can be our birthing partners. They remind us to look beyond the pain and keep the creative vision alive.

Are you afraid of labor? If so, ask the angels to be your birth partners. Think about the times in your life when you created or birthed something new that you were proud of. Was the pain worth it? Don't be afraid of pain. Go into labor and be born again.

An Angelic Reflection: I realize that to grow and prosper I must labor with love in my heart and give birth to new wonders.

GOING TO EXTREMES

An Angel Reminder: Irrational acts never achieve rational results.

One of the biggest disasters in China's history occurred when Mao Tse-tung declared war on the sparrows. Denouncing the birds as the "enemy of the people" because they were eating the grain, Mao suspended all work and ordered everyone in China to mobilize. From rooftops across the nation, billions of men, women, and children screamed, banged gongs, fired rifles, and so frightened the sparrows that, having nowhere to land or hide, they eventually fell to the ground, dead of exhaustion. Mao did succeed in virtually decimating China's sparrow population. But the angels could have told him that because the ecological balance was so severely disrupted, there would be nothing to combat the worms the following spring. And indeed the worms devastated crops throughout the country, throwing China into a terrible three-year famine that killed perhaps as many people as Mao killed sparrows.

The next time you are tempted to go to extremes and act out of anger or fear rather than waiting until you have calmed down and carefully thought out the situation, remember Chairman Mao and the sparrows. Then ask the angels to help you restore the natural balance in your life by finding a more rational and helpful solution to your problem.

An Angelic Reflection: I do not allow my emotions to cloud my reason.

𝒫ROMISES

**An Angel Reminder: Your
relationship with the angels is very
promising.**

A promise is a declaration assuring
that you will or will not do something.
In these changing times, we have to
be careful what we promise others
and what we promise ourselves. What
really holds promise—the ranting of commercials, the big talk of people, or the
promises of God? God has promised us the
chance to make our lives worth something while we
are here. God has promised that the angels will watch
over us. God has promised that there will always be
beauty to feed our souls. Promises from people may wither
and fail, but the promises of God stand true forever.

*Think about what God promises to you personally. Are you
willing to accept and trust in God's promises? Do you feel the
future is promising or threatening to your evolution? Do you
believe there is a promised land? Are there any guarantees
that this life isn't just a big joke? Think about what you
promised yourself long ago before you entered the earth
plane. Be easy on yourself. You are a promising star rising to
shine before others.*

**An Angelic Reflection: God has promised me beauty, hope,
joy, and angelic protection to guide me in all my ways on
earth. I promise to accept these gifts freely.**

$\mathcal{M}$ODERATION

An Angel Reminder: Moderation affords us the mental and physical stamina necessary to live life to the fullest.

When older people are asked their secret to a long life, their most frequent answer is that they have always done things in moderation. Consciously or not, these people understood and respected an important truth: that because many of the body's systems work within limits, moderation is an essential protective mechanism. We need food, water, air, sunshine, exercise, play, rest, and work to survive; yet each one of these done in excess puts stress on our bodies, which in turn blocks creative energy and endangers the health. Moderation may not be a fashionable philosophy; excessiveness has always been seen as more daring and alluring. But in order for the divine intelligence of the universe to flow freely through us, we must respect our physical and mental limits. The angels encourage us to enjoy but not overindulge in life's pleasures, while always keeping its pains in perspective.

We often respond to stress by doing the very things that create more stress. Instead of resting, eating sensibly, or meditating, we might push ourselves, eat too much sugar, drink alcohol, smoke, or seek out other stimulants that give us temporary comfort. Think about your own response to stress, and ask the angels to give you suggestions for practicing moderation in a creative and life-enhancing way.

An Angelic Reflection: Through moderation I achieve a sense of mental and physical balance and harmony.

RELATIONSHIPS

An Angel Reminder: Instead of trying to make a relationship work, let it evolve.

The degree of satisfaction in our relationships depends on how willing
we are to let them evolve at their
own pace, in their own way. Often
without even realizing it, we base our
relationships on a set of preconceptions
and expectations that demand conformity
instead of embracing uniqueness. As a
result, instead of manifesting reality, relationships
become the illusory projections of our own dreams and
fears. We fall in love and try to make the other person
conform to our ideal of the perfect mate. We map out
sensible paths for our children to follow and are disillusioned when they choose instead to live their own lives.
We give advice to friends and are hurt when they don't
take it. The angels remind us that a relationship is not an
inanimate lump of clay that we can mold to our specifica-
tions but is rather a living, breathing, ever-changing entity in its own right. A relationship needs freedom and
space in order to grow and mature.

*What sort of relationships do you cultivate in your life? Do
you allow others the right to be themselves? Do you allow
yourself to be yourself? Do you try to control the direction of
a relationship, or do you enjoy the delights and surprises the
relationship brings?*

**An Angelic Reflection: I respect the uniqueness of each
relationship in my life.**

MESSENGERS

An Angel Reminder: The angels reach our hearts and souls through our eyes and ears.

The angels are messengers, emissaries from heaven, and they bring us their messages in many ways and guises. Our lives often change through what might be considered events of chance or coincidence. People may appear unexpectedly, bringing gifts of wisdom, friendship, opportunity, or help. We may open a book or switch on the TV or radio at random to a passage or situation or song lyric that directly applies to something we're currently experiencing. Remember that the angels work through synchronicity and that if we remain open, not closed, to all possibilities, we may receive their messages of insight, love, and hope through virtually any channel of earthly communication. All we have to do is keep on watching and listening.

Can you recall instances in your life in which you may have received a message from the angels? Have certain people entered and exited your life suddenly, for what almost appears to be a specific purpose? Have you ever been inexplicably saved from a tragedy or dangerous situation? Begin to pay closer attention to incidents that you might have previously attributed to chance or coincidence, and be open to new thoughts, insights, and information. It just might be the angels trying to reach you.

An Angelic Reflection: I am aware of and open to all sources of help, guidance, and information. I allow my good sense and intuition to help me decide which ones are for my highest good.

OMNIPRESENT

An Angel Reminder: The sun is always shining, and God is always loving.

Omnipresent means all-present or present everywhere at the same time, met with constantly. God and the angels are thought to be omnipresent. Our selves are omnipresent to us, because everywhere we go we are met with our selves. We carry baggage with us everywhere. Some of it probably isn't necessary for every trip we take; on the spiritual path it is best to travel light. Love is omnipresent; you will find it wherever you go if you train yourself to look for it beyond your reactions. As soon as you are truly willing to see and feel without a doubt in your heart, you will find that the angels are present everywhere, especially in the beauty of nature.

What does everywhere *really mean? How can there be an* everywhere? *If you want to play with an abstract concept, think about this: everywhere is really nowhere, no space.*

An Angelic Reflection: Everywhere I go I will be present to myself.

$\mathcal{W}$ORK

An Angel Reminder: "We ought not to get tired of doing little things for the love of God, because He looks at the love rather than the work."

Brother Lawrence, The Practice of the Presence of God

The seventeenth-century French monk Brother Lawrence was only a monastery kitchen attendant without education. But his practice of the presence of God through menial labor had a profound impact on the history of spirituality. Although he initially detested kitchen work, Brother Lawrence learned to find—and communicate— joy and purpose in each and every one of his actions, from doing dishes to picking up a single piece of straw. As human beings with unique abilities, talents, and perceptions, we all have the power to make our work an enriching and rejuvenating experience and to influence others through our attitudes toward our occupations, whatever they may be. The job or career itself is of secondary importance; whether we are rich or poor, famous or anonymous, in the foreground or in the background, our angelic task is the same: to connect to our higher selves and inspire others through recognizing the true value of service.

The next time you are at work, try practicing the presence of God in any task for a few minutes each day. Whatever the job—painting a house, typing a letter, answering phones, handling a large project—take pride in doing it well and reflect upon how it will help someone else while helping you to grow in mastery and self-discipline.

An Angelic Reflection: I know that the universe is my true employer.

*T*HE SOUL'S REFLECTION

An Angel Reminder: A tiny mirror can reflect a strong beam when it faces the light.

Our souls are beautiful mirrors that seek to reflect the light of God. We cannot see our souls' reflections, but if we could we would see many different degrees of light. Some of us have a light bright enough to forever illuminate our path and the paths of those with whom we come in contact. Others, who are not in touch with their spiritual selves, have dulled their inner light and so its reflection is dim. The light of God is the light of truth; the intensity of the light we reflect depends on the amount of truth that we are willing to accept and practice in our lives. The more we live in truth, the more light we reflect back to the world. The angels are pure light and pure truth. With the angels in our lives our light naturally becomes brighter.

Imagine that you are a light in the darkness of the world. How could you brighten up the world around you? How could the angels help?

An Angelic Reflection: I am a mirror for the light of truth. The clearer my mirror is, the more light I reflect to illuminate the darkness.

*I*NSULATION

An Angel Reminder: The angels help insulate us from the tensions of the world without blocking the natural flow of energy.

Insulation, by definition, blocks the passage of energy. Insulation is a popular commodity in today's world. We insulate ourselves from the elements of nature by conditioning the air in our homes and clothing our bodies. We insulate ourselves from reality by letting others do the dirty work, such as taking care of the dying, picking up and disposing of our trash, raising our children, housing the criminals, baking our daily bread. The energy of reality can, of course, be overwhelming, but by the same token, if we block too much of that energy we will feel less than alive. The angels want to help us insulate ourselves in a natural way so that we see reality and know where we can intelligently help humanity without allowing negative forces to drain us. The angels encourage us to use creative energy to make our lives interesting, and they will insulate us from the harshness of reality through the energies of hope and humor.

How do you insulate yourself from reality? Does this have a positive or negative effect on your life? Think about how the angels use insulation for positive purposes: offering heavenly protection, preventing the passage of negative energy, affording us the warmth of divine love. Yet the angels never block the energies that encourage us to be awake and alive members of society.

An Angelic Reflection: I will brave the elements and embrace life with only the angels as my insulation.

$\mathcal{A}$VENUE

**An Angel Reminder: There is a wonderful
avenue that starts in your own backyard.**

The journey through life does not have to be
a straight and narrow path. There are many
enchanting avenues, lined with angels and
hope, that we can travel on and explore.
The avenues we choose will help us define
our journeys and lead us to the people and
places we must encounter. When the feeling sets
in that the avenue we are traveling has become
boring and tedious, it is crucial to find out why. It
may be that it is time to change avenues, or it
may mean that a surge of creative energy is needed to
change our perceptions and find ways to make better
use of what we have.

*An avenue is a means of reaching something, achieving a
goal, and making progress. What avenues are you traveling to
achieve your goals? Are they avenues that make you happy
and help you live with mental peace? The scenery on your
avenue is important. Surround yourself with lots of roses to
smell, and light the way with angels.*

**An Angelic Reflection: I will stay off the avenues of
boredom and resentment, and I will travel the avenues of
light and laughter with the angels by my side.**

FRUSTRATION

An Angel Reminder: Frustration is a gift waiting to be opened.

Frustration is wonderful. It can be the beginning of creativity, the power behind creating what you truly want to create. Frustration is a sign that raw energy is at your fingertips, waiting to be dealt with. We have many choices to make when we feel frustration. We can let it sink down to the tombs of resentment we keep in the dark recesses of our shadows, or we can use the energy to give us a positive kick in the pants. Frustration often signals the moment before a breakthrough, and if we stick with the frustration and work it out, our insights will expand tremendously.

The definition of frustrate *is to prevent from accomplishing a purpose or fulfilling a desire. At the first sign of frustration, ask yourself what you could do to use the raw energy in a creative way. There is always an answer. Sometimes we get frustrated because we are struggling to attain something we don't really want, so we must identify what we truly want. The angels will help you find a creative use for frustration. It is up to you then to funnel the energy into a new form.*

An Angelic Reflection: Frustration will not get the best of me, for I will get the best from frustration.

*I*NTEGRITY

An Angel Reminder: Integrity is a personal declaration of independence from mediocrity.

Integrity by definition means wholeness or soundness, honesty and incorruptibility. To be honest and whole takes knowing yourself and what you stand for. When you are true to your values, you are true to yourself—whole and sound. Can you put a price on your integrity? If someone came along and offered you big money to give up one of your values, would you do it? Would you give up hope for a price? Courage? Intelligence? If you can put a price on something, then you really don't value it. If you put a price on something that you do value, then you have corrupted that value and compromised your integrity. When we live in integrity, we commit ourselves to excellence. We upgrade our lives and the lives of those with whom we come in contact. When we live in integrity, we will always be striving to attain even greater harmony with the laws of the universe. We will not be a little lower than the angels; we will be eye to eye with them.

What are your values? If you are not sure, make a list of the things that bring meaning to your life, things you would protect and stand up for. Some of your top values may be: God, education, children, family, creativity, freedom, hope, health, peace. Ask yourself if you are true to your values in your everyday life. If not, how can you begin to live with more integrity?

An Angelic Reflection: My values embody the principles of integrity. I know that the angels are the wind beneath the wings of integrity, carrying the vision of all people as whole and sound.

$\mathcal{E}$XPRESSION

An Angel Reminder: Life is the expression of God's love.

Expressing ourselves to those who really care is not very easy in these busy days. How often do you feel satisfied that you have expressed who you are and been accepted and listened to? One reason Twelve-Step programs are so ingenious is that they allow people to express who they are and what they have been through, and the people who listen understand and support them. Expression is important. If you rarely get the chance to do it, you will lack harmony in your life and try to express yourself in ways that are not appropriate to people who don't really care. We can express who we are in many ways, and it is good to explore many possibilities. We learn about who we are by expressing who we are.

How do you express yourself? The arts are a good outlet. Joining a support group is a good way to express yourself and learn more about who you are. Don't ignore the importance of expressing yourself and allowing others to express who they are. The angels help us express ourselves in new and beautiful ways when we allow them to express love through us.

An Angelic Reflection: I know who I am, and I will express who I am to people who care.

ᎭOSITIVE CONSCIOUSNESS

An Angel Reminder: Thinking is thinking; consciousness is awareness.

So much has been written about the power of positive thinking that the entire concept has become a cliché. Viewed superficially, positive thinking has too often been misinterpreted as denying the negative and closing one's eyes to reality. It has been touted as a panacea for all ills; just "think positively," we are told, and everything we want will come to us. Instead of positive thinking, the angels would like us to develop positive *consciousness*. With positive consciousness we do not deny the negative or try to manipulate the universe into doing our bidding. Instead, we work at replacing negative thoughts with loving thoughts, and we view whatever comes to us as helping us to grow. As our consciousness shifts from negative to positive, as our perceptions become more loving and nonjudgmental, we begin to attract joyful and fulfilling experiences to us.

Make a list of the most frequent unhelpful thoughts you have, and in a column beside it list an uplifting alternative thought for each one. Whenever you find yourself thinking in a negative or critical manner, stop and replace these thoughts with their loving and nonjudgmental equivalents. As your consciousness changes from negative to positive, note any corresponding changes in your life.

An Angelic Reflection: As I begin to see the world through the angels' loving eyes, I attract their positive energy into my life.

*P*OSSIBILITIES

An Angel Reminder: Let's stop answering the questions for which only God has the answers.

One popular question posed to angel-ologists is, "When a loved one dies, could she or he become an angel and watch over loved ones from the other side?" Most angelologists answer no, on the basis that angels are separate beings created by God, not humans who have died. Yet how do the angelologists re-ally know? The best way to answer our questions about the angels is to identify the feeling we have in our own hearts and to acknowledge that with God all things are possible. Maybe God changes and updates informa-tion; who are we to say yes or no to possibilities? Limiting God limits our perception of what the angels can do for us. If you want to limit yourself, keep answering God's questions; if you want to live in the realm of unlimited beautiful possibilities, then let go of strict answers and let God have the last word.

Next time you need an answer about the rules and regula-tions surrounding angels, remember that all things are possi-ble. What is true in your heart may be different from what is true for another. Consider the possibility that ultimately everything is true. Ask the angels to help you play with your ideas and to help keep you from getting attached to strict rules concerning the truth.

An Angelic Reflection: When I have a question concerning the truth, I will let my heart answer.

I NTUITION

An Angel Reminder: When searching for truth, do not despair; let intuition lead you.

The angels have supplied us with all the navigational equipment we need along the journey of life. Perhaps the most powerful item is our intuition—our inner knowing that, if we trust it, will keep us on the right track, out of the brambles of distraction and toward our soul's purpose. Intuition is a multipurpose tool. It can help us with indecision and confusion, alert us to danger, and point the way through the unfamiliar and sometimes frightening territory of new experience. Our intuition is always available to us, whether or not we choose to heed it. How many times have we disregarded that little warning voice inside and done something we later regretted? Or how many times have we followed our hunches, with surprising success? Learn to listen to your intuition. The quieter you become, the louder it will speak. Then do not be afraid to follow it. It will always lead you in the right direction.

How strong is your sense of intuition? Do you listen to it? The next time you need an answer to a problem or more clarity in a situation, grow calm, breathe deeply, and tune in to your inner guidance, your gut feelings. Write them down and reflect upon them. The answer you are seeking will come.

An Angelic Reflection: My intuition is one of my most powerful natural resources. The more I trust it, the surer will be my footing on the life path.

$\mathcal{F}$ ASCINATION

An Angel Reminder: Life is a fascinating journey.

Fascination is an irresistible attraction to something. It means being enchanted. We have to be careful about what enchants us; sometimes we are fascinated by things that are not for our highest good. If we can be fascinated by the process of life and not so interested in defining it as good and bad, life will be more interesting.

When we are fascinated by life, we become fascinating to others. We have to be careful not to be too fascinated with the angels themselves, for they want us to be fascinated with God.

An easy way to get out of the black-and-white world of good and bad is to look at what fascinates you and to be aware of the dangers of enchantment. Be fascinated without an investment, be interested and wise about what interests you. What exactly fascinates you about the angels? Think about it.

An Angelic Reflection: I am irresistibly attracted to the wonder of life.

$\mathcal{M}$ORALITY

An Angel Reminder: A lazy mind will never grasp the true spirit of morality.

In cartoons we have probably all seen the little angel that sits on one shoulder telling the person of the virtues of goodness, while on the other shoulder sits a little devil telling this person to be bad. Recognizing the distinction between right and wrong in regard to behavior and motives is the work of the conscience. Out of the conscience arises morality. Morality has received little attention in recent history because we don't take time to understand how important it is. Morality does not exist to control our behavior from the outside, although many religions would have you think it does. Morality comes from having inner discernment of what is right or wrong for yourself. It involves making choices that are best for you and for the advancement of the whole.

Choosing to allow a sense of morality to rule your motives and behavior can mean delaying gratification or even sacrificing something you truly want to have or do. For this reason morality has become so unpopular, because we have been told that "if it feels good do it," and many of us have based our decisions on that very cliché. But clichés change, and we need to change with them. Next time you get the urge to do something because it feels good, think of those little beings on each shoulder and listen to what each one has to say about it. Then make your choice.

An Angelic Reflection: I will make the noble effort to listen to the voice of the angel on my shoulder.

$\mathcal{V}$OICES

An Angel Reminder: Don't lose your voice.

We have heard the tales of people throughout history who heard voices and were punished harshly for it. After all, people who hear voices are crazy, right? There is no such thing as "crazy," and all of us hear voices all day long. We often hear the voice of the critic, especially when we are doing something creative. The voice of the adult or parent comes to us often to remind us to get ourselves together and grow up. The voice of childhood calls out to us to drop everything and run outside to play. We can manage these voices if we balance our lives properly. Trouble comes when one of the voices is shouting and drowning out the rest. When this happens the angels can't get their messages through and life becomes stressful. We have a strong voice, and we have the power to tell the voices we don't want to hear to be quiet.

The idea that hearing voices is a sign of mental weakness probably came about because hearing unwelcome voices usually happens when people are tired and worn-out. Their batteries are worn down and their power low, so outside influences seem to have power over them. We are amazingly resilient if we take the time to recharge our batteries with proper food, rest, sunshine, and angel love.

An Angelic Reflection: I will listen to the voice of heaven, and I will know what to do.

$\mathcal{F}$EELINGS

An Angel Reminder: Occasional reality checks are a good idea.

Feelings are sometimes complicated affairs. We strive to be in touch with them, and at the same time we often fear becoming overwhelmed by them. As a result, we may deny our feelings or run from them—or we may become altogether enmeshed in them. In order to keep ourselves emotionally balanced, we need to remember that feelings are not facts but *responses* that require both listening and monitoring. If we feel fearful or angry or depressed, for instance, we need first to acknowledge the feeling. Then we need to separate it from the situation. We can say to ourselves, "While I am having this feeling, it is not an unalterable condition. It is a response to a particular situation. It may be a warning, or it may be an unfounded fear. In order not to become overwhelmed by my feelings, how can I change the situation or my response to it?" The angels want us to rejoice in the whole range of our emotions, while at the same time maintaining a sense of clarity and balance.

Are there any feelings that you'd like to be more in touch with, or less at the mercy of, in your life? Write them down. Now try to identify any fears that may be blocking your ability to feel or your inability to extricate yourself from your emotions. Are you afraid of intimacy? Afraid of losing your sense of feeling? Whatever the fear, talk to it. Ask it why it is there, what it is trying to tell you. Pay attention and let awareness replace fear.

An Angelic Reflection: I allow my feelings to guide me, not control me.

$\mathcal{U}$NLEARNING

An Angel Reminder: "The chief object of education is not to learn things but to unlearn things."

G. K. Chesterson

Education is a funny thing, especially if it has been shaped by schooling. Mark Twain once said, "I never let my schooling interfere with my education." Art students provide a good example of having to unlearn things. Just the idea of art school is rather absurd if you think about it. In some art classes students are encouraged to draw exactly what they see, to learn the skill of duplication. Yet when we consider what is fresh and interesting in art, it is rarely a duplication, and often the art we are attracted to is a primitive interpretation of what is seen. The process of unlearning is paramount to finding new and interesting ways of doing things. Unlearning is a process of giving yourself artistic license to live life.

Ways to foster unlearning: Let go of formulas. Break the rules—just a little at first, then allow the dam to break if you need to. Let go of straight lines, linear thought, and answers. Never be a textbook case. Remember that the best teacher is nature. Ask the angels for insight and new perceptions whenever you feel stuck.

An Angelic Reflection: I know that true learning is a process of discovering my own thoughts and feelings about life.

$\mathcal{H}$UMOR

An Angel Reminder: Blessed are those who have a sense of humor, for they will laugh with God.

When we were created, God equipped us with a built-in safety valve to keep us from exploding in the pressure cooker of life. That safety valve is a sense of humor. Humor in this context is not mere silliness or frivolity; it is actual power. Studies have proven that people in leadership positions who maintain a sense of humor and use it to disarm their adversaries are much more well-liked and likely to be elected, reelected, or promoted than those who are incapable of laughing at themselves. Norman Cousins and others have proven that laughter can actually help to cure life-threatening illnesses by empowering the immune system and restoring our mental and emotional stability. It is when we cease to be able to laugh that we risk becoming unbalanced and overwhelmed by negativity. The angels want us to remember not to take ourselves too seriously. Even—and especially—when our troubles seem too much to bear, humor can help to defuse the despair, give us a new perspective, and gently remind us that the clouds never overtake the sun—only temporarily obscure it.

The next time you find yourself coming down with an attack of severe solemnity, call on the angels, who find humor, hidden or obvious, in all sorts of places and will direct us to situations and people who will automatically lift our spirits.

An Angelic Reminder: With humor as my constant ally, I emerge victorious over the negative forces of life.

COURTESY

An Angel Reminder: "A man without courtesy . . . might as well cease to be."

Confucius

In today's fast-paced world, courtesy seems to be a virtue of a bygone age; it is practiced and valued less and less. Yet courtesy is actually a primary requisite of humanity. With it we are ever mindful of our true place; in according others respect, acting with decency, and practicing good manners, we are in effect maintaining the balance of harmony in the universe by honoring the Divine in everyone and everything. Without courtesy, says Confucius, we are "mere beasts who might as well die, death being end of no decency." Courtesy is, in short, one of the attributes that most clearly defines our humanness, separating us from the beasts and uniting us with the angels.

Begin noticing when and where courtesy is practiced around you, and seek to be courteous whenever you can. Note how, as courtesy tends to beget courtesy, you can actually upgrade the level of harmony and mutual respect in the world.

An Angelic Reflection: I am considerate of others and respectful of my place in the divine scheme of things.

$\mathcal{M}$IRACLES

An Angel Reminder: Each time we transform negative thought into positive awareness, we have prepared the ground for a miracle.

Many people equate the angels with the miraculous. But we don't need the angels to appear to us in a clamor of bells and whistles to experience a miracle. Instead, the angels want us to ponder the question "What is a miracle?" The standard definition focuses on an event that defies the laws of probability and seems to issue from the supernatural rather than the natural. To the angels, however, the natural and the supernatural are part of the same package. They do not divide the universe into categories of metaphysical and physical, miraculous and mundane; to them, life itself is miraculous, and miracles—whether as simple as the existence of a blade of grass or as earthshaking as a vision, premonition, or astounding synchronicity—are a natural part of life and lie within the realm of our own creation.

The world is full of people who, by changing their attitudes, beliefs, and awarenesses, suddenly begin to experience miracles in their lives. The first step toward a miracle is to open your mind and heart to the angels' presence and to incorporate their loving and positive qualities into your thoughts and actions. The second is to become more aware and appreciative of all the miracles around you, not the least of which is the miraculous organism that is you. And the third is to simply expect a miracle. You won't be disappointed.

An Angelic Reflection: With an attitude of gratitude, faith, awareness, and expectancy, I create my own miracles.

*N*OBLESSE OBLIGE

An Angel Reminder: Come forth nobly born and accept your rightful place in life.

Noblesse oblige is kind and generous behavior considered to be the responsibility of persons of high birth or rank. Privilege entails responsibility, and noble people must behave nobly. You may be thinking that talk of the nobly born does not involve you, but it does. We are all nobly born children of the Great and Noble Spirit of Life. The angels are an important part of our nobility, and they look to us to honor the Great Spirit with our own noble behavior. A noble person possesses excellent qualities that please the angels. Be noble and keep yourself free from pettiness or meanness in any situation you encounter, and the angels will admire you.

Are you a good example of one who is nobly born? Begin to realize the importance of your noble birth. Think about it often. What could you do to improve your attitude? Instead of reacting with judgment to situations you encounter, stand back and allow a sense of nobility to guide your instincts. Life will be much more tolerable, and you will find you cherish the Great Noble Spirit that flows through all of life, regardless of rank or file.

An Angelic Reflection: The more admirable I act in life, the more noble I will feel.

$\mathcal{N}$O COMPARISON

An Angel Reminder: Only God and the angels have the whole picture of another's life.

How often do you play the comparison game? We compare ourselves to others and their situations and then judge ourselves and them accordingly. We believe that if only we had what other people have, if only we were as lucky as they, we'd have it made in the shade. Aren't we forgetting that luck really has nothing to do with the good things we have in our lives, that fortune is the result of making the proper choices and keeping our values intact? Don't we understand that each and every one of us has our own life lessons to learn, our own soul's journey to pursue? We cannot begin to be content until we have released the urge to compare ourselves to others. The angels love us just the way we are and would never judge us against one another. Rather than indulge in comparison, they ask us to be grateful for and aware of all that we have and are and to value each aspect of our lives as a means for growth.

Do you often compare yourself to other people? What do they seem to have that you don't? Have you ever thought about what you have that others don't? Begin now to appreciate your life as a gift that is uniquely yours.

An Angelic Reflection: I am grateful for who I am and for what I have in my life. God's infinite creativity assures that no two experiences are ever the same.

$\mathcal{H}$OSPITALITY

An Angel Reminder: We are not permanent residents on earth but guests for the night.

Hospitality is a wonderful attribute; it is also an attitude. Truly hospitable people regard their homes—and hearts—as open hearths to those who may pass through needing physical, emotional, or spiritual sustenance. In so doing, their lives become a metaphor for heaven. The angels want us to understand that the entire universe is constructed according to the laws of hospitality, for aren't we all, ultimately, guests of God? As guests, we are beholden to our host to be properly grateful and to extend, when we are able, the same hospitality to others. When we are truly hospitable, from the heart to the hearth, we are not disillusioned if our hospitality is taken advantage of or not returned, for we know that true hospitality is not merely an action but an attitude, our natural response to the generosity we ourselves have received from the universe.

Hospitality is one part gratefulness and one part generosity. If you would like to develop an attitude of hospitality, begin by being grateful simply to be a guest here on earth. Think of your needs that have been taken care of, your wants that have been answered. Then try extending a little more hospitality toward others by being more generous with your time, your support, your interest, your love.

An Angelic Reflection: I receive hospitality without greed; I extend hospitality without fear.

$\mathcal{V}$ICTIM

An Angel Reminder: Don't be a victimized victim.

One popular notion—most likely reached without a lot of deep thought—is that there are no victims. A victim is a person who suffers because of an injury inflicted either by another person or by an event such as a natural disaster. Some people believe that we attract every event that happens to us and we create anything bad ourselves, so therefore there are no victims. It is difficult to imagine that an innocent child has attracted abuse or that a few people killed in a natural disaster brought it on themselves. This way of thinking puts the victim at the center of the universe, running the show. One problem with the idea that there are no victims is that it lets off the hook those who consciously choose to victimize others. We each have free will, so when someone chooses to trick, swindle, or injure us, we have to consider that that person chose the action and could have chosen not to follow through with it. Someone has to stop the buck. Why do the innocent have to take the blame?

If you become a victim, one choice you do have is not to allow the traumatic event to further victimize you; you can shape your attitude to give you the courage to get back up in the saddle. With the angels in your life you have less chance of becoming a victim, and they will always be there to help you out if you feel you have been a victim.

An Angelic Reflection: Regardless of the choices others make for my welfare, I will fare much better if I keep the angels near.

*A*PPRECIATORS

An Angel Reminder: Nothing of beauty would have lasted through time had it not been for appreciators.

Being an appreciator means that you intelligently enjoy creations of truth and beauty. Appreciators are those who respect, cherish, treasure, prize, value, and are thankful for what they see, hear, and feel. Sometimes we act as creators, and at other times we are the appreciators. Both are equally important. Great art and poetry need to be recognized by creative souls who fully realize and respect the true value of greatness. Appreciators practice the art of seeing. True appreciators are grateful for the chance to appreciate beauty and will allow themselves to have a peak experience at the recognition of great art. The art and practice of appreciation will give you renewed respect for the people you love and the gifts of beauty that surround you.

You cannot be a great artist without appreciating the beauty of God in nature. And you will get nowhere if you do not appreciate the art of your colleagues. If you feel that you don't really know how to appreciate truth and beauty in art and nature, the angels are great teachers. Great art is everywhere. You may find it in the architecture on the nearest corner, the fountain in the park, the masterpieces in the museums, and wherever trees are found. Most importantly, learn to appreciate the people you love.

An Angelic Reflection: I will appreciate the beautiful expression of life.

*M*ORE THAN MEETS THE EYE

An Angel Reminder: "I had, from boyhood, known all the stars of the heavens perfectly."

Tycho Brahe

One evening in 1572, the great Danish astronomer, Tycho Brahe, discovered a new star. Because Brahe subscribed to the prevailing Christian doctrine that celestial bodies could not alter in size and number, he was convinced that the heretofore unseen object he was observing constituted "a miracle indeed." Actually, what Brahe witnessed was a stellar explosion. And as for knowing "all the stars of the heavens perfectly," well, how could he know that several centuries later new telescopes would be developed that would make visible millions of stars that had been there all along? The angels remind us that there are always two realities: the one outside of us and the one inside. And so, in order not to make too many invalid assumptions, we must constantly remember there is always far more to life than meets the eye. The universe extends far beyond our limited perceptions; there will always be stars we haven't yet met.

Do you feel you know all there is to know about a particular subject? How often do you divide the world into absolutes of right and wrong? Begin to open your mind to the possibility that you neither see nor know everything there is to see and know, and note how your view of the world changes correspondingly.

An Angelic Reflection: I accept the fact that my perceptions are just my perceptions, and I leave room for other conclusions.

*I*MAGINATION

An Angel Reminder: "Imagination is more important than knowledge."

Albert Einstein

While our rational, logical society discounts things of the imagination as unreal, in fact the imagination is our direct line to true intelligence and greatness. It is in the womb of imagination that the great inventions of the world are conceived, the great works of art envisioned. It is through our imaginations that we connect with the future and meet the angels in their purest form. When we are in an imaginative state we are completely open to all sorts of possibilities and highly receptive to angelic guidance. And that guidance, if followed, tends to turn imaginings into happenings. Your most impossible dreams are, indeed, all in your imagination— just waiting to become reality.

Imagine something that you want to happen in your life. Now, use your imagination to think of all the ways your dream could materialize. Discount no possibility as being too ridiculous or impossible; in the realm of imagination, all things are possible.

An Angelic Reflection: I will not be afraid to unleash my imagination, for within its borderless realm lies the master plan of my life.

UTUMN

An Angel Reminder: We sow, we reap, we harvest, we prepare.

The autumn is the season of harvest. As such it is tinged with a bittersweet quality, for it involves both maturity and decline. Traditionally harvesttime is a time of gathering of both crops and people; all come together in joy and goodwill to help one another pick the fruits of the earth and to share in the bounty. But even as we rejoice in the gifts and beauty of fall, we are aware that the glorious colors of the changing leaves have already begun to fade. The dusk is coming sooner, the air growing colder. So autumn contains both joy and urgency as we harvest and we store, making the necessary preparations that will give us sustenance during the long winter nights ahead.

Are you entering autumn in any area of your life? What are you harvesting? What do you need to store, to take you through a period of coming decrease and waiting, so that you will once again be ready for the spring?

An Angelic Reflection: I prepare for the inward times even as I partake of the sociality of the harvest.

*L*OVE-LINK

An Angel Reminder: Our relationship with the angels is one of give and take, not just take.

A love-link is an object or experience we use to connect us to our guardian angels. Angelologist K. Martin-Kuri suggests the following: "You can do something once in a while for the angels in your life. You can put some flowers in your house as a love-link, or listen to a beautiful piece of music. Every time you see or hear something beautiful, consciously give it to your angels to distribute. Then it can be given to somebody who may be in need of it. It's a form of energy: you translate an experience into energy which can then go into the care of your angel and be used."

Make a conscious effort in your life to designate love-links with the angels. Do something each day to strengthen your relationship with your guardian angel. There are many ways to expand the love you have for the angels and to keep the relationship thriving. Remember to give back to them and thank them each day.

An Angelic Reflection: I will allow my relationship with the angels to grow stronger in love each day.

𝒫ERFECT LIFE

An Angel Reminder: Were you to trade your life for another's, you'd only be trading one set of joys and sorrows for another.

A woman with four cats is constantly amused by their behavior at dinnertime. She feeds the cats exactly the same food, in exactly the same quantity, only to watch them play a game of musical feeding bowls as they go from dish to dish, certain that one has something the other hasn't. Eventually they end up eating one anothers' meals; whether or not they recognize that they had nothing better or worse in their own bowls is their secret. The angels consider this a parable for all of us to ponder, for how many times have we envied someone else's life, certain that person had it better than we do? What an illusion! Because we can never know the private struggles and difficulties of another human being, things are usually never as they seem on the surface. And besides, the person who today may seem on top of the world could be at the bottom tomorrow. The angels want us to remember that when it comes to the perfect life, no one has it and everyone has it. The universe has dished out the same thing to all of us—a bowl full of lessons that are perfect for *us*.

Are there people whom you envy because they seem to have it all? Who are they, and what do they seem to have that you desire? Try to see the whole picture—what they had to go through to get what they have, what problems they might have that you don't.

An Angelic Reflection: I really do have the perfect life for me.

*M*OTIVATION

An Angel Reminder: The angels are motivated only by God's love for humans.

A motive is an impulse that causes motion, stirs us to action. When we are motivated to do something, an energy behind us is carrying us forward. It is important that we identify the original impulse that is providing the energy and inspiration for us to act. If we grew up without a lot of money, we may be motivated to do things that bring us money and material comfort. If we are lacking love in our lives, our motive is to find love. When the angels motivate us, inspiration and energy come from the impulse to achieve higher love in our lives. When we achieve higher love, then we will want to motivate others to experience this gift for themselves.

Are you aware of what motivates your actions? If your motivations could use some refining, ask the angels for a new impulse. Think of yourself as a motivational force of delight in the universe.

An Angelic Reflection: I am motivated by the angels, and I am guided by higher impulses.

$\mathcal{G}$RATITUDE

An Angel Reminder: The angels immediately respond to the summons of gratitude.

The gratitude attitude is a remarkably powerful force that, when unleashed, turns everything into a joyful experience. Yes, everything. The reason is quite simple: when we develop a consciousness of gratitude, the negative ceases to exist. The gratitude attitude involves thanking everything that is in your life, including the negatives. This may seem at first ridiculous, but here's the magic: when you thank something negative for happening or thank a negative thought for being there, you've just negated the negative and turned it into positive energy. At this point, miracles start to happen. The more thankful you become for all the abundance around you, the more that abundance will flow into your life and the more easily the angels can communicate with you. So thank everything, even when you're not so sure you are grateful for it. In time you will be.

Spend a day thanking everything that you come in contact with. When you open your eyes in the morning, thank the night for your rest and the day for its promises. When you take a shower, thank the water. When you drink your coffee, thank the plant that produced the bean, the person who picked the bean, and those who fashioned the cup you are drinking out of. And, of course, thank the angels for all the good they're bringing into your life.

An Angelic Reflection: I continually pause in gratefulness for the amazing process of life.

INSTRUMENT OF PEACE

PRAYER OF ST. FRANCIS

> Lord make me an instrument of Thy peace—
> Where there is hatred, I may bring love;
> Where there is wrong, I may bring the
>   Spirit of forgiveness;
> That where there is discord, I may bring
>   harmony;
> Where there is error, I may bring truth;
> Where there is doubt, I may bring faith;
> Where there is despair, I may bring hope;
> Where there are shadows, I may bring light;
> Where there is sadness, I may bring joy;
> Lord, grant that I may seek rather to
>   comfort than to be comforted;
> To understand, than to be understood;
> To Love, than to be Loved;
> For it is by self-forgetting that one finds;
> It is by forgiving that one is forgiven;
> It is by dying that one awakens
>   to Eternal Life.

Many people who resonate to angel consciousness feel that they have a deep connection to St. Francis. How do you feel about St. Francis and his prayer? Are you inspired by this prayer? Are you willing to be the angels' instrument of peace? Next time you feel a lack of direction, meditate on this prayer and ask the angels for guidance, and soon you will know what to do.

An Angelic Reflection: I will live my life as an instrument of peace, and the angels will be my guides.

$\mathcal{L}$ONELINESS

An Angel Reminder: Loneliness is a search that begins outside and ends inside.

Loneliness is a feeling of disconnectedness. When we are lonely, we feel unwanted, unloved, unsupported, even unnecessary. We feel disconnected from the outside world, when in reality we are disconnected from ourselves. When we begin to understand that loneliness has nothing really to do with our relationships to others, and everything to do with our relationship to ourselves, we begin to understand that we are, in truth, alone—alone responsible for our connectedness. Others come and go in our lives; we can't count on them to always be with us. But we can get to know ourselves, feel comfortable with ourselves, and reach out to others from a place of strength and serenity, not fear and despair. We can choose to connect to life once again, in the spirit of gratefulness rather than neediness, giving rather than taking. Then we are never alone.

If you've been feeling lonely, hold a conference with the lonely part of yourself. Ask it why it is feeling disconnected and sorry for itself. Tell it that you love it and so do the angels. Ask it if it is ready to reach out to others instead of waiting for others to reach out to it. List some ways that you could relieve yourself of loneliness by giving to others from your strong center. Could you do volunteer work? Start a group or workshop in one of your areas of interest? The more positive connectedness you initiate, the more will flow into your life.

An Angelic Reflection: In my loneliness, I discover the strength of my aloneness.

*H*UMILITY

An Angel Reminder: "Everything belongs to the people. I was just privileged to use it for a while.... It was only lent to me, and by that I'm includin' the power of the Presidency."

Harry S. Truman, from Merle Miller's Plain Speaking

Perhaps Harry Truman's ultimate purpose in life was not merely to become president of the United States, but to serve as a model of genuine humility for the world. Humility is a difficult concept for some of us to grasp because it is so often confused with self-effacement. Yet true humility is a combination of awareness, modesty, and gratitude. When we are truly humble, we are aware of our talents and accomplishments and we do not need to broadcast them. But at the same time, we are always grateful to a higher source of power and wisdom for the gifts that we possess. The genuinely humble person identifies with his or her abilities, but not with the position or the power that might go along with them.

Think of the gifts and abilities that you possess. Are you able to be proud of them without being prideful? Or are you too critical of yourself? Ask the angels to help balance your perception of yourself and to give you equal measures of confidence, modesty, and gratitude for all that you have to offer the world.

An Angelic Reflection: I am loved by God and the angels for who I am, not for what I have accomplished.

AMATEUR

An Angel Reminder: "Three things I avoid: poems by a poet, paintings by an artist, cooking by a chef."

The Zen master Ryokan

These days we seek things that seem homemade, taste homemade, and feel homemade. The reason is that homemade things are made by those who seem to love what they are doing, and the love appeals to our hearts. The word *amateur* comes from the Latin word for lover, *amator.* We often assign a higher status to professionals, yet amateurs may have the edge in enjoyment. Professionals do something because they are trained to; it is their job. Amateurs do something because they love doing it; it is often a pastime. An amateur carpenter may have all the skills, perhaps more, that a professional has yet will take the time to build a house with the essence of love and caring. Wouldn't you rather eat a great meal cooked with love than a fancy dish a chef whipped up without effort? Start to look beyond the professional world and seek out those who love.

If you find that you have become an uninspired professional rather than an enthusiastic amateur toward the game of life, look for more things to love. Professionals may also love what they are doing, so this is only an idea to play with. Allowing creativity to touch all that you do will help you love what you do, and the angels will be your assistants.

An Angelic Reflection: I will never forget that the essence of greatness follows those who love.

*T*HE GATE

An Angel Reminder: "For the gate is small, and the way is narrow that leads to life, and few are those who find it."

Matthew 7:14 (New American Standard Bible)

Why does the proverbial gate that leads to eternal life have to be so narrow? If you believe in the theory that God gave each human free will, then you will understand why the gate appears to be so small. Free will means we were not sent to earth with a set of instructions on how to live our lives. We are free to choose which rules to follow and which rules to discard. So when a human being finds the gate, recognizes it, and steps through of his or her own accord, all of heaven rejoices. Choosing to use our gift of free will to love God in our own creative way takes us through the gate. We are on our own, yet never alone; the angels will always be joyfully at our sides, playfully inspiring us onward to everlasting life.

If you want to make a spiritual choice in your life but feel that maybe you are not worthy or ready, think again. One can never make a mistake when choosing life; we may stray, but ultimately we will find our own ways to salvation, living life through the consciousness of our higher selves.

An Angelic Reflection: The gate may be small, and the path narrow, yet I know in my heart that it is large enough to accommodate all of the angels.

*E*LIMINATE THE NEGATIVE

An Angel Reminder: How many negative thinkers have you been inspired by lately?

It is important to understand why eliminating negative thoughts is vital to our health and well-being. Negative thoughts depress our immune systems, make us tired, and influence those around us in a negative way. Thinking negatively about a situation will send you searching for negative outcomes. You will then waste your time preparing to cope with a possible negative situation instead of pursuing positive goals and living a creative life. Negative thoughts bore the angels, and you wouldn't want to chance that. Once you realize the tedious nature of negative thinking, you can create a built-in warning system that will identify negative thoughts, allowing you the chance to choose a better way.

It is important to recognize when we have negative thoughts. Use the following questions as a negative-thought checklist: Is the thought life-defeating? Does it encourage excess worry? Is the thought hard to get rid of? Does thinking it make you feel uncomfortable? Would the angels view the thought as a waste of energy? If you answered yes to the above questions, then chances are the thought is negative. Two more questions to think about: What does the thought inspire in others? Is this thought the way you really want things to turn out?

An Angelic Reflection: I will make it my goal to eliminate the negative and affirm the positive, loving aspects of the angels.

DON'T SWALLOW IT WHOLE

An Angel Reminder: Don't believe everything you read, and never accept a label.

We wouldn't swallow a mouthful of food without chewing it, and we don't need to swallow a "mindful" of information without assimilating it properly. We can choke on food and also on information. Just as we can choose what food to put in our mouths, we can choose what information will be food for our thoughts. Humans possess the power of analysis, the power to separate the whole into constituents and examine and interpret it for a deeper personal understanding. Analyze all information you receive, regardless of the source, and think things through for yourself. In the final analysis, the most important thing is to come to your own conclusions and keep your mind free from litter.

Begin to use your power of analysis, and don't ever stop. Be conscious in your analysis, and don't overdo it or torment others with it. All things require balance. The angels will help you pull the parts away from the whole, so you will understand more fully the way things work. Understanding is our greatest power tool.

An Angelic Reflection: I will consciously look to nourish myself in mind, spirit, and body by understanding what I am swallowing.

$\mathcal{A}$NGEL APPEARANCES

An Angel Reminder: When it comes to angel appearances, the angels, like the Boy Scouts, encourage us to "be prepared."

Angel appearances are part of virtually all cultural and religious traditions. Whether the winged gods of the Greek pantheon, the celestial beings of the Hindus, the hairless youths of the Old Testament, or the haloed heavenly messengers of Christianity, angels have commonly been depicted as out-of-the-ordinary beings whose identity could definitely not be mistaken. But in addition to inhabiting what is commonly referred to as the celestial realm, the angels often move among us here on earth, taking the humble forms of other human beings just like us. We can encounter angels in friends, strangers, coworkers, passersby; the sign of their presence will be the sudden helpfulness, insight, protection, inspiration, or beneficence they impart to us and the joy, wonder, and peace we consequently experience. The angels enjoy popping up now and again to make life interesting. They want us to be prepared for the unexpected so that we are always open to the gifts that are handed to us without our knowledge.

Think about people you know or have encountered who might have been angels. What qualities did they possess that would alert you to their angelic nature? If you'd like an angel to appear in your life, ask to have one sent your way. Then be prepared *by fine-tuning your powers of awareness, and adopting an attitude of joyful expectation.*

An Angelic Reflection: I welcome the angels to make an appearance in my life.

$\mathcal{M}$OUNTAINTOP

An Angel Reminder: Cream rises to the top.

A mountaintop is a symbol of spiritual awareness, spiritual exaltation, and of getting closer to heaven. Moses ascended Mt. Sinai to receive the Ten Commandments, and Jesus went to the mountaintop to impart his greatest teachings, knowing that only the most sincere believers would follow him up. Each of us has our own symbolic mountaintop to reach, where we will receive a pure awareness of heaven. Our spiritual path is not always the easiest climb, but each time we reach a new height, our view is more magnificent. Our goal is to reach the top without missing the beauty and lessons each part of the mountain provides us on the way up. When we reach the top on our own, we can rest in the glory of God and enjoy the company of angels.

How far up the mountain have you climbed? Has the climb been difficult? Remember that when the climb seems too steep, the angels can help lighten you up and free you of the excess baggage you are trying to drag up with you. Stay on the path. The higher you go the easier it gets.

An Angelic Reflection: I know that the air is cleaner at the top of the mountain. I long to reach the top and breathe in the pure breath of divine inspiration.

OFF THE BEATEN PATH

An Angel Reminder: If we refuse to step off the beaten path, we will never notice the angels in the bushes.

All too often we treat life as though we've seen it all before. We go through our daily routines like robots, substituting habit for curiosity, unconsciousness for awareness. We're like hamsters in a little wheel, going round and round, thinking we're moving but always ending up, it seems, in the same place. While structure and established patterns of behavior have their advantages in terms of comfort and security, they become dangerous when they blind us to the beauty of fresh experience. The angels want us to look around us with new eyes, to discover the treasures that we bypass in the methodical trance we too often mistake for living. This is why they will often nudge us off the beaten path onto untried roads that will, if we follow them, lead to a heightened level of consciousness and joy.

Next time you're traveling a familiar route, allow yourself enough time to make at least one detour off the beaten path. Stop, look, listen. See—really see—everything around you. Take a new turn, explore a new street, a new path. If you're driving, get out of the car and walk around. Explore the environment. Let yourself meet someone new. (Who knows, she or he may be an angel.) Reflect upon how the experience might be a metaphor for your life and changes you may want to make.

An Angelic Reflection: As I open my eyes to new realities, I open my mind to new possibilities.

LANGUAGE

An Angel Reminder: We invented language to speak our minds. The angels communicate with our hearts.

Do the angels have a language, and if so, which language is it? Do they understand English? Of course they understand our language, regardless of its origin, but it is not the words they follow; it is the intent and the impulse that we generate that they pick up. Some think the angels have a language that is actually a series of strange symbols. Others think they use color as their language. Divine communication with the angels happens when we meditate, when all thoughts leave our minds and we enter the gap, which is bliss. When you reach this moment of no-thought, it is incredibly powerful and healing. You will want to go there often.

Try communicating with the angels through no-thought. It may seem strange to say you are communicating if you are not receiving and generating thoughts, but play with it. Practice meditating and losing all your words. When you reach the moment of blissful no-thought, you will have merged with the source, where all knowledge originates. You will know you have communicated with God and the angels. Even though words are not exchanged, much knowledge will be gained.

An Angelic Reflection: I will learn the language of love. I will then communicate with the angels from heart to heaven.

*C*OSMIC CONSCIOUSNESS

An Angel Reminder: "He sees that in the infinite ocean of life the soul of man is as immortal as God is . . . and that the happiness of every individual is in the long run absolutely certain."

Richard M. Bucke, From Self to Cosmic Consciousness

In 1901 Canadian psychiatrist Richard M. Bucke wrote a groundbreaking treatise entitled *From Self to Cosmic Consciousness*, in which he described a "new faculty" of beyond-self-awareness experienced by a few men and women throughout history. Comparing such luminaries as Jesus, Buddha, Muhammad, Walt Whitman, Dante, and Francis Bacon, among others, Bucke found them all to have been recipients of a "clear conception or vision of the drift and meaning of the universe" that inevitably resulted in an all-pervasive sense of joy. The angels want us to know that cosmic consciousness is not the domain of the privileged few; it is within the reach of each and every one of us. In fact, it may be just a breath away.

Do a cosmic consciousness meditation. Go into your relaxed state, close your eyes, and breathe deeply and rhythmically. With each inhalation, feel your body, mind, and soul being filled with the light of immortality. Feel your soul filled with divine love and peace, as it becomes one with the Eternal One. Breathe deeply, restfully and joyously, until you feel ready to open your eyes.

An Angelic Reflection: I love life and do not fear death, for I know that I am one with God.

${\mathcal{D}}$IGNITY

An Angel Reminder: When we protect our dignity, we honor our divine individuality.

Although dignity is one of our birthrights, we often neglect to protect and uphold it. Sometimes we don't even realize our dignity is in jeopardy. We want so much for things to be comfortable with others that when they take advantage of us we may allow denial to obscure reality. True friends will always accept and honor our needs and decisions and will never try to make us feel guilty when they don't get their way. But if someone begins abusing or coercing us, we need to realize that this person is not a true friend. The angels work hard to safeguard our dignity. Make it a little easier on them by standing up for your self-worth. When you feel worthy and honorable, you will be a strong force in favor of angel consciousness. Your life will inspire others, and you will forever have many true friends in high places.

Become aware of the times when your dignity feels attacked or compromised. What are you afraid of losing by honoring your own needs and convictions? What do you stand to gain?

An Angelic Reflection: I will be true to my own feelings and beliefs, and I will treat others with the same respect I expect from them.

SENSATIONAL

An Angel Reminder: Life is not a three-ring circus where the angels perform great feats to entertain us.

The angels are sensational in the true definition of the word. They create excitement, admiration, and eager interest in many people, especially now. It is easy to get carried away with the sensational aspects of the angels, but this is not what the angels want. Many people first become interested in angels because they hear of or have experienced for themselves an amazing incident that defied all logical law. Perhaps the angels saved a human from imminent danger. This is exciting and does lead people to find out more about angels, but the ultimate reason the angels save someone or intervene in a life is because God sanctioned it. The angels are not looking for credit for what they do, and they never want to have a circus form around any incident they are involved in. Let go of any attachment to the sensational, and you will be like the angels, free to perform great acts for the Creator.

Are you interested in the angels for the wisest reasons? Be aware that the real energy behind your interest in the angels is leading you toward the true wisdom and sensation of God. The angels never say, "Hey, look at us, see how great we are, look at all the magical things we can do." They say instead, "Look past us; we are pointing upward."

An Angelic Reflection: I will pay more attention to the wise message of the angels and less attention to their supernatural powers.

$\mathcal{B}$IRDS

An Angel Reminder: "Mother Nature has the angels tell the birds to go check on the humans to make sure they are okay. The birds tell the angels if we are in danger. That's why birds fly over your car and why you see birds everywhere."

Orianne Thompkins (age five)

Birds live in the strangest places. Birds could make their nests in parks and forests, yet you often find them under freeway passes and in crowded cities under the eaves of buildings. Unlike other wildlife, the birds stay close to humans. Birds have often been thought of as divine messengers. Maybe they have a message for you. Next time you hear a bird sing, think about how much you are loved in heaven. Imagine that birds are the eyes and ears of the angels. Watch birds play and frolic. They are natural comedians and will bring you laughter.

Pay attention to birds. Become a bird-watcher, and each time one is near stop to appreciate it. Once you become more aware of the birds in your neighborhood, they will entertain you with their spirits and they may relay a message from the angels. You will find that you are attracted to some birds more than others. You might want to get a bird feeder to attract your favorites to your window.

An Angelic Reflection: I will appreciate the sweet song of the birds, and each time a bird touches my heart I will remember how loved I am in heaven.

SOARING

An Angel Reminder: "Oh! I have slipped the surly bonds of earth and danced the skies on laughter-silvered wings. . . ."

John G. Magee, Jr.

How many of us have felt the sensation of soaring? Of letting go, breaking free, transcending limits? John G. Magee, a young British fighter pilot who was killed in World War II, was privileged to soar in his work, which became not a job but a joyous and profoundly spiritual experience. To allow ourselves to soar takes courage. Many of us have been brought up with the limiting belief that if we experience too much happiness, it might be taken away. If we fly too high, we might crash. So we cautiously remain earthbound, leaving it to the crazy daredevils to do the things we've dreamed of and the things we haven't. The angels, however, want us to soar, to "slip the surly bonds of earth" and move past the fears that keep us from reaching our highest potential. The traditional image of angels as winged beings carries a pointed symbolism; as manifestations of pure spirit, living in tune with their inner wisdom, they are, at last, free to exult in their true power and purpose.

Are you feeling blocked, frustrated, or unfulfilled in some areas of your life? If so, it may be time to think about soaring. Where have you been earthbound? Where would you like to soar? What's holding you back? What will happen if you allow yourself to soar? What will happen if you don't?

An Angelic Reflection: I am the pilot of my own plane; I have the power and the will to take myself anywhere I want to go. I welcome the unknown, for once I am there it becomes the known.

$\mathcal{I}$NTERPRETATIONS

An Angel Reminder: Relax; it's only an interpretation.

When an event or crisis takes place we immediately try to figure out why it happened. The problem is that the reasons we come up with are usually not accurate because they are filtered through our views of ourselves and our perceptions, which are based on how we feel at the moment. When we feel good we interpret what happens in our lives as good. When we feel bad, then events usually feel bad. The lesson is to not get attached to interpretations. Things are never exactly as they seem.

When we feel good and worthy then we will interpret hardships or undesirable events as positive challenges. We will know we have the power to control our emotions and reactions for the best outcome. So the key is to feel good most of the time. But we can't expect to feel good all the time. The real key is to ask the angels to help us interpret events through the eyes of heaven.

An Angelic Reflection: I will not interpret events based on how I feel. I will not be attached to my initial perceptions. I am open to the gift of life without reasons.

*L*AW OF THOUGHT

An Angel Reminder: "The lamp of the body is the eye; if therefore your eye is clear, your whole body will be full of light."

Matthew 6:22 (New American Standard Bible)

What we focus on is what we will see. What we think about often enough is created in our lives. Energy follows thought, and where we put our thoughts is where we accumulate energy. If we worry and fret over life's problems we give our energy to them and that creates torment for us. Does thinking about how bad you feel over a financial debt pay the debt for you? No, but if you spend your time thinking creatively and giving your mind a rest from disturbing thoughts, an answer to how you might erase the debt will have the chance and the room to grow. Our minds can be our greatest assets or our greatest liabilities; it all depends on what type of thoughts we fill them with. Our mind's eye is the lamp of our body; if the lamp is burning the bright oil of the angels' clear, inventive, and positive energy, then our bodies and our spirits will be full of light and joy.

Have any worries or difficulties been consuming your thoughts lately? If so, each time you begin to worry, say "Stop!" out loud. Then close your eyes, breathe deeply, and concentrate on the image of your inner lamp. See the angels filling it with their beautiful golden oil of positive thought; see it radiating peace and illuminating your unconscious. Forget about your problems for the moment and let the angels bring you creative ideas and solutions.

An Angelic Reflection: I own my mind; what I fill it with is what I choose.

*F*OUNDATION

An Angel Reminder: A life founded on love becomes a spiritual stronghold with the angels acting as guards and overseers.

What constitutes the underlying foundation that your life is built on? How do you support yourself? You may start to answer, "With the money I make." That may pay for your shelter, your meals, and your worldly entertainment, but it does not support your life. A life is best supported by spiritual love, based on a loving higher power that we trust. All things are passing; what remains constant is God's love. Build your life on the foundation of higher love and you will remain strong in the darkest hours. You are never alone when love is the foundation of your life.

When we truly understand that our foundation is God's love, we can consciously do things to strengthen that foundation. Think of ways to strengthen your own foundation in life. Prayer, spiritual practice, and attuning to the angels can help add a few solid corners to your life's foundation.

Your life is a unique creation, and with the angels guiding you, you will find your own strongest areas to build on. Never forget to call out to God when you feel like your foundation is crumbling.

An Angelic Reflection: Love is the solid rock that I stand on in the midst of a turbulent sea. God will never fail me no matter how rough the waters get.

ℱOLLOWING THE DREAM

An Angel Reminder: The angels love enthusiasm far more than perfection.

In the 1940s lived a stellar example of a woman who followed her dream. Her name was Florence Foster Jenkins, and her dream was to give operatic recitals at Carnegie Hall. It didn't matter that Florence was in her seventies when she finally attained her dream, and it didn't matter that she was one of the most terrible coloratura sopranos who ever lived. Her enthusiasm, flair, and unwavering devotion to her dream made up for her glaring lack of vocal talent. She had a grand time on that stage, dressing in lavish costume, throwing roses to the audience, living her dream to the hilt. Florence died not long after she attained her dream, undoubtedly with a sense of complete satisfaction that most of us would be lucky to experience. The public adored her and so, of course, did the angels. To them, her off-key arias were the sweetest paeans of praise to the Divine because she had the courage to brave the brambles of the critics and the scoffers in the blissful pursuit of her soul's fulfillment on earth.

If you have a dream and aren't following it, what are you allowing to stand in your way? If you fear that you aren't good enough or might be rejected, simply think of Florence Foster Jenkins, up there on the stage of Carnegie Hall, happily screeching her way to immortality.

An Angelic Reflection: I have the courage to pursue and attain the deepest desire of my heart.

Glamour

**An Angel Reminder: All that glitters is not gold—
or angels.**

Glamour is an illusion, an erroneous perception of reality,
a misleading visual image. Glamour calls to us by saying,
"Look how exciting, magical, and beautiful I am. Come
and be a part of this enchantment." Glamour is elusive,
seeming to be just out of our reach, and it wastes our energy grasping for a piece of that pie in the sky. We think
that we have been cheated out of the good life when we
are seduced by glamour. Glamour doesn't exist; the play-
ers that we envy in the game of glamour envy someone
else. They have not found happiness in all the supposed
magic and beauty they are surrounded by, and we
wouldn't either. A true state of magic, enchantment, and
beauty comes from being happy with what you have and
who you are now. The angels cannot be impressed with
glamour, because they do not see glamour; they see only
truth.

*Are you seduced by glamour? Are you willing to let go
of your attraction to the illusion of glamour? Glamour imprisons, and if you want to be
free, you must see the truth in all
things. Do this by paying more attention to the issues of the day, and
ask the angels to help you focus on
true happiness without reason.*

**An Angelic Reflection: I will look
beyond the illusion of glamour and
find truth.**

$\mathcal{D}$ISCIPLINE

An Angel Reminder: Discipline yourself to have more fun!

Just the idea of discipline is exhausting for many of us, because we immediately relate it to work and difficulty. We often set ourselves up for failure when we set out to practice a discipline that simply doesn't fit comfortably into our daily schedule. No one likes to fail, so we associate discipline with disappointment. It is time to change our view of discipline and use it to our best advantage. Discipline is not punishment; it is simply a means of training that produces a skill. The angels want us to use discipline in gaining the skill of working less and enjoying life more. Then the world will no longer pass us by like the scenery out of a fast train's window. The angels will guide us to do less, make it count, and enjoy it more.

Think of ways you could discipline yourself—train yourself to be skilled at—doing less in your life. Think of meaningless activities you could either drop or do with more enjoyment. For example, if you have to drive in traffic each morning, discipline yourself to listen to an inspiring story on tape. Wake up five minutes earlier and have your coffee with the angels. Stop setting unrealistic work goals for yourself, and each time you get that uneasy feeling that you are doing too much, stop and ask the angels for the permission to do less. They will never turn you down.

An Angelic Reflection: I realize how fun it is to be a disciple of the angels, who want us to slow down and live, not race ahead and fall.

$\mathcal{F}$RIENDLINESS

An Angel Reminder: If you want to have a life full of friends, be friendly.

Friendliness creates an aura of warmth, comfort, and favor. A friendly soul is someone you want to be around, someone you feel you know and can trust. Being friendly is not reserved for extroverts; introverts are equally friendly, they just may not advertise it as loudly. And being friendly does not mean you have to have millions of friends. It is better to have a few good friends whom you trust and value than many friends you don't know well. The key is to seek people you resonate with, whose heartstrings vibrate to the same beautiful angelic tones that yours do. In this way your friendliness will attract kindred spirits and your life will be rich in the rewards of true and inspiring friendship.

Not everyone will be our friend, and that is what makes friendship special. Use your sense of intuition and impression to sense whether you are in friendly territory or not. Ask the angels to guide you in being a friendly soul who is strong and wise in matters of friendships. We always have the choice to go out into the world with a friendly attitude, and with the angels by our sides we can make the world our friend, not our enemy.

An Angelic Reflection: The world is a friendly place when I am with my friends.

$\mathcal{H}$EALERS

An Angel Reminder: When you awaken to angel consciousness, you enter the realm of the healer.

The very act of choosing this book to read means that you have awakened your angel consciousness and now have the choice to accept it fully into your life. By accepting angel consciousness, you are accepting the responsibility of being a healer. Healers in the angel consciousness tradition go back to basics. They know that healing simply means making whole again, restoring balance and harmony. In each situation we encounter we always have the choice to make it better in our own creative ways, and this is what healing is all about. Angel healers don't set out to change people, only to initiate awareness. Angel healers cure with love and never for gains or recognition.

Whatever situation you find yourself in, you can practice healing. You may work for a company that needs your love, or you may be an artist who sends their healing love out with the beauty of a painting. You may be living with someone who is dying, where all you can do to heal the situation is give love. Regardless of your situation, the angels are present to help you initiate healing. They will never let you forget that you have entered the realm of the healer, and in your own special way you will heal each situation you encounter with the divine energy of love. Are you ready? All you need is love.

An Angelic Reflection: I realize that one moment of pure love, offered freely and divinely, is a healing force far stronger than any substance found in a plant or pharmacy.

SPEED

An Angel Reminder: The only reward for going the fastest through life is being the first one at death's door.

Speed is great, when you're running a race or being chased by a monster. But is it necessary to be the fastest when you are living your life? To some people, life is a race to the top, a competition for position, money, or power, a push to succeed or to get things done. But the angels know that there are no trophies at the end of the race of life, because the only ones we can run against are ourselves. If we feel that life is a race, we need to ask ourselves what purpose it serves to be way ahead of everyone else. We don't need to be fast to catch up with the angels. They are always in the right place at the right time, and they've never gotten a speeding ticket. As a wise person once remarked, "God is slow, but he's never late."

Do you find yourself scurrying through life? Do you need to be faster and better than everyone else? Are you consumed by your work or your deadlines? Then it might be time to screech to a halt and rethink your priorities—and your life. Ask the angels to help you gain some perspective and insight into why you're racing through life. Then ask them to pace you so that you have the time to truly live.

An Angelic Reflection: I am never in a race against time. It is safe to walk slowly and freely through life.

$\mathcal{G}$IVING UP

An Angel Reminder: "You can't, but God can."

Emmet Fox

The term *giving up* is usually associated with admitting defeat. When we give up, we simply can't take one more breath or run one more step. We're at the end of our rope, which to the angels, of course, is always the beginning. The angels see giving up in a positive, not a negative, light. To them, when we give up, we give "up." We hand our worries over to God. We are not defeated; we are merely ready to relinquish our need to push ourselves beyond where we can or should be pushed and to let the angels fill in for us until we're ready to once again forge ahead. There is no disgrace in giving up; in fact, it is the mark of true wisdom to know our limits, to know when to put forth effort and when to conserve our resources. As the great spiritual teacher Emmet Fox observed, as the operator of a freight elevator doesn't use his own muscles but relies on electric power to effortlessly do the job that's beyond his limits, so it is with knowing when to give up and allow divine power to take over for us.

Are you carrying a difficulty that makes you want to give up? If so, practice giving it up to the angels. See yourself as carrying around a big burlap sack, inside of which is the problem that has been weighing you down. Now hand the sack over to the angels, who fly with it up and away. Finally, take a deep breath, release it, and allow divine power to work at helping you to come up with a solution to the problem or to get rid of it altogether.

An Angelic Reflection: It is in giving "up" that I realize the source of my true strength.

𝒟IVINE LULLABY

An Angel Reminder: A lullaby gives our minds a rest and guides our souls to dreamland for a chance to play with the angels.

A lullaby is a magical song of love, sung to lull babies softly off to dreamland, where they are free to play with their close friends, the angels. Lullabies are a comfort to our souls. Perhaps we were sung to sleep as children, perhaps not. It is never too late to discover the magical quality of a lullaby. As adults, we need to take a break from the many heavy responsibilities that can so often consume us. A lullaby will remind us that we are really only babies in the eyes of God and the angels, seeking the natural comfort that gives peace to our souls and new energy to our lives. We all have a Divine Mother who has never left our side; she will sing to us whenever we need her soft, sweet voice. All we need to do is call upon her.

The next time you lie down to sleep, play a lullaby or sing one to yourself. Imagine that the angels are singing with you, and when you hear them, close your eyes, grow quiet, and let them continue to sing to you. Try to recapture, for a moment, babyhood, with the pure essence of heaven vibrating in your soul. Connect with the love you were one with then, and realize that the love has never left you. Your soul is still vibrating to the pure tones of heaven's song.

An Angelic Reflection: I will never be too old to be lulled to dreamland by the sweet voices of the angels.

$\mathcal{T}$RUST

An Angel Reminder: "Trust thyself: every heart vibrates to that inner string."

Ralph Waldo Emerson

Mastering trust is difficult. By definition trust means relying on and placing our confidence in someone or something. Trusting others is great in theory, but it's almost impossible to put into practice. Why? Because most of the time we trust people only when they do exactly what we want them to do. When they act otherwise, we feel disappointed and think they can no longer be trusted. But true trust is not about relying on others to meet our expectations. True trust means learning to rely on ourselves instead, which will help us accept others for who they are, not for who we want them to be. When relying on others, don't get attached to outcomes; cultivate faith, and never put all your eggs in one basket. Above all, cultivate trust in yourself, for therein lies true confidence.

Think about how important trust is in your relationship to the angels. Without trust how would we really know the angels? How often do you trust yourself and the angels when your rational mind is saying "doubt"? Use your relationship with the angels to teach you about trust, and use your relationships with other people to teach you about love, honesty, growth, integrity, and nonattachment. In other words, reserve the issue of trust for your relationship with yourself.

An Angelic Reflection: I know that I can rely on the angels to teach me more about the true value of trust.

Observations

An Angel Reminder: Each of us is a unique observatory.

We would be in big trouble if we did not possess the power of observation. For example, if we were not able to observe a stoplight changing to red, we might start to cross the street during the wrong signal. Sometimes we have to observe things in our lives that bring us pain and discomfort. Observing the tumultuous news headlines is rarely enjoyable, observing loved ones go through rough times is never easy, and noticing the beautiful aspects of society continue to decay can make us sad. We could try to hide our heads in the sand and not observe these things, but we would miss our chance to live in the truth and do our part to make things better. The angels help us observe the truth with an element of detachment. They teach us that all our observations are passing and that if we keep them in perspective, happiness has the chance to bloom in our lives.

If your observations are getting you down, remember that all things pass. What you observe now will look different tomorrow.

An Angelic Reflection: I will observe yet be unattached to the changing world around me. I know that the angels will teach me to observe the truth and beauty that are present everywhere.

$\mathcal{A}$SPIRATIONS

An Angel Reminder: Surrender ambition and you will know how to really live.

Aspiration, like ambition, is the strong desire to achieve something. Aspiration and ambition are similar, but they part ways on one important point: manipulation. Manipulation means controlling the action of something, adjusting it to suit one's own selfish purposes. Ambition brings the temptation to manipulate, because with ambition comes the inordinate desire for power or attainment of a goal. Those who are ambitious are not thinking clearly or conscientiously, for they are thinking only of reaching their goal and doing whatever it takes to get there. The angels do not think of ambition as something to be proud of. It is good to have aspirations, to aim high and improve your life, as long as you keep the whole picture in perspective and use your aspirations to make the world a better place.

Have you ever wanted something so badly that you were willing to compromise your values and the welfare of others? Take the time now to appreciate the fine line of balance we must respect in aspiring to be great. There is nothing great about having power and money when other people had to suffer for it. What are you aspiring to be? Ask the angels to help you clear your mind and strive for aspirations, not ambitions.

An Angelic Reflection: I will aspire to lose my ambitions and improve my life with conscientious motives.

GIVING

An Angel Reminder: That which we withhold is withheld from us; that which we give is given back to us a thousand-fold.

The most interesting aspect of giving is how much we get out of it. When we don't give—out of selfishness, greed, or fear—we are only cheating ourselves by creating an atmosphere of withholding around us. Stinginess is not appealing to the angels or to anyone; if we resist giving, others are not likely to be quick to give to us. In addition, if we try to hoard, we will, in effect, impoverish ourselves; as the French philosopher Montaigne so wisely observed, "Once you have decided to keep a certain pile it is no longer yours, for you are unable to spend it." The angels remind us that when we are generous with whatever we do have and maintain faith in the abundance of the universe, we create an opening for that abundance to flow back into our lives. So giving becomes not a depletion but a circulation of prosperous energy that, as we enrich others, continually enriches us.

What are your attitudes and beliefs about giving? Practice releasing any fears about loss or deprivation that you might have associated with giving, and know that by circulating wealth, more of it is available.

An Angelic Reflection: I give without fear.

$\mathcal{E}$DIFYING

An Angel Reminder: An edifying moment has an everlasting angelic place in your mind.

Edification is one of those noble concepts from the angels that seems to have little importance in society today. When something is edifying, it encourages moral improvement and has an uplifting influence on our minds. Unfortunately, edification today has been increasingly overlooked in favor of quick and easy escapes from the boredom and emptiness of unedified lives. How often do you feel edified by reading a newspaper or watching TV? Where disaster, triviality, and materialism abound, few opportunities exist to be edified. So it's important to create uplifting and enlightening experiences for ourselves. Reading good, thought-provoking books, listening to good music, watching an inspiring movie, discussing spiritual ideas with a friend, meditating, creating things of beauty, helping others to seek out the truly edifying aspects of life—these are just a few of the ways in which we can improve our connection to the angels, who are always seeking to provide us with moral and spiritual inspiration.

How does your environment contribute to or detract from edification? How can you change or improve your environment—the people you choose to associate with, the activities you engage in, the priorities you have or haven't set? Ask the angels to help you spend at least one hour a day edifying your life.

An Angelic Reflection: I am able to make behavior choices that are comfortable and positive for me and beneficial to the world.

$\mathcal{H}$OME ENVIRONMENTALIST

An Angel Reminder: Ecology starts in the home.

Ecology is the scientific study of living things in relation to one another and to their environment. An environmentalist is a person who seeks to protect or improve the environment. Often when people speak of the environment they are referring to the areas of nature that have been designated to be left wild and protected from human intervention. Most of the ecological problems in the wild don't happen in the wild; they happen a few miles away where the humans are living and manufacturing their comforts. True environmentalists work to improve the relationship they have with their own immediate environment. The angels teach us to live in harmony with the environment by living in harmony and peace in our home base.

Because we are as much a part of nature as the birds that make their homes in the treetops, we too need a natural, clean environment in which to live and breathe. Simplify your daily home routine. Recycle anything that you can use again. If there are living things in your home—children, pets, a spouse—think of ways you can take better care of them and promote harmony and consciousness in your relationships. Ask yourself if the angels would be comfortable in your home environment.

An Angelic Reflection: I know that I am part of a vast environment of divine purpose, and my purpose is to improve my immediate environment.

$\mathcal{E}$LEMENTALS

An Angel Reminder: It is all elementary.

Within the angelic hierarchy are the elementals, important beings who represent one of the main four elements of nature: earth, water, fire, and air. The elementals exist in and are vital to every part of nature, including us. Elementals are actually the primal energy forces with which all of nature is built. We have a special connection to the elementals; they work with us to balance our own elements. If we learn to work with them, we will develop a deeper understanding of attuning with nature, and in turn we allow them the opportunity to move higher within the angelic hierarchy. The way in which you work with the elementals will depend on your lifestyle and how creative you are willing to be in your relationship with them. One thing is certain: when we develop a deeper understanding of the elements of nature, we allow ourselves a deeper experience of life itself.

You can attune to the various elementals around your home by recognizing wind patterns, water patterns, and how the earth looks and feels around you. When you use fire you will have a deeper understanding of its properties if you attune yourself to the elementals of fire. Some teachers suggest that when you fly on an airplane you ask the elementals to help replace and heal the air currents that are interrupted by the airplane's high speed.

An Angelic Reflection: Next time I witness the wind blowing gently through the trees, the waves crashing on the shore, or the beautiful flames of a fire, I will stop and honor the elementals.

*S*PIRITUAL CRISIS

An Angel Reminder: A spiritual crisis is also a time of spiritual growth.

A crisis is a time of difficulty or danger or a period of shortage, like an energy crisis. A crisis creates suffering for us until we accept it as a spiritual challenge and a time to reset the button, be kind to ourselves, and stop and reassess the situation and our lives. Many people lead lives of suffering due to physical or emotional pain, unconscious patterns of behavior, or mental blocks, not understanding that they have the power to transcend their misery by viewing it as a chance to grow spiritually. We need to remember that suffering is meant to awaken us, not cripple us. Next time you find yourself going through a time of suffering, intense or mild, realize it as a time of spiritual crisis. Just acknowledging that our suffering has a spiritual origin starts the healing process, because then we have taken the first step toward understanding. The angels are with us always as spiritual helpers, and they point us toward the light of hope on the horizon.

Is any situation in your life creating suffering for you? Write it down. Now write down the changes it has brought into your life and some ways it may be helping you to grow spiritually stronger and wiser. What has it taught you about yourself, your needs, your attitudes, your priorities, and changes you might need to make in your life?

An Angelic Reflection: I am willing to give up suffering and start growing.

$\mathcal{T}$IME TO GO

An Angel Reminder: Like the trains of Mussolini's Italy, death is always on time.

If you've ever watched *The Twilight Zone,* you know that death comes not in terror but in gentleness, and always on time. Episode after episode of that remarkable series, which is high on the angels' must-see list, depicts death either in the form of a compassionate, understanding being who comes to free us or a persistent figure whose inevitable presence we must accept. In his book *Zen Flesh, Zen Bones*, Paul Reps tells the story of a precocious young boy who broke one of his teacher's most cherished possessions, an antique cup of great value. Fearing the teacher's wrath, the boy pondered what to do. When the teacher came in, the boy said, "Master, why do people have to die?"

"Because it is a part of the natural process," the teacher replied. "Everything has its allotted time on earth."

"Well, then," said the boy, handing the teacher the pieces of his precious cup, "it was time for your cup to die."

If you have been faced with the loss or impending loss of someone dear to you, imagine that this was or is that person's time to go. It is the right time, the perfect time. The best way to send your loved one on is to release him or her in peace and total trust to the expert care of the angels.

An Angelic Reflection: I accept the timing of the universe in death as well as in life.

$\mathcal{F}$RICTION

An Angel Reminder: Friction brings fatigue.

Friction is caused by the resistance of one surface moving over another or the rubbing of one thing against another. The friction of rubbing two sticks together for a long enough time creates fire. When we become the one surface that resists moving over another surface, such as the river of life, we cause friction, and if we don't stop there we end up in the fire. We can always rebuild and rebirth, but it makes more sense to stop the friction before we are engulfed in flames. Friction also brings fatigue. Fatigue makes us suffer and think that nothing wonderful ever happens. Fatigue does not go away with a good night's sleep; fatigue comes from a tired spirit that can be replenished only when we let go of the turmoil and friction that are wearing us down.

Are you moving smoothly over the surface of life? If not, what is causing the friction? What are you resisting? The answer most likely has to do with change. Resisting change brings on friction. Become more aware of friction points and let them be warning signals alerting you to a new way of being. Next time you become overly tired, look for a friction point and think of ways to file it down. Fatigue means we have lost the fight with ourselves, so the key is not to fight but to turn instead toward acceptance.

An Angelic Reflection: I will no longer fight with the universe. I will go with the natural flow and remove friction from my path.

$\mathcal{I}$DEALISM

An Angel Reminder: There is no particular way things ought to be.

Letting go of idealism is not easy, because we may confuse idealistic thinking with positive thinking and with the action of keeping hope alive in our lives. But idealism translates into dissatisfaction rather than hope. It is okay to ask "Why not?" as long as we don't get attached to our own idealistic answers. We could spend all day seeing the world as we think it ought to be, but there is really more value in seeing the way things are and accepting the whole. By accepting the whole, with all its ambiguities and outrageousness, and not judging it or fighting it, we will have the spiritual eyes to see the true wellsprings of hope.

It may be uncomfortable at first to give up your ideals, but don't be afraid; it is actually quite freeing. If the world were the way it ought to be, we might never grow into the unlimited humans we are meant to be. Ideals exist only in the mind. Our standards of perfection are ours, and few others may share them. Giving up ideals does not mean you are giving up your values; always stay true to your values. Ask the angels for insight.

An Angelic Reflection: I will accept the whole picture, with all its ambiguities and outrageousness, and I will look for humor, not oughts.

$\mathcal{L}$IMITS

An Angel Reminder: Limits should define us, not limit us.

Many times we find it difficult to set limits with others and with ourselves. We may take on too much work or too much responsibility because we don't know our own limits. Or we may allow others to take advantage of us, to get us to do things we don't feel comfortable doing, because we need approval or are afraid to risk confrontation—to show our true, strong selves to the world. But learning about limits is an important part of angel consciousness. The angels show us how to set limits, not with belligerence but with confidence and love. In becoming more comfortable with our own limits, we naturally become more honest with ourselves and others. We learn what we are capable of accomplishing without jeopardizing our emotional or physical health. We learn what behavior we will and will not tolerate from others. When we begin to value ourselves as the angels do, we will not be afraid to set limits—to protect and honor the loving and lovable selves we have come to know.

Envision the life you would be most comfortable and at peace with. What limits would you have to set in order to realize that life? Would you have to say no more often to requests and situations that make you uncomfortable or demand too much of your energy? How would you expect and require others to treat you?

An Angelic Reflection: I am not afraid to honor my self-worth and my needs.

CREATIVE ENERGY

An Angel Reminder: We are all blessed with an endless supply of creative energy.

Energy demands movement and expression. Creative energy seeks an unblocked channel in which to flow. We all possess the ability to channel creative energy; it is as much a part of our systems as breathing. Because creativity is so natural to human life, blocking the flow of creativity will result in pent-up energy and frustration. The angels encourage creative energy to flow. When the angels alight in your life and you begin to expand your angel consciousness, you will not be able to resist the urge to do something creative. Eventually you will have to surrender to your own unique creativity; the angels will see to that.

What happens inside of you when you think about creativity? What feelings surface when you hear the word creativity? *Your reaction to creativity reveals where you are at with your own creative energy. If you feel jealous or insecure when you think about creativity, it means you are not using your talents. If you think you are not a creative person, you may feel a sense of longing. If you resonate with joy thinking about creativity, you are allowing creativity to flow in your life. Creativity is an energy that can be expressed and used in all that we do. Art, music, cooking, sewing, speaking, nesting, birthing—the list goes on forever.*

An Angelic Reflection: With the angels' help, I will create love forever and always.

ℋUMAN FAMILY

An Angel Reminder: The only race we should be actively engaged in is the human race.

Imagine what would happen if we all woke up one morning without skin. We would all look virtually identical, and we certainly wouldn't know who belonged to what race. Being skinless isn't a pleasant thought, but the problems that human skin has caused for the last few thousand years are equally unpleasant to contemplate. For some unknown and disturbing reason, humanity has endowed the physical body with an inordinate amount of power. We are so often judged by the way we look, not by who we are. We can think of all humanity as one big family, united by the same basic concerns and capable of the same basic emotions. The main thing this gigantic family needs to get along is respect based on understanding. But respect and understanding can come only when we cease cataloguing human beings according to race and begin to see them as the angels do—past the body, into the heart and soul. Humanity is a colorful bouquet of possibilities, and the angels see us in colors of light, not in shades of skin.

How are people really different from you? What are the commonalities you share with those who seem foreign to you? Try practicing the angelic art of appreciating each and every individual with whom you come in contact as an important and valued member of your family.

An Angelic Reflection: I allow others to teach me about themselves and their worlds.

$\mathcal{D}$ON'T KNOW MIND

An Angel Reminder: You don't know until you know.

In a largely futile attempt to know the unknowable, we spend a lot of our time trying to second-guess life. We fantasize what people are doing or saying when we're not around. We project our desires and fears onto others; we predict what they may be thinking and adjust our worries accordingly. Of course, this kind of elusive—and "illusive"—mind-play generally only increases our sense of confusion and frustration. When we start driving ourselves crazy over our inability to control what we have no power to control and no business controlling, the angels suggest that it's time to enter into what Zen practitioners term a "Don't Know Mind." In accepting the fact that we can neither know nor control what others are thinking or doing or what hasn't yet happened, we free ourselves to concentrate our energies fully on the moment, the only true place of knowing.

Is there something you want to know that you can't possibly know, or an outcome that you want to control and can't? If so, surrender to the moment and get into a state of "Don't Know Mind." Allow yourself to not know—and to not care about knowing—what will be revealed to you when and if it is supposed to be revealed.

An Angelic Reflection: I will let the angels guide me to know only what is important for me to know.

$\mathcal{D}$ISCERNMENT

An Angel Reminder: The road to hell is paved with good intentions that have not been balanced by good sense.

One of Aesop's fables tells of a woman who brings a frozen snake into her home, thaws it, and treats it well, only to have the snake bite her when he regains his powers. While dying from his poison bite, the bewildered woman asks him how he could do such a thing after she had taken such good care of him and shown him so much kindness. The snake reminds her that he is a snake and that is what snakes do. The snake in this fable is a wonderful metaphor on several levels; not only is he, like many people, dangerous by nature, but his venom is the poison we feel when those we intended to help take advantage of us. Like Aesop, the angels want us to be wise and discerning when giving to and caring for others. Many times we get into trouble when we give too much to those who have never asked for our help or who, having asked for it, are likely to take advantage of it. The angels give constantly, but they never get into trouble because they only give when asked by those who are ready to receive their gifts.

Have you taken in any snakes lately? Have you allowed someone to take advantage of your kindness or sympathy, or shared your soul with someone not interested in your highest good? When you have doubts, stop and ask the angels for insight and help. They seek to protect you from snakes, but they can do so only if you cooperate by respecting and safeguarding your own gifts.

An Angelic Reflection: With the help of discernment, I can safely act with kindness and compassion.

$\mathcal{H}$OPE

An Angel Reminder: Hope was all that remained in Pandora's box; the angels must have saved it out of love for humanity.

Some intellectuals love to argue about hope. They argue that hope exists in the future, not in the now, and that we must disregard anything that takes us out of the now. Without hope, both the future and the now can be color-less and dim. If you feel hopeless, then you need hope. It is that simple. Heaven is not impressed with humans who continue to feel hopeless in an attempt to experience the now. The now is pure awareness, and when your awareness is tainted by heavy feelings, you are not experiencing a pure now. Hope is very important to humans, especially *now*.

Next time you feel an ache of hopelessness in your heart or a dark cloud over your spirit, ask the angels to give you a blast of hope. Hope has its own energy, and it will warm that ache out of your heart and pick up your spirits. Feel the energy of hope, cherish it in your mind, and use it as a tool on your path through life. Make a little hope chest for yourself. Draw it on a piece of paper, then make a list of the things that give you hope. Next time you feel hopeless, open your hope chest and ask the angels to join you in a little old-fashioned hope.

An Angelic Reflection: When I feel hopeful for the future, I am positively positioned to help life unfold in a naturally beautiful way.

*E*MPATHY

An Angel Reminder: With sympathy we foster pity; with empathy we gain understanding.

Empathy is different from sympathy. Empathy involves listening; sympathy involves reacting. When we empathize with others, we understand their feelings without getting involved in them. When we sympathize with others, however, we identify with their feelings to the point where we take on their pain. The empathetic person asks questions; the sympathetic person may be moved to offer advice and solutions rather than allowing others to come to their own realizations. The angels want to make us aware that we are not meant to suffer when others do; their suffering can aid their growth. But we *are* meant to be there for others with a loving and supportive heart. The highest gift we can give others in a difficult situation is a chance to express themselves and to reach their own—not our—conclusions.

When you find yourself in the position of empathic listener, do as the angels do and simply listen unconditionally with love in your heart, aiming to understand the person's feelings and to help him or her to understand them also. Although you may be tempted to agree ("Yeah, Ralph sure is a jerk!") or give advice ("You ought to get yourself a good lawyer!"), ask constructive questions instead, allowing the other person to discover her or his own solution to the problem.

An Angelic Reflection: I listen to others as I would like to be listened to—with an ear tuned to their highest good.

CLOUDS

An Angel Reminder: When our heads are in the clouds, we are nearer than ever to the angels.

Clouds have a strong influence on us. In many ways they mirror humanity; full of shifting moods, they echo the many different parts of our makeup that can, at any moment, cause us to experience either storms or calm. Clouds also orchestrate the symphony of nature, bringing us rain and snow, filling daybreak with the soft glow of expectation and sunset with the passionate hues of memory. Clouds are masters of imagination; when the sun shines through a cloud made up of ice crystals, for instance, we see little rainbows of pastel color, which some people call sun birds. The angels want us to remember that we too orchestrate nature—our own. Our many moods are nothing more than passing clouds that disappear with a breath of new wind. And like the clouds we can create our own beautiful daybreaks, passionate sunsets, and lives filled with imagination and wonder.

The next time you're outdoors, take at least five minutes to watch the spectacular, free air show that is always going on above us. Remember to thank the angels for touching you through the clouds, the warmth of the sun, the softness of the breeze, the coolness of the rain, and the many images of heaven that inspire your soul.

An Angelic Reflection: I will appreciate both the importance and the ephemerality of my moods while I continue always to look heavenward.

DEPRESSION

An Angel Reminder: The angels allow us to be depressed, but they never allow us to remain depressed.

There's nothing wrong with depression; it's a human safety valve, constructed to keep us from burning out. The real trouble comes when we remain depressed after the warning lights flash and the angels have told us it's time to get back on the energy track. When we're depressed, we draw our energy inward, imprisoning it in the deepest recesses of our being. But energy cannot exist without movement. If we do not allow it to rise upward and outward, it will kick around inside of us like a cornered colt until it either beats down the stable door or expires for lack of an outlet. So the best cure for depression is movement, which is energy directed outward. This may seem somewhat paradoxical, since when we're depressed we feel that we have no energy to do anything. But we *do* have energy. All we have to do is let it out by moving—to a new activity, exercise, or whatever action will shift our focus from inside to outside ourselves.

If you have been depressed lately, call on the angels to energize and revitalize you. Meditate on their joy and enthusiasm. Then think of ways to draw this energy into your own life.

An Angelic Reflection: If I feel depressed, I accept it as a natural phase while looking for ways to move onward.

$\mathcal{W}$ILLPOWER

An Angel Reminder: "Will is the ability to direct your energy where you want it to go."

Sanaya Roman, Living with Joy

The concept of willpower usually gives us a shudder. We don it like a suit of armor as we go into battle with the adversaries of bad habits and addictions, and we despair of ever having enough of it to emerge victorious. But what we don't seem to realize is that, far from being something outside of us that we must strive to attain, willpower is an ever-available inner power source. The angels prefer to reverse the negative idea of willpower into the positive concept of "power of will." Our will is not a burdensome suit of armor; it is a positive energy that we can point like a laser beam in any direction, penetrating issues and dissolving obstacles with confidence and enthusiasm rather than trepidation and displeasure.

Close your eyes and visualize your will as a power source inside of you that is constantly generating all the positive energy you need to accomplish whatever you choose. Now direct your will like a laser beam to whatever you would like to accomplish, and see all barriers to your progress evaporating. Continue to do this visualization daily, and watch your goals begin to materialize.

An Angelic Reflection: I befriend my will and am constantly empowered by it.

$\mathcal{F}$RAILTY

An Angel Reminder: If we stop trying to cure and eradicate our problems, we can integrate our problems and mistakes into our lives in a positive way.

Some positive can be found in anything that we have labeled negative. For example, the issue of codependence has many people going to great lengths to stop being codependent. But some of the qualities that go hand in hand with codependence are quite positive. Take neediness, for instance. We do need one another; we cannot deny that. Because neediness is sometimes painful and not admired, we want to get rid of it, pull it out like a sore tooth. Humans are frail, easily broken, yet easily put back together if the truth of our weakness is accepted. Our frailty is what ultimately makes us great. So instead of getting rid of all your problems, ask the angels to allow you a view of the positive side of human faults.

The human condition is just that—human. The only way to cure the ills of being human is to stop being human, and we can't really do that. We are here to experience the human condition with all its faults and frailty. Out of our weakness are born beauty and grace and the ability to feel deeply. Make a list of your faults and weaknesses. Look at your list with the angels and see how each fault is actually the result of simply being human. Think of the things on your list you wish you could eradicate, and begin to accept them as a part of your larger being.

An Angelic Reflection: I will learn to love my problems, and through love they will bloom into assets.

$\mathcal{H}$ARP

An Angel Reminder: The harp is an instrument of divine music.

Angels are often depicted in paintings playing harps. The harp as a symbol has come to represent songs and music in honor of the Divine. Its tones are soft and soothing, not loud and jarring; its music speaks not simply to the emotions but to the soul. In mythology, the harp has been used as a symbol of disarmament, calming and neutralizing anger and danger with its gentle voice. Angels honor the Divine and disarm its adversaries with the gentle strains of unconditional love. So the harp is a natural symbol to think of in connection with the angels. We can be harps that the angels play to honor God. Our lives can be sweet songs that melt down anger into understanding and compassion. Let's stop harping on the negative and begin to play the divine music of hope and light in our lives.

Try listening to some beautiful harp music. Breathe gently with it, until it begins to become a part of you and the vibrations of your soul. See yourself as the harp. How can you tune up your life so that the angels can play divine music on your strings?

An Angelic Reflection: The music of heaven sings in my soul and resonates throughout the universe.

CARETAKERS

An Angel Reminder: The angels are caretakers of the human soul.

Our souls are the parts of us that are immortal and connected to the realm of the angels at all times. It is said that the soul is the real self and the personality is the mortal part we represent here on earth. We feel the best when our personalities are closely aligned with our real selves—our souls. The soul knows its true mission and seeks to bring that mission into expression through the personality. When the soul's impulses are ignored and when we act against them, we bring unhappiness to our lives. The angels are the caretakers of our souls. The angels are most concerned with helping us create qualities and virtues in our lives that allow the soul to express its mission and help the angels disperse their wonderful love everywhere.

To nourish the soul, first recognize that you have one, then acknowledge and value it. The angels know the soul very well and will help us when we are ready to get to know its importance. The imagination is the doorway to soul knowledge. Certain things feed the soul; these will be different for everybody, but the nourishment will always be of divine quality. The Bach flower remedies are one way to treat the soul, so if you are interested in learning more about the qualities of the soul, here is a place to start.

An Angelic Reflection: I know that the angels are taking good care of my soul, and I will do my part to align my personality with the qualities of my soul.

FRAME OF MIND

An Angel Reminder: Frame your mind with angel consciousness.

Our minds sometimes get stuck in a frame. A frame of mind is only temporary, but when we enter a dark and gloomy one, it seems like it will last forever. It is good to recognize what frame of mind we are in. When we feel comfortable and positive, it is important that we protect it. We can frame our minds however we want by being consciously aware of our attitudes. A frame is only a structure, and an attitude is simply a way of approaching life; we are allowed to switch frames and attitudes. Better yet, when you let the angels in on your frame of mind, your attitude will lift naturally.

Think of what helps you stay in a positive frame of mind. To protect a positive frame of mind, you have to take action and be willing to put forth the effort. If others want to engage you in a negative conversation, gently explain to them that you are not in the frame of mind to listen to anything that would ruin your peaceful frame of mind. Start keeping a mental note of when your mind changes from feeling peaceful to feeling disturbed. When you can identify the crossing point, you will be able to cross back over quickly. The angels will help; they want you to be happy and peaceful.

An Angelic Reflection: I will know my mind in a new and intimate way; I will frame it in love and approach life with peace.

$\mathcal{D}$ESIRES

An Angel Reminder: Taming desire does not mean destroying passion, personality, and spirit.

Our desires often define us. This can be positive for us or not, depending on which desires we are allowing the world to see. When we desire peace on earth for all beings regardless of race, creed, or gender, this desire appeals to humankind's higher nature. On the other hand, when we desire to hoard money, pleasure, or too much food or drink, these desires define us in a negative light to most people. It doesn't matter so much what people think of our desires, but it does matter if the desires bring us pain. This is an issue of excessive wanting. How often do you hear yourself say or think, "I want. . . ." This leads to the "if onlys," followed by the "why me" syndrome. Sometimes we confuse desires with passions and personality traits. Some things in life we will feel passionate about, and this is okay. Do not spend energy trying to curb your passions, destroy your desires, or to stop enjoying something that gives you pleasure. Seek understanding. Start to understand what your desires represent, and know that the angels recognize what we really desire deep in our hearts.

Mental peace is what we truly desire down deep, and the angels help us attain it whenever we are ready to give up excess desire. So the next time you find yourself wanting something with a burning desire, ask the angels to help you replace it with mental peace. Mental peace will help us even out and sort through our desires.

An Angelic Reflection: I will allow the fire of my passions to warm my heart but not scorch my wings.

NATURAL LAWS

An Angel Reminder: Natural laws can be neither changed nor broken, only obeyed or disobeyed.

Great spiritual teachers have often used metaphors and parables about the natural world to teach us about basic spiritual principles. For example, from the river we learn the law of flowing with, not against, the current of life. From the willow tree bent by the wind, we learn strength through flexibility. The four seasons—summer, fall, winter, and spring—teach us the laws of harvest, preparation, death, and rebirth. Natural laws cannot be broken or changed; they are immutable. They are not meant to be mindlessly obeyed but rather honored and respected. If we ignore a natural law, no cosmic police will pull us over and cite us for a violation. Instead, our ensuing unhappiness will be our punishment. The angels operate in the realm of natural law and are of great service to those who seek to live in accordance with the timeless principles of the universe.

Next time you get stuck in a dilemma, take a moment to ask whether there is a natural law that, if followed, might help you in your situation. Ask the angels to help guide you to a realization.

An Angelic Reflection: I will allow natural laws to guide me in making the highest choices in each situation I encounter. I seek to align myself with the highest principles of the universe.

Worries

An Angel Reminder: Worry is a state of mental uneasiness.

It is natural to worry about things, but it is unnatural to let the worries take up permanent residence in our bodies and minds. Do you have a stiff shoulder, a headache, stomachache, backache? It could be that a worry has decided to take some of your precious energy and torment you with it. The natural way to worry is to allow time to think creatively through your worries and come up with solutions. If immediate solutions are not available, set the worry aside or put it in the angels' out-file. The angels love our worries and can help us put our worries in proper perspective. Like most problems, if we take care of small worries when we first notice the uneasy feeling they cause us, they won't grow into a pain in the neck.

Worrying is a drain on energy. If we direct the energy we are using for worrying into some activity designed to change the energy, then our worries will be transmuted. When we worry it is good to have something in our hands to fidget with. Make your own set of angel worry dolls or angel worry beads. Next time you worry, get your beads or dolls, call in the angels, and tell each doll or bead one of your worries. Then ask the angels to take the worries far out into the universe where they will be lost among the stars, and all that you will have left is solutions.

An Angelic Reflection: When I worry, I will remember to take it easy on myself and not let the worries manifest themselves as aches and pains in my body.

GRIST FOR THE MILL

An Angel Reminder: "We can take our lives exactly as they are in this moment; it is a fallacy to think that we're necessarily going to get closer to God by changing the form of our lives. . . ."

Ram Dass

The phrase *grist for the mill* means making use of everything. Grist is grain that is ready to be ground in the mill. When grain is milled into flour, it has many new uses. Many things in our lives can be grist for our spiritual mills. Everyday events like washing the dishes, solving problems in our relationships, playing with our children, or doing our jobs can become a means of getting closer to God and the angels. We don't need to do anything fancy or strict; we don't need to change our religion, diet, or career; we only need the willingness to use everything we already have to bring us one step closer to God. We can use our own unique creative energy to recognize the grist, then grind, refine, and sift through it for new and beautiful uses.

Think about the grist in your life right now. Think of any issue, dilemma, or routine you are bored with, and come up with a way to grind it into spiritual flour for a new spiritual use. The angels can help you see all of your life as a spiritual route to enlightenment.

An Angelic Reflection: I will recognize the wider dimension of the mundane and use my everyday life to get closer to God and the angels.

CENTER

An Angel Reminder: Calm and peace are available at the center.

We all have a point within us that we can call our center (of gravity). When we feel centered, it means that our energies are in balance. Often, centering involves grounding those energies. One definition of grounding is good basic training. Entering spiritual basic training with the angels as our drill sergeants is a very different experience from entering the military. Instead of commanding us to adhere to a prescribed structure, the angels encourage us to hang loose and cultivate flexibility. In place of grueling exercises that force us to the edge of pain and exhaustion, the angels provide us with the means to enjoy ourselves and move freely at our own pace. Instead of striving to become what others want us to be, the angels invite us to discover and be faithful to who we are. When we are truly centered, we feel confident, flexible, tolerant of others, and at peace with ourselves, because we know that as long as divine love warms and illuminates our lives everything is in perfect balance.

Take a reading of your energies at this moment and get a sense whether or not you need to ground any excess energy. Focus on being in your body and releasing any thought or feeling that does not contribute to your inner peace by imagining an energy pathway that goes directly into the earth, taking your unwanted thoughts and feelings and transmuting them into positive energy for the universe.

An Angelic Reflection: I am here to receive basic training in life.

ᴾARTNER

An Angel Reminder: A partner is not so much an answer to our prayers as a stimulant to our growth.

Who, exactly, is our perfect partner? Is it someone who makes us totally, blissfully happy at all times? Does he or she take care of all our needs? Do we expect the perfect partner to be perfect—to meet every single one of our criteria for eternal contentment? If so, the perfect partner doesn't exist. But if we change our perception of *perfect* to mean right for our situation and our growth at the present moment, then—theoretically, anyway—every partner is the perfect partner. Of course, we may be in relationships that are not satisfying, which means that we are being shown that we need either to readjust our expectations if they are unrealistic or to honor our needs and our self-worth by allowing ourselves to have a loving, caring, fulfilling partnership. The angels do not ever want us to remain with an abusive partner; they know that the truly perfect partner will be there with proud and unwavering support to help us to realize our soul's highest aspirations.

Examine your beliefs about your perfect partner—your hopes, dreams, expectations. If you haven't yet found the person you are looking for, ask your soul what sort of partner would be best for its growth. Then stop searching and let the angels lead you to this person.

An Angelic Reflection: I seek and find the person who honors the needs of my soul.

CHANGELS

An Angel Reminder: Change is not a threat to your life but an invitation to live.

Change is life; life is change. Changels are angels who help us welcome and enjoy change as a natural part of life. Change means that from moment to moment things become different and new. Change is also growth. When we grow spiritually we experience changes within, and here is where difficulties may arise in adult minds. Spiritual growth is not easy because we all have a natural human resistance to the unknown. We often want to keep things the way they are and cling to the familiar, even if the familiar is less than satisfying and far from happy. Although change is often threatening to us, we have nothing to fear and everything to gain by accepting it in our lives. The changels encourage us to let go of the familiar and embrace the unknown with trust and openness. Changels teach us that as we welcome change, we will be able to make the best choices in each moment.

The unknown is far more difficult to handle when we worry too much. Next time you find yourself fearing or worrying about change, sit back, relax, and ask the changels to help you see the potential change from all perspectives and vantage points. If you are facing a major change, such as a job change, a divorce, or a move, write down the pros and cons of the situation. How will the change make your life more difficult? What new and positive opportunities might it bring to you?

An Angelic Reflection: Change is fun, change is fresh, change is challenging, change is life.

$\mathcal{L}$OVELIGHT

An Angel Reminder: We all have starring roles in the divine comedy, whether we realize it or not.

Limelight was once used to illuminate the stages of theaters. A brilliant light resulting from burning lime, it transformed the actors on stage in such a way that the audience knew they were witnessing something very special. Limelight is not used anymore, and perhaps some of the magic it produced lies dormant. The angels have a magic light they use to illuminate our lives, and when it shines on us others know they are witnessing something special. The angels call it lovelight, and they shine it on the stages of real life. There are many theaters of life to act in and many different plays and productions. When we choose to act out the divine play, something special happens.

Think about the stage you have created in your own life. Next time you need some extra illumination in your life, ask the angels to shine the lovelight on you. Study your role in the divine play of life. Play with the idea of living a theatrical life. Ask yourself: Who is directing my life? Who are my other leading actors? Who is producing or backing the show?

An Angelic Reflection: I am an important actor on the stage of life. I have my own story, and I am developing my character to be great.

$\mathcal{I}$NSIGHT

An Angel Reminder: Genuine seeing is a process of awareness that does not depend on visual proof for validation.

The word *insight,* which means to see into something, is really a function of seeing with one's inner eyes, or what the Bible terms the "eyes of understanding." It isn't always easy to be insightful. We may be distracted and deceived by appearances. We might judge others too quickly, react too defensively. True vision, however, demands that we see beyond actions into their source—and then beyond the source into the soul. The angels ask us to practice seeing with the eyes of understanding. They challenge us to see beyond the frustration, irritation, or disappointment of the moment into the underlying reasons for behaviors or events. They also challenge us to see into ourselves—to monitor our responses and reaction patterns, to consider why we create certain situations in our lives, to explore ways in which we can turn apparent misfortune into an opportunity for growth and, ultimately, good fortune.

In what areas of your life could you use a little more insight? Could certain relationships be improved? Career moves become clearer? Into which of your own behaviors would you like to gain more insight? Begin by trading judgment for nonjudgmental observation and reaction for thoughtful response, and your eyes of understanding will begin to open.

An Angelic Reflection: When I see with my heart and soul, though the night is dark, my true path will always be visible.

ENRICHMENT

An Angel Reminder: We all have the means to enrich our lives.

We can improve and enrich the quality of our lives by adding new things to our programs each day. It doesn't have to take a lot of money, just effort. Travel is a great way to enrich our lives; visiting new places around town, eating new foods, and exploring nature all enrich our lives and expand our horizons. Adding the angels to our everyday lives makes us far richer than a fat bank account. Rich experiences are everywhere waiting to be found by adventurous humans, and with the angels nearby, you will be rich in love.

Think of the ways in which you are truly rich. Now think about your current situation and look for new ways to enrich your life. The angels are enrichment agents. If you are at a loss for ideas, ask them to lead you on an enriching journey. Just be open to the rich rewards of experiencing a full life, and you will find hidden treasures right in front of your eyes.

An Angelic Reflection: I make life richer for myself and those I love by following the angels through life.

ℰTHERIC

An Angel Reminder: The universe responds to the light and delicate touch of the angels.

Ether is the clear sky, the upper regions beyond the clouds, beyond the earth's atmosphere. It is the substance of heaven—light, delicate, highly refined. The word *ethereal* is often used to describe the angels or something angelic. Not only do angels exist beyond the physical, beyond time and space, they also use the ether to communicate to us. Just as at one time ether was thought to be an invisible medium for transmitting the waves that filled all of space, so ether is a medium for transmitting messages from the angels. The angels are always encouraging us to develop the etheric side of our nature. Being ethereal can make us more lighthearted, free of the worries and burdens of the earth, able to fly with the angels in soul and spirit. The mysteries of the etheric realm must be respected, however. Because the earth is such a dense place, being too light and delicate may cause us to detach from our earthly experience. While of the earth, we must learn to function in it, to balance the physical and the ethereal in our lives. The angels can help us to keep our heads in the clouds and our feet on the ground.

Visualize yourself becoming a part of the etheric realm—shedding the denseness of your physical self, breaking free of imagined limitations, flying with the angels. Now see yourself coming back to earth, feeling both grounded and free.

An Angelic Reflection: When I balance the ethereal with the material in my life, I have the best of both worlds.

New Day

An Angel Reminder: The news is good in heaven.

Days can be very useful when we need to start anew. Each day we awaken to the chance to learn something new, see something new, and do something new. We can find new things in our own backyards; we don't really need to travel all over to find something new to be interested in. We can even *be* something new. Humans thrive on new things. Think about how fascinated we are by news. When we greet our friends we ask, "What's new?" News is information, and humans are information gatherers. One thing is for sure: we won't run out of new things. A new moon cycle is always coming our way, babies are being born all the time, and we wake up as new people each morning when the angels are in our lives.

What's new with you? Do you feel interested in life? Is there enough new information coming your way to keep your mind fresh? If you need something new to happen, think about what you want. Sit down with the angels and contemplate newness. Think about how you can renew your interest in the simple and beautiful process of life happening all around you.

An Angelic Reflection: I wake up with the angels each morning, and I am new and improved.

CRISIS MENTALITY

An Angel Reminder: There are far more satisfying ways to have fun than manufacturing crises.

Some people wouldn't know what to do without a crisis. So they remain at the control tower, binoculars in hand, on the lookout at all times for the next major disaster. When no crisis looms on the horizon, they magnify small problems into events of enormous proportions. If the sea is calm for the moment, with not even a small difficulty to liven things up, they simply focus on worrying about something awful that hasn't happened yet but might at any moment. They are also talented at becoming involved in other people's crises, jumping right in to offer advice and even carry the load as if it were their own. The reality, of course, is that the only crisis such people suffer from is boredom. They generally need a great deal of excitement and drama to give them a sense of importance and control, and they use crises to provide them with the stimulation they can't find in ordinary, everyday existence. The angels are gently amused by people with a crisis mentality and are always ready to show them how to find genuine excitement through concentrating on joy instead of sorrow, humor instead of drama, calmness instead of chaos.

If you find that crises, or people who are constantly involved in them, take up a lot of your time, ask yourself what payoff you're getting from them, and if you could get the same payoff from other, more positive, sources.

An Angelic Reflection: I can feel alive and important without a crisis.

Sᴘɪʀɪᴛᴜᴀʟ

An Angel Reminder: We are spiritual beings having a human experience.

A spiritual life is one in which we are in the world but not of the world and its many problems of competition, trials, and material gains. Think about the values of the world and of heaven. In the world money is our reward, and in heaven the reward is manna, spiritual food, and delight. In the world we do things for recognition from people; the heaven way is to do things for our higher purpose. Possessions, financial investments, and security are what we depend on in the world; our personal integrity and virtue allow us to stand tall in the light of heaven. To relieve stress in the world we choose chemicals and technological advances; the heaven way is to pray, meditate, and connect with the peace of God within. You can be a part of the world and be spiritual. Keep your awareness keen and you will move beyond duality.

To be spiritual means to be as concerned with spirit or soul as with physical world or body. Being spiritual does not mean that we ignore the world or our bodies; rather, it means that we take better care of them. Think of ways to increase spirit, and do it the heaven way.

An Angelic Reflection: I solve my problems the heaven way.

$\mathcal{N}$ERVOUSNESS

An Angel Reminder: "Each cell and tissue in the nervous system is a living, intelligent structure. Life energy can always renew it."

Paramahansa Yogananda

The nervous system doesn't know the difference between our thoughts and reality. So if we are disturbed by certain thoughts, our bodies respond as if something is threatening us physically, activating our nerves to carry information and impulses that pump adrenaline through our bodies and exhaust our energy. Although this uncomfortable state of being may seem an inevitable result of our fast-paced, stressed-out lives, it is not a natural way to live. The angels want us to remain calm and centered. They want us to understand that we can train our minds to replace fear with positive and uplifting thoughts. As the intelligent nervous system processes this new information, it will send a message of life energy to all of our cells, and nervous tension will give way to a sense of joy and peace.

Our nervous systems need special care. From now on, notice how many negative and stress-producing activities you have in your life, and try to reduce them with a new schedule and new priorities. Above all, give yourself a set amount of time each day to do absolutely nothing except renew your nerve fibers with divine life energy by focusing on the angels, who are models of tension-free living.

An Angelic Reflection: Every day I find ways to reduce the stress and increase the peace in my life.

HEALING

An Angel Reminder: Healing means making peace with life.

Healing is a personal voyage that we each embark on in our own way. The healing of illness does not mean that you won't face death, and it does not mean you have failed to follow some magic formula of behavior. Suffering from illness does not mean you are being punished; it could be a gift to your overall life plan. Before Anthony Perkins died from AIDS, he composed the following statement to be released after his death. His words relay the true message of healing. "Many believe that this disease is God's vengeance, but I believe it was sent to teach people how to have compassion. I have learned more about love, selflessness, and understanding from the people I have met in this great adventure [AIDS] than I ever did in the cutthroat, competitive world in which I spent my life."

Healing does not mean curing; being healed means being made whole and sound. We are whole and sound when we accept the process of life as a gift. Have you made peace with life? If not, begin the process now and ask the angels to help you.

An Angelic Reflection: I know that the angels are guiding me to make peace with my life so that no matter what I encounter here on earth, I will be ready to learn more about love.

CONTEMPLATION

An Angel Reminder: "Contemplation is the only proven way of changing human behavior radically and permanently."

Aldous Huxley

To contemplate means to muse, ponder, and consider. When we practice a contemplative life with the angels, we renew our relationship with the Divine. Although contemplation and meditation are headed in the same direction, the two are not the same. The goal of meditation is to touch divine truth by transcending the distraction of thought, whereas contemplation moves us closer to God through specifically directed thoughts. Contemplation is a productive endeavor; great geniuses have been known to sit for hours just gazing into space, and when asked what they are doing they reply, "Thinking." Contemplation is a natural human activity; when allowed the chance, children instinctively contemplate all the wonders of nature. We all need time to contemplate, to delve beneath our surface thoughts, to go deep within our souls and listen to our inner wisdom.

How often do you sit just thinking, musing, and pondering? Take the time to practice contemplation for ten or fifteen minutes each day. Start by contemplating angels. Let your mind wonder about them. Don't try to control your thoughts or achieve specific results. Simply allow the contemplative process to take you where it will. Eventually certain thoughts may call to you, inviting further reflection.

An Angelic Reflection: I will allow myself a rich inner life through contemplation.

Qualities

An Angel Reminder: The angels lead a quality life.

Angels possess only positive qualities, qualities that enlighten rather than darken consciousness. The list of qualities that interest angels is quite long and may include some you haven't thought of. Of course, the typical angelic qualities that immediately come to mind are love, hope, faith, compassion, peace, and gratitude. Other qualities equally important to the angels are mirth, joy, openness, imagination, humor, delight, lightness, and playfulness. After all, what good is faith without joy, or love without playfulness? How can we have true peace without openness? And could we ever separate gratitude from delight? You can tell when you have attracted the angels to you by the appearance in your life of such unfailing signs as peace of mind, hope, fortunate coincidences, favorable meetings, and an irrepressible urge to enjoy life. You can then become an angelic messenger yourself, as you radiate these positive qualities to those with whom you come in contact.

What characteristics do you possess that especially attract the angels? Make a list of qualities you would like to develop that would attract the angels. The angels are available as quality control agents; not only are they attracted to certain qualities in humans, but they also help us to develop the true essence of great qualities.

An Angelic Reflection: With the angels in my life, I discover the secret of unconditional joy.

𝓕ACE-LIFT

An Angel Reminder: The only direction in which we need to lift our faces is up.

Western society looks with amused incredulity at so-called primitive cultures that believe in the supernatural power of healers, shamans, or folk remedies and rituals to cure illnesses. But we too have some strange beliefs. For instance, in our society people actually believe that there is a cure for old age. We are convinced that with a magical operation known as a face-lift we can regain our lost youth and beauty. How absurd this notion would seem to our supposedly less-advanced neighbors! They would never think to bypass the necessary stages of life, since they associate age not with the loss of beauty and power, but with the attainment of wisdom. The angels too are unimpressed with flawless skin. They know that there is as much, if not far more, beauty in a face that bears time's noble imprint with grace and dignity. And because the angels see only the soul, we do not need to hide behind a youthful countenance in order to attract them. We only need to lift our faces up, in the direction of heaven.

Are you afraid of getting old? Or do you accept the natural progression of life with enthusiasm, gratitude, and humor? Think of older people you know who have not had face-lifts but who would nonetheless be considered beautiful. What beautifully ageless qualities do they possess?

An Angelic Reflection: Reflecting joy, compassion, and wisdom, age gives my face a whole new dimension of beauty.

Opposition

An Angel Reminder: Opposition is not a wall to batter down but a doorway to walk through.

Wouldn't it be great if we could just glide through life, never having to face opposition, everything always going our way? Heavens, no! Without the challenge of opposition, we would never learn our true greatness. Learning to handle opposition inventively is the beginning of wisdom. This may seem like a tall order, but we are all capable of it, especially with the angels as our consultants. The first thing to do in any situation involving opposition is to think carefully and listen to your inner voice before taking action. Take stock of your advantages and your gifts; get to know yourself. Then assess the situation. What would be the most advantageous action to take? Moving forward? Retreating? Waiting patiently for the right moment? Finally, concentrate on being creative rather than competitive. How can you turn opposition into a positive rather than a negative experience? The angels remind us that it is in overcoming opposition that we truly come in contact with our creative power.

Where are you facing opposition in your life? Write down some strategies you could take to understand and overcome the opposition. What angelic qualities would be particularly useful to cultivate at this time?

An Angelic Reflection: I take the creative approach to opposition and surprise myself by my own ingenuity.

$\mathcal{P}$EARLS

An Angel Reminder: "Do not give what is holy to dogs and do not throw your pearls before swine, lest they trample them under their feet, and turn and tear you to pieces."

Matthew 7:6 (New American Standard Bible)

The emphasis in the familiar biblical passage above has traditionally been placed on the swine—those people in our lives who are incapable of appreciating all that we have to offer. But the angels prefer to emphasize the pearls—the treasure troves within us that house our unique and priceless spiritual energy. The angels remind us that while we should choose our friends wisely, not wasting our talents and gifts on those who will misuse or reject them, we should also be aware of our inner pearls. Most of us are not in touch with the beautiful radiance we possess, the amazing transformative energy that too often lies buried in the mire of unconsciousness. The angels exhort us to be the first ones to appreciate our wonderful qualities, the first ones to whom we cast our pearls. Only then can we wisely share them with others.

Make a list of all the unique and precious abilities and qualities you possess. Now, for each item you listed, put a pearl (real or simulated) in a special jar or box. Begin now to appreciate your worthwhile qualities and to reserve them for those who respect their value.

An Angelic Reflection: I am aware of and grateful for the many wonderful qualities that I possess, and I know that I am precious in the eyes of the universe.

Spiritual Guides

An Angel Reminder: Listen carefully for the knock at the door of your soul.

We all have spiritual guides, angels who take us to higher levels of consciousness and knowledge. We will feel the influence and/or presence of these guides as we become more aware of our inner yearnings. When we suddenly feel compelled to learn about a religion or we feel an almost inexplicable pull in a metaphysical or spiritual direction, our guides may be making contact with us. Our guides may take on physical presence in a dream, during meditation, or in the form of a spiritual adviser or teacher whom we may unexpectedly encounter. Or they may make themselves known simply through new interests and ideas that come to us. However they reach us, our spiritual guides always bring us into closer contact with our inner goals and our higher selves.

Have you felt any yearnings or desires to explore a new spiritual direction? What or who sparked your interest? Can you think of any instances in your life in which your spiritual guides might have been—or might be—trying to reach you?

An Angelic Reflection: I am open to my spiritual guides, and I greet them with excitement, respect, wonder, and love.

$\mathcal{P}$RODUCERS

An Angel Reminder: We are the producers of the flop or the blockbuster of our own lives.

What are you producing in your life? What are you creating and bringing forth through your mental or physical effort? If your answer is "not much," perhaps some debris is inhibiting your productivity and needs to be cleared out of your life. Sloth and envy are two of the main slowdowns we need to avoid. Sloth is simple laziness—knowing what you need to do and then letting time slide by. Envy is discontented desire that is fueled by the false belief that others have something much more valuable than you do. Envy is a big trap; it is like a field of flypaper that we have to artfully and consciously avoid stepping into. There is only one cure for sloth and envy and that is doing your life's work—not just thinking about it, but doing it. If you don't yet know what your life's work is, that's okay. Just keep engaging in meaningful and productive activities and eventually you will discover the one thing that will make your life fun, enjoyable, and productive. The angels know what you are here on earth to produce, and they will gently guide you into full production as soon as you are ready and willing.

If your life were a movie, what would you like it to say or reflect? What would you like to accomplish and be remembered for? Start to think of yourself as the producer of your own life, with the angels as your associate producers.

An Angelic Reflection: I make a big production out of my life.

$\mathcal{G}$ETTING SILLY

An Angel Reminder: Every once in a while, silliness just might be next to godliness.

Getting silly can be a very worthwhile pastime. When we truly get silly, we give ourselves over to the joyously uninhibited side of our natures. In the throes of an attack of pure silliness we can find side-splitting humor in anything. We are beyond judging whether we should or shouldn't laugh at something or be just a little more serious about life. We just laugh from the deepest, most helpless, most ridiculous parts of ourselves. The angels are not above being silly from time to time, and they invite us to join them whenever we feel like it. For through silliness we can release an enormous amount of tension, cleansing our systems and restoring them to sanity.

How do you feel about getting silly? Does it embarrass you? Do you think it's childish or stupid? Or do you rather like the idea? How might a little bit of silliness improve your life?

An Angelic Reflection: I am not afraid to abandon myself to joy.

$\mathcal{P}$LEASE TAKE NO FOR AN ANSWER

An Angel Reminder: No means no.

If people say no, they most likely mean no; otherwise why would they say it? Yet in our culture, if no is not the answer we want to hear, we take no as an invitation to use our best convincing acts to change the answer to yes. A saying that seems to roll off the tongues of almost everyone is: "I won't take no for an answer." The only thing that results from convincing another to do something she or he doesn't want to do is that you have gotten your way and the other person's wishes were not respected. Whatever you wanted will suffer in some way, and the person convinced will also suffer. This is not the way of angel consciousness.

Next time someone says no to you, accept the answer and be done with it. Don't start convincing the person to change his or her mind. Respect the other's wishes; if that person's mind changes on its own, then renegotiate. If you can take no for an answer and trust that all will turn out in your highest favor no matter what, your goals and desires will find the most magnificent way of coming to fruition. The angels have a secret for us: when we accept a person's answer, that person will be so amazed and interested in who we are that she or he will want to find out more about us. Perhaps it will even inspire the other to reconsider the answer on his or her own.

An Angelic Reflection: I will respect the answers that I receive and learn to take no for an answer if that is what I am given.

*F*ESTIVAL

An Angel Reminder: "By finding the right festival mood, we will once again link human existence to divine existence."

Rudolf Steiner

A feast is a day of special observance and rejoicing, such as a religious holiday; a festival is a celebration of a feast. A festival gathers together communities or families in gratefulness for some aspect of life. The four seasons have a special influence on our spiritual growth, and therefore many traditional festivals center around the changing of the seasons and the midpoint or height of the season. The angels want us to lead more festive lives, joining with others to celebrate our divine heritage. When we experience a more festive interaction with the world around us, we draw closer to the mirthful energy of the angels. For the angels, rejoicing is not simply an activity reserved for special days but a way of life.

Think of ways to create your own festivals or to support the traditional ones in new ways. Look into your family history and discover feasts and traditions that you may want to resurrect. Or design a festival around something that is particularly meaningful in your life. Bring your friends and family in on the planning, and begin experiencing unbridled delight in creation.

An Angelic Reflection: My soul and spirit were created to master the art of celebration.

 REJUVENATION

An Angel Reminder: Energy is never lost, only misplaced.

Every living thing on earth ages, matures, and is eventually reborn. The babies we once were have evolved many times over into the adult forms we are now. But even though our bodies may age, our spirits and souls remain young and full of pure energy. Sometimes as we experience the natural aging process, we become tired and weary, forgetting that we have an eternal fountain of youth at the core of our being. We believe that it is natural to slow down and weaken, when in reality the most natural part of us is our boundless inner well of enthusiasm and hope. The angels are natural rejuvenation experts. If we ask their help in restoring our original vitality, we will both feel and look younger. And we will understand the unique principle of youthful energy, which is that the more of it we use, the more we will have.

Chi *is the Chinese word for energy. Practitioners of tai chi— the art and practice of activating and uniting spiritual and physical energy—do not peak until age sixty-five, and many tai chi masters teach well into their nineties. They know that energy doesn't diminish with age, as long as it is used and allowed to flow through the body. Think about your age in years and then think about how old you really feel. Does energy flow freely through your body and mind?*

An Angelic Reflection: I know that the angels enjoy energies of hope, joy, and youthful enthusiasm. As I allow these energies to rejuvenate my mind and body, I experience the fullness of life at every age.

*D*ECISIONS

An Angel Reminder: Decision making and personal truth go hand in hand.

Sometimes it's tough to make decisions. We're afraid of doing and not doing; we stick with the devil we know for the devil we don't as long as we can, before he pursues us to the edge of the abyss. The angels can be a great help when we have important and difficult decisions to make, for they can work with us to clarify the situation and get in touch with our personal integrity, which is the base from which all our decisions must be made. We can ask the angels to guide us in self-awareness and self-respect so that we can make decisions based not on fear or ignorance but on realistic assessments of who we are; what we need and don't need; what will further our purposes in life; and what will be in accord with our highest selves and our highest good.

If you have an important decision to make, think about what you really want to achieve. How will your decision increase your happiness and productivity or contribute to the growth and welfare of others? If you have to make a decision that is painful but necessary, ask the angels for the strength you need and trust in their loving support at this meaningful juncture in your life path.

An Angelic Reflection: When my decisions are the product of my integrity and inner wisdom, I am at peace with them and with myself.

$\mathcal{I}$SHI

An Angel Reminder: "He was kind; he had courage and self-restraint, and though all had been taken from him, there was no bitterness in his heart."

Dr. Saxton Pope, referring to Ishi

One of the most inspiring stories about the triumph of goodness in human nature concerns Ishi, "the last wild Indian in North America." Ishi's people, the Yahi, were systematically exterminated by the white man in the late nineteenth and early twentieth centuries. He alone escaped the final massacre and was found wandering, bewildered and grief-stricken, in Oroville, California, in 1911. Eventually Ishi ended up a resident of the museum of anthropology at U.C. Berkeley, where he won the hearts of all who came in contact with him. He was the soul of gentleness and gentlemanliness. He was cheerful, industrious, hospitable, and generous. One of his favorite pastimes was to visit the nearby hospital, where he would make his own self-appointed rounds, singing Yahi healing songs to the surprised and delighted patients. Ishi never spoke of himself or the horrors he had endured. Instead, he gave all that he could of himself to others. When he died, all who knew him felt both profound loss and profound gratitude, for Ishi had shown them what an angel was.

Have you come across any Ishis in your life? If so, what effect did they have on you? What are some of Ishi's qualities you would like to cultivate in your life?

An Angelic Reflection: I find inspiration in those who have maintained their sense of joy and kindness in the midst of suffering.

$\mathcal{B}$UTTONS

An Angel Reminder: Robots need buttons; human beings don't.

In the nuclear age the idea of pushing buttons has attained life-death significance. If the person with his "finger on the button" happens to push it, the human race will be history. This is why buttons are so dangerous to our health. If we let others push ours, we go into reactive mode, which means irrational behavior that is either defensive or offensive. The result is a loss of control over ourselves and our sense of self. The angels want us to understand the difference be-tween reacting and responding. Reacting is un-thinking, automatic behavior; responding is behavior based on awareness and choice. As we become aware of our buttons and begin to deactivate them, we vastly increase our chances of living in harmony and under-standing.

What are your buttons? Who has their fingers on them? Re-flect upon why you have given certain people the power to push your buttons, and start noticing the types of situations that cause you to react rather than respond. Awareness alone will begin the deactivation process.

An Angelic Reflection: I live neither offensively nor defensively, but in the spirit of peace.

$\mathcal{P}$LAY

An Angel Reminder: The world is the angel's playground.

Have you ever watched kittens at play? To them, play is a serious business. Play is movement and exercise, toning and skill building. It leads to a healthy appetite and deep, restful sleep. Above all, it is the doorway to joy, wonder, and appreciation of all the little mysteries and surprises that add up, at the end of the day, to life. Unfortunately, most of us grown-ups spend so much time at work and worries that we are unable to allow ourselves to indulge in anything as "unproductive" as play. This distresses the angels, who are masters of playfulness. An angel's work is actually play; play is free movement that does not restrict or control anyone. The angels prefer to guide us by freedom of movement, allowing us to make our own choices while introducing us to the unexpected, encouraging us to be more spontaneous and reminding us that we too can fly—as long as we take ourselves lightly.

When was the last time you really loosened up and let yourself have a ball with life? If you are reading this meditation, chances are the angels are telling you to give yourself regular playtime. Schedule a time at least once a week to indulge in your favorite activities and enjoy the simplest pleasures. Then observe the changes in your work and relationships.

An Angelic Reflection: Play is a gift that allows me to touch my limitless capacity for enjoyment of life by becoming more in tune with my body, my surroundings, and the angel spirit within.

Options

An Angel Reminder: In the human package, options are always included.

When we have decisions to make or problems to resolve, we should never feel backed up against a wall. Regardless of whether or not they are immediately evident, options are *always* available. Alternative ways of thinking and doing can always be found. We may see only one way out, but the angels see all the possible combinations and permutations of our beliefs and actions. If we feel angry, frightened, or trapped, we need to stop, rethink the situation, and enlist the angels' aid in helping us to see things from their larger perspective. We need to ask ourselves what it is that we really want and what we can and can't give up in order to get it. We need to be honest with ourselves as to our real motivations, assessing whether or not our wants are in alignment with our genuine needs. Then we can either find or create the necessary options that will free us to take the right action, which comes not from desperation but from inspiration.

If you can see only one solution to a situation or difficulty, think about why. What beliefs or opinions are you clinging to that could be changed in order to give you more options? Think about what you really want to accomplish and why, and create alternative scenarios of achieving your goal.

An Angelic Reflection: I exercise my freedom of choice in clarifying my situations and resolving my problems.

*F*EARLESSNESS

An Angel Reminder: "In the Shambhala tradition, discovering fearlessness comes from working with the softness of the human heart."

Chogyam Trungpa, Shambhala: The Sacred Path of the Warrior

In Western society, we often confuse fearlessness with physical power, believing the dubious principle upon which our civilization seems to be based: might makes right. But in the realm of the angels, true fearlessness has nothing to do with building strong muscles on your body. Rather, it involves building strong muscles in your mind and heart. To the angels, fearlessness means having power that is so well integrated into your being that the power itself is hidden. When you are fearless, you possess the courage to be tender and the inner fortitude to withstand all circumstances. According to Shambhala, the Tibetan principles of enlightened warriorship, those who are genuinely fearless have moved past the fear of rejection and disillusionment that lies at the heart of the human quest for physical power. Therefore, true warriors are no longer afraid to be gentle, because they are at peace with their inner natures.

See your heart as strong, invincible, and completely open. Feel the strength of your interest in and compassion and enthusiasm for life. See this strength as a powerful light radiating from your heart center to the outside world, touching others and opening them, melting the barriers of fear that separate us from one another and prevent us from living fully.

An Angelic Reflection: As I free myself to be vulnerable, I am liberated from fear.

WINTER

An Angel Reminder: Without winter, how could we possibly appreciate the spring?

Winter is the season of reflection and challenges. In the rhythm of natural cycles, it corresponds to that part of us that must conserve our resources, draw inward, and allow ideas and situations to hibernate and awaken in their own time. Winter is a time of opposing forces that teach us beauty through harshness. The cold both chills and invigorates us. The snow and ice can be fierce in their fury or breathtaking in their pristine purity. The long hours of darkness make us yearn for the day while appreciating the stillness of the night, the warmth of the evening fire. Through winter we learn the art of patience and the joy of discovering new inner strengths, as we wait for new growth to emerge.

At times in your life when you experience the chill of winter—the freeze on activity, the harshness of painful experience, the despair of the lengthening darkness—the universe may be telling you to draw inward, to look within for understanding and solutions, and to release the old in order to prepare ground for the new.

An Angelic Reflection: I rest in the night to be ready for the day.

COURAGE

An Angel Reminder: "Just as one's heart, by pumping blood to one's arms, legs, and brain enables all the other physical organs to function, so courage makes possible all the psychological virtues."

Rollo May

Courage is a word that stirs up images of bravery, strength, and warrior confidence when facing danger. Courage is much more than facing dangerous situations with bravery; it is a quality we develop that allows us to control or use fear in a positive way. The word *courage* comes from the Latin word *cor,* which means heart. To control fear, we must lighten our hearts and rise above the sinking feeling fear brings. The angels help us do this by their very nature. The angels are light and uplifting, so in those times when bravery is needed, ask the angels for the courage to lighten your heart and face life with buoyancy. Centered at the heart of your soul are all the courage and support from the angels you'll ever need to go beyond and above fearful situations.

Courage is an energy that gives us the chance to go beyond our limits. We are not perfect, and it is not always easy to practice courage. It takes patience and trust and the willingness to allow the angels to help you go beyond a fearful situation. Allow this truth to bring you courage for whatever you want to do in this life.

An Angelic Reflection: I will allow my heart to pump courage through my being so I can go beyond and above fearful situations.

ᏢROGRESS

An Angel Reminder: Progress is not always visible, but it is always in progress.

Sometimes progress is such a subtle process that we don't know if it's happening to us. Things may seem unchanged at the surface; we may become doubtful or frustrated by an apparent lack of movement. But the angels remind us that progress is a process of moving slowly and surely. It does not happen in an instant; it does not announce itself with grand fanfare and excitement. Rather, each action we take toward our goals is like carefully setting brick upon brick, building slowly and steadily until one day we step back and realize that the house is completed.

If you have been working steadily toward a goal but wish you could make faster progress, think about how far you have already come and trust in the process.

An Angelic Reflection: Even though it may not always seem like it, I am always progressing.

$\mathcal{B}$URNOUT

An Angel Reminder: We help no one, least of all ourselves, by courting burnout.

We probably all know about burnout, that unforgettable experience in which we encounter exhaustion at its most profound level. When we're burned-out we have come to a crisis state caused by our neglect of ourselves. We have become overwhelmed by pressure and the demands of others and are drained of all energy. We can no longer function, on or off the job, because we have nothing left to give to anyone or anything. Burnout is not a necessary or inevitable condition; if we heed the warning signs that always flash well in advance, we can prevent it. If we find ourselves experiencing repeated bouts of illness, depression, anxiety, and unhappiness in our work and relationships as a result of pressure in some area of our lives, it's time to listen to what our bodies and our souls are trying to tell us: that we need to remove ourselves from the offending situation and put a new priority on our own well-being. The angels remind us that it is not in depleting ourselves but in valuing our emotional and physical health and knowing how and when to conserve our energies that we can be of most help to the world.

Have you experienced or are you experiencing burnout? If so, think about why you let yourself get to this stage of depletion. What changes in your attitude and lifestyle would you have to make in order to restore your energy and vitality and prevent burnout in the future?

An Angelic Reflection: I protect, honor, and defend my right to physical and emotional well-being.

RECOGNITION

An Angel Reminder: "If you judge people, you have no time to love them."

Mother Teresa

Humans want to be recognized, noticed, and appreciated. Through the power of recognition we become strong in who we are. Not all of us receive the recognition we feel we deserve, and this can cause us to seek it in frustrating ways. We often recognize in others negative things that we ignore or refuse to accept in ourselves. Whatever we recognize is what we know; *recognize* means "to know again." By recognizing God instead of negative traits in others, we bless them and strengthen them spiritually. In turn we are strengthened and others will recognize God within us.

Reserve a day to recognize God and the love that is present in every person you encounter. After this day ask yourself if you feel you could continue it. Be mindful of what it is you recognize in each person. It will teach you many things.

An Angelic Reflection: I will take the time to recognize God in others, and I will know again that love is what we are here for.

$\mathcal{A}$NIMALS

An Angel Reminder: Animals have an instructive nobility.

Although we often condescendingly refer to those who commit savage acts as "animals," this is an insult to our four-legged friends. An animal would never commit the ingenious and grisly crimes that human beings have invented. Animals are not grasping or avaricious; they are grateful for food, water, shelter, and love. They know nothing of vanity, and they do know a great deal about loyalty to their young, their owners, and often, one another. They live in constant awareness, are not deceitful, and always make full use of instinct and intuition, their most valuable and reliable resources. They do not desecrate the environment; they live according to the principles of nature, do not complain when they are ill, and quietly go off to die when their times have come. Many other cultures have traditionally revered animals as supernatural beings with special kinds of wisdom. The angels suggest that we pay more attention to animals and what they have to teach us. It just might make us more human, in the best sense of the term.

If you live with any animals, become aware of their unique personalities and the things you can learn from them. Write down the qualities you love about them, and note that, according to psychology, the way you perceive your animals is the way you perceive yourself.

An Angelic Reflection: I listen closely to the silent wisdom of my animal friends.

STOP THE BUCK OF DENIAL

An Angel Reminder: We can't correct our mistakes until we admit them.

It's not always easy to take responsibility for something we're not proud of having said or done or caused. But in the long run it takes a lot less energy to stop the buck of denial than to keep on passing it. Stopping the denial buck puts the brakes on the negative energy that has already been created and allows the repair work and the healing process to begin. It gets us back in touch with reality and our own sense of integrity, which is a far stronger base of power than denial and dishonesty. In being able to admit our errors in judgment and our vulnerability, we may even inspire respect and admiration from others, for the angels are hard-pressed to find someone who has never been afraid to own up to a mistake. In short, when we stop denying, we stop running—and start living.

Have you avoided taking rightful responsibility for any mistakes? Have you tried passing the buck instead? If so, what did it cost you? If you need to stop the buck, ask the angels to help you face your fears and discomfort, and know that you will come out ahead.

An Angelic Reflection: I take responsibility for my actions and live in the freedom of integrity.

RIGHT SPEECH

An Angel Reminder: We should regard our words as instruments of healing.

According to the Buddhist principle of right speech, one should always know when to speak the truth and when to refrain from speaking it in order to spare someone unnecessary hurt. The intention of right speech is to make sure our words are used only in a helpful, not a harmful, manner, which involves speaking at all times with discretion and compassion. Of course, we will find right speech difficult to practice if, like most humans, we indulge in the fascinating activities of gossiping about, judging, analyzing, and advising others. Right speech is also a challenge if we are convinced that we can clean up the world with the mop and pail of our knowledge and opinions. In other words, right speech involves a certain degree of deflation. When we become conscious of how and when we use or don't use words and the effects of our choices upon others, we are compelled to turn our attention inward rather than outward—to become interested in our own behaviors and motivations as we work to master the difficult, delicate art of looking before we speak.

Become conscious of how you use words. Try practicing the art of right speech for just one day, refraining from talking about and judging others or saying anything that could hurt someone unnecessarily. Notice how your thinking and listening skills increase as your verbal activities decrease.

An Angelic Reflection: I choose my words with care, knowing that they will take root in the minds and hearts of others.

$\mathcal{W}$HOLENESS

An Angel Reminder: We are, above all, seekers of wholeness.

All of our quests can ultimately be traced to the search for unity with ourselves and the Divine. The angels encourage us to explore our desires and to pursue them when they fulfill the needs of our higher selves. But if we are looking to someone or something outside ourselves to complete us, we will inevitably be disappointed, for wholeness can be experienced only within the self. To become truly whole, we must meet and marry our inner natures. We must allow that which lies hidden to emerge without fear; we must strive to discover the essence—the pure spirit that often lies buried beneath the dense layers of our personalities—and express it to the world. It is then that we can begin to experience the wholeness of union between self and soul, soul and divine.

If parts of you feel incomplete, send love to them and think about where the sense of incompleteness comes from. Reflect upon actions you could take and attitudes you could change to feel whole within.

An Angelic Reflection: I allow the light of wholeness to enter and heal my entire being.

ENCOURAGEMENT

An Angel Reminder: The angels only encourage, never discourage.

A young man who had been in a gang, had taken drugs, and was serving time for robbery not only felt that his life was over but that it had never really begun. In prison he underwent a spiritual transformation, during which he understood that only he could change his destiny. Upon his release he decided to enroll in remedial high school classes. The very thought filled him with fear, for he had known only contempt and discouragement in school. But he went to class, worked hard, and received his first A. This was the second major turning point in his life. Encouraged by his teacher and by his own newly discovered abilities, he got his high school diploma and went on to a highly respected university, where he became an honor student and, in his spare time, developed and implemented a volunteer program that encouraged kids who had lost hope to find meaning and purpose in life.

What role has encouragement or discouragement played in your life? Do you practice encouragement with yourself and others? If not, try to become aware of the fears that may be blocking you, and ask the angels to help you release those fears and become an encouraging presence.

An Angelic Reflection: I fill myself and others with the courage to realize the best that is in us.

Seriousness

An Angel Reminder: "Angels can fly because they take themselves lightly."

G. K. Chesterton

Seriousness is an illusion that humans naturally buy into. With all the problems in the world, if we don't take them seriously we will all be doomed, right? Wrong. We have been taking the world's problems too seriously for too long. So long, in fact, that politicians and the news media have us convinced that serious is the only way to be. Maybe it is time to start having some lighthearted fun in our own lives. This isn't easy to do when we have so many survival issues to take care of each day, but the angels will teach us to trust more and worry less. This will allow us to not take everything so seriously, especially ourselves and our seemingly monumental problems. In the overall scheme of the universe, is it really that important and serious that you were stood up for a date? Could it really ruin your whole life if you lose your job? Only if *you* let it.

Make a list of your serious issues and rate each of them in seriousness from one to ten. Then ask yourself what the angels would think of each of your serious issues. Think of how amusing we humans are to the angels when we take insignificant issues so seriously.

An Angelic Reflection: When I take myself lightly my thoughts will fly with the angels.

INDEX BY TITLE

$\mathcal{T}$ERRY LYNN TAYLOR is the bestselling author of four books written to encourage angel consciousness: *Messengers of Light, Guardians of Hope, Answers from the Angels,* and *Creating with the Angels*.

$\mathcal{M}$ary Beth Crain has written for numerous publications, among them the *Los Angeles Times,* the *Chicago Sun-Times, Redbook, Cosmopolitan, L.A. Weekly, L.A. Style,* and many others. She is the coauthor, with Joel Edelman, of *The Tao of Negotiation* (HarperCollins) and the editor of the humorous guidebook, *The Best of L.A.* She wrote the foreword to *Messengers of Light*.